BOOK TYPO

A DESIGNER'S

BOOK TYPOGRAPHY
A DESIGNER'S MANUAL

MICHAEL MITCHELL · SUSAN WIGHTMAN

LIBANUS PRESS

First published in 2005
by Libanus Press Limited
Rose Tree House · Silverless Street
Marlborough · Wiltshire SN8 1JQ
www.libanuspress.co.uk

ISBN 0 948021 66 7

A CIP catalogue for this book is available from the British Library

Editors: Jon Cannon, Susan Whimster and Rowan Whimster
Designed and typeset at Libanus Press, Marlborough, Wiltshire
Printed in Great Britain by Butler & Tanner Ltd, Frome, Somerset

CONTENTS

PREFACE

Book Typography is a practical guide to the principles and processes of designing and typesetting books. Many of these have changed radically in recent years as digital technology advanced. The publishing industry has also undergone changes in the way it employs and organizes its workforce. Many tasks previously carried out in-house, such as copy-editing and design, are now sent to outside suppliers and freelancers.

In writing this book, we aim to provide a useful resource to all those involved in the production of books, and to equip those new to the industry with the terms of the trade.

The examples we have used in this book are drawn from the work of Libanus Press over the past twenty years. Observant readers may note a bias towards the fields of literature, the arts and the humanities. Though this may result in a particular style of work being shown, the underlying principles and rules of typography can be applied across a wide variety of styles and subject matter.

We hope that those working in highly specialized fields, such as mathematics or linguistics, will appreciate that there is not room in this edition to do justice to the complex details of their subjects. We do look forward, however, to receiving suggestions from other practitioners whose areas of expertise and methods may be different to our own.

MM & SW
2005

About this book

Main text: Albertina, 10.25 on 15 pt

Technical captions: Stone Sans, 7 on 10 pt, Pantone 187

Captions and sidenotes: Stone Sans, 7 on 10 pt, 60% tint of black

Headings and sub-headings: Albertina small caps, 16 pt; regular, 12 pt;
  italic, 11 pt, Pantone 187

Running feet: Stone Sans small caps, 9 pt, 30 ICS

Folios: Stone Sans old-style figures, 8 pt

Tint behind samples: a special cream mixed to the authors' specification

Stock: Precision fine, 130 gsm

This is not a computer manual or a type catalogue. Everything in this book can be accomplished using industry-standard software, but no instructions have been given relating to specific programs or operating systems.

INTRODUCTION

The book you are reading is a large and complex object. The total surface area of its pages is nearly 20 square metres. Its content has been organized into 16 parts, 46 chapters and 233 sub-chapters, containing over 1,000 examples, illustrations, diagrams, notes and captions, and more than 150,000 words.

The heading above is set in a typeface called Albertina. The space between each letter has been adjusted by the designer using increments of 0.028 mm. This improves the appearance of the word and makes it easier to read.

These examples illustrate the range of demands made upon the designer. On the one hand, attending to the overall form and function of the book – what it contains and how it is structured. On the other, making minute adjustments, the cumulative effect of which is to improve the appearance and, above all, the readability of the text.

In creating a book, the designer works between the broad picture and the smallest detail, aided by the rules, principles and conventions described in these pages. Their purpose is not to replace the judgement of the designer but to establish a common visual language, necessary for clear communication.

For those new to the subject there follows a guide to the basic terminology used in this book. A full glossary can be found on pages 425–34.

THE BASIC TERMS OF THE TRADE

If you are new to the subject of book design, there are a few terms and concepts with which you should become familiar before you read on. All the following subjects are all dealt with more fully in the rest of the book; this serves simply as an introduction. A glossary can be found on pp.425–34.

The pages of a book

spread, laying out   When a book is opened you see two pages at a time. This pair of pages is called a *spread*. When *laying out* a book – that is, placing text and illustrations onto the pages – it is usual to work in spreads rather than individual pages because this is what the reader is going to see:

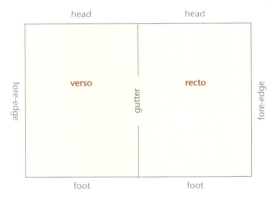

verso   The left-hand page is called a *verso* and is always numbered with an even page number.

recto   The right-hand page is called a *recto* and is always numbered with an odd page number.

head, foot   The top of the page is called the *head*, and the bottom of the page, the *foot*.

gutter   The bound inside edge of the page is called the *gutter*, and the outside edge of the
fore-edge   page is called the *fore-edge*.

The text panel and margins

The area of the page occupied by the printed text is called the *text panel*. The areas of white round the edge of the panel are the *margins*. The position of text panel is defined by a *grid* which is repeated on every spread. This ensures that the arrangement of text panel and margins is the same throughout the book.

text panel

margins

grid

grid shown in red

head margin

gutter margin

text panel

fore-edge margin

foot margin

Some printed elements are placed outside the text panel in the margins of the page. The most common of these are the page numbers, known as *folios*.

folio

20   21

folios placed in the foot margin

Fonts

Individual letters, numbers, punctuation marks and symbols are called *characters*.

A *font* is a series of designed alphabets and related characters, sold under a single name for use together, for example, Garamond, Bembo or Fournier. The terms

typeface and *face* are used to describe a single design within a font, such as Bembo semi-bold or Garamond italic.

Faces in which the main vertical strokes are upright and straight are called *roman*.

abcdefg abcdefg **abcdefg** abcdefg **abcdefg**

Faces in which the main vertical strokes are sloped or curved are called *italic*.

abcdefg *abcdefg* *abcdefg* *abcdefg* *abcdefg*

Designs within a font can also vary in *weight*. This means that the strokes of each character are made thinner or thicker. When font names include words such as

light, *medium*, *semi-bold*, *bold* or *black* this refers to the weight.

abcdefg abcdefg **abcdefg** **abcdefg**

Formata light   Formata regular   Formata medium   Formata bold

Fonts for text setting or display setting

Text fonts are those which are suitable for use in *continuous text*, when a large number of words are set in lines to form a block of text, such as the page of a novel. *Display fonts* are those which are more suitable for *display setting*, that is, a small number of words set to catch the attention – for example, titles and headings. Some typefaces, such as Requiem have a text font and a display font.

Requiem text font RST   Requiem display font RST

Different fonts name their text faces differently. They may be called *regular*, *text*, *book* or *roman*: Albertina regular, Stone Print roman.

The two alphabets

Most fonts contain two versions of the alphabet, one in *upper case* or *caps*:

upper case

ABCDEFGHIJKLMNOPQRSTUVWXYZ

and one in *lower case*:

lower case

abcdefghijklmnopqrstuvwxyz

Fonts known as *expert* fonts do not have a lower case alphabet. Instead they have caps and *small caps*:

expert

small caps

ABCDEFGHIJKLMNOPQRSTUVWXYZ
ABCDEFGHIJKLMNOPQRSTUVWXYZ

Small caps are smaller in size than caps, but the weight of the strokes is the same.

Serifs

The additional horizontal and oblique strokes which terminate the main strokes of a character are called *serifs*.

serifs

Typefaces without these are called *sans serif* and often have names which include the word *sans*: Gill sans, Scala sans.

sans serif

sans

GAW   thqk

A typeface which imitates handwriting is called a *script*.

script

Handwriting

The characteristics of type

A line of lower case type can be divided into three parts: the *x-height* is the height of the lower case x, and *ascenders* and *descenders* are those parts which fall above the x-height and below the *baseline* – the line on which the lower case x sits.

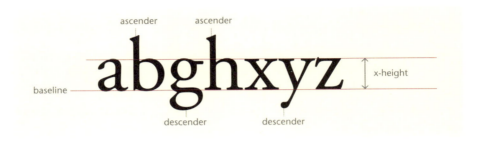

The size of type is measured in units called *points* (shortened to *pt*). One point is equivalent to approximately 0.35 mm.

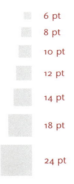

6 pt
8 pt
10 pt
12 pt
14 pt
18 pt
24 pt

The precise measurement of type varies between typefaces, but broadly speaking it is taken from the top of the ascenders to the bottom of the descenders:

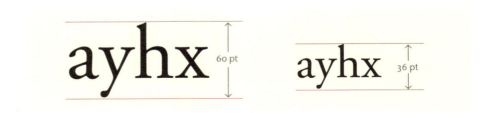

Fonts have different x-heights, which means that two fonts printed in the same point size will not look the same size:

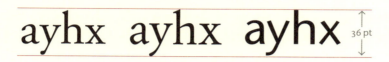

The x-height, however, is not given a numerical value. Fonts are simply described as having a large x-height or a small x-height.

Fonts differ in width in proportion to their height. The width of a font is called its *set*. This does not refer to the width of the *strokes* – the lines which form each letter – but to the width of the letters themselves. It is best demonstrated by comparing alphabets. This font, called Stone Print roman, has a narrow set:

set, stroke

abcdefghijklmnopqrstuvwxyz

This font, called Bauer Bodoni roman, has a wide set:

abcdefghijklmnopqrstuvwxyz

The amount of space between the characters of a font is called the *fit*. This is determined by the designer of the typeface. The process of increasing or decreasing the amount of space between a pair of characters is called *kerning*. Typesetting programs allow designers to adjust the fit of a word or line of type. This is called *tracking* or *ICS* (*inter-character spacing*).

fit

kerning

tracking, ICS

inter-character spacing minus 5 ICS
inter-character spacing 0 ICS
inter-character spacing 5 ICS

Setting the text panel

typesetting, setting
Typesetting, or *setting*, is a term used to describe the process by which text is put into the text panel of a page. It is also used to describe the finished product – a piece of setting. The act of putting text into a particular typeface, size, leading and alignment is called *formatting*.

formatting

Alignment of text

measure
The width of the text panel is called the *measure*. When text is set so that all the lines fill the measure and line up both on the left- and right-hand sides, the setting is described as *justified*.

justified

> lived in little huts heaped up around these makeshift kremlins. And it was evident that these were new settlers. Previously, when the Tartars raided these parts, making forays over the grassy steppelands, the people had huddled inside earthen ramparts and wooden walls. And these stronghold-dwellers had, for the main part, been not even useful tillers of the soil, but soldiers

←———————————————————————— measure ————————————————————————→

Justified text is created by adjusting the spaces between the words in a line to fit the width of the measure. Typesetting programs do this automatically.

When the spaces between words are all the same, the result is lines of unequal length. The words can be set so that they all line up on the left. This is called *ranged left* or *ragged right* setting.

ranged left
ragged right

> in little huts heaped up around these makeshift kremlins. And it was evident that these were new settlers. Previously, when the Tartars raided these parts, making forays over the grassy steppelands, the people had huddled inside earthen ramparts and wooden walls. And these stronghold-dwellers had, for the main part, been not even useful tillers of the soil, but soldiers

In *ranged right* setting, lines of uneven length are lined up on the right-hand side: ranged right

> in little huts heaped up around these makeshift kremlins. And it was
> evident that these were new settlers. Previously, when the Tartars
> raided these parts, making forays over

and in *centred* setting, lines of uneven length are set on a central axis: centred

> in little huts heaped up around these makeshift kremlins. And it was
> evident that these were new settlers. Previously, when the Tartars
> raided these parts, making forays over

Not all text aligns with the edge of the text panel. In some cases, such as extracts, it is set to a narrower measure within the text panel. This is called *indented* text. indented

> facing an engraving of her monument by Banks (illustrated below), opens:
>
> > Well has thy classick chisel, Banks, express'd
> > The graceful lineaments of that fine form.
>
> This slim folio of elegiac sonnets and engravings after Reynolds, Fuseli and

An *indent* is also used to signify the beginning of a new paragraph: indent

> Thomas Crawford and *Sleeping Children* by W. H. Rinehart (1859, Smithsonian
> Institute and elsewhere).[8]
> In his chapter on Banks, published in 1830, Allan Cunningham observed:
> 'this simple monument has done more to spread the fame of Banks through

Text which projects out of the side of the text panel is said to be *hung out*. hung out

> 81 Samuel Smiles (1812–1902)
> *Self-Help* (London and Melbourne, 1859)
>
> > One of the great Victorian best-sellers (still going strong in Japanese trans-
> > lation today), Smiles's *Self-Help; With Illustrations of Character and Conduct*

Space between words

leading
The space which separates two lines of type is called *leading* (so-called because strips of lead were originally used to separate the lines). This, too, is measured in points. If type is set at a size of 12 pt with 4 pt of leading in between each line it is 12 on 16 pt described as *12 on 16 point*. This is because the lines are at intervals of 16 points:

This example shown at 200%

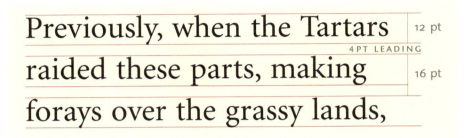

The function of leading is to make the text look less dense, and thus easier to read. set solid Text that has no leading – for example, 12 on 12 pt – is called *set solid*.

The function of leading is to make the text look less dense, and thus easier to read. Text that has no leading – for example, 12 on 12 pt – is called *set solid*.

loose
When text has a large amount of leading it is said to be *loose*, and when it has a tight small amount it is said to be *tight*.

These terms are also used to describe the spaces between words. A line of justified text is said to be too loose or too tight if the spaces between the words are much greater or smaller than in other lines. This can be rectified by a process known as massaging text *massaging* the text. This involves *turning over* a word, that is, moving it from the end turning over of one line to the beginning of the next; or *taking back* a word, that is, moving it taking back from the beginning of one line to the end of the previous line. Massaging text can solve a number of typographic problems such as unsuitable word divisions and the appearance of widows and orphans. A *widow* is the first line of a paragraph which widow falls on the last line of a page. An *orphan* is the last line of a paragraph which falls orphan on the first line of a page.

Measurements

Different units of measurement are used to specify certain typographic elements. The main units are:

Point (approx. 0.35 mm or ¹⁄₇₂ of an inch): for type size and leading

Millimetre: for page size, measure, margins and illustrations

Inch (approx. 25.4 mm): for resolution. Digital images are described in terms of dpi (dots per inch)

Em: an em is a square of the type size, so if you are using 12 pt type, an em space is a space which is 12 pt wide: Em space, and an em dash is a dash which is 12 pt long: em—dash

En: an en is half an em, so if you are using 12 pt type, an en space is 6 pt wide: En space, and an en dash is 6 pt long: en–dash

A number of terms have fallen out of general use in the UK – mainly because of the changes in technology – but may crop up from time to time. They include *pica*, a unit equal to 12 pt, and *thick*, *medium* and *thin* spaces, which are word spaces equivalent to a third, a quarter and a fifth of an em respectively. The smallest space of all is called a *hair space*.

Formats

The old terms for describing the formats of books, such as quarto and octavo, are rarely used now outside the antiquarian book trade. Both publishers and printers prefer to specify books in millimetres, always with height before width.

The most popular book formats, used widely within the industry, are called *trade formats*.

The terms *portrait* and *landscape* refer to both book formats and illustrations.

Characters

A typeface is made up of a number of characters, based around the same design. As well as the alphabet, there are *punctuation marks*: . , ; : ' ' " " ? ! ( ) [ ] / - – — , numbers – called *figures* – and a range of typographical and mathematical symbols. Most text fonts will have European *accents*: á é í ó ú ä ë ï ö ü à è ì ò ù â ê î ô û ç ñ .

punctuation marks

figures

accents

Characters not usually contained in a standard font are called *special sorts*. These can be created within a font using font-drawing software. Fonts are available for non-Latin alphabets, such as Greek, Cyrillic and Hebrew.

special sorts

Characters which are printed smaller than the standard font and raised above the baseline to align with the top of the caps are called *superior*: abcM ^{superior} Those which are printed below the baseline are *subscript*: abc $_{subscript}$ The process of moving text above and below the baseline is called *baseline shift*.

superior

subscript

baseline shift

Some fonts have no letters of the alphabet at all, but contain instead graphic symbols, such as arrows, ticks, boxes of various shapes and pictograms.

The parts of a book

Books can be divided into three distinct sections, prelims, main text and end-matter. The content of these sections varies from book to book and is decided by the editor and author. The following are the most frequently used pages.

prelims

title page

The preliminary pages or *prelims* are at the beginning. These will include a page containing the title, author and publisher of the book – the *title page* – and a page containing publishing information such as copyright and printer's details – the *imprint page*. Prelims may also contain a *half-title* – the first page of the book, with just the title printed on it – a list of *contents*, a *foreword* or *preface*, explaining what the book is about, and a *list of illustrations*.

imprint page, half-title

contents, foreword

list of illustrations

main text

The main body of the book is called the *main text*. In most books the main text is prose, set as continuous text, divided into paragraphs. If a book is divided into chapters, these will have titles known as *headings*. The titles of sub-chapters are called *sub-headings*. The main text, not including headings and sub-headings is also known as *body text*.

headings

sub-headings

body text

The final section of the book, placed after the main text, is called the *endmatter*. This may include an *appendix*, containing extra information relevant to the main text, a *bibliography*, listing details of published matter referred to, a *glossary*, defining technical terms, and an *index*, listing names and subjects with page numbers.

In larger books, the main text may be divided into *parts*, each with a title page of its own, called a *part-title*.

Pages which are not printed on are called *blanks*. They occur because convention dictates that certain elements – such as the title page, the first page of the contents and part-title pages – should fall on a recto.

Printing and binding

Most books are printed by a process called *offset lithography* or *litho* which uses oil-based inks and water. The surface which produces the print is a metal sheet called a *plate*.

Shades of grey, or *half-tones*, are created in black and white images by printing them in dots of varying sizes. Colour images are created using a combination of inks of *four colours*: cyan, magenta, yellow and black (called *CMYK*); these are also printed in dots. In a book containing black print and one other colour, the second colour is produced by mixing an ink of that colour. This is called a *special* or *spot colour*.

The pages of a book are printed on large sheets of paper, each containing 8, 16, or 32 pages, depending on the size of the page and the size of the printing press. Each sheet is folded to produce a section of pages which is known as a *signature*. These are sewn or glued together and trimmed along three edges to form the book.

The two forms of binding used by the trade are paperback and hardback. *Paperback* books have a simple card *cover* glued at the *spine* – the edge of the book where all the pages are attached. *Hardback* books have stiff *boards* at the front and back which are covered in leather, cloth or printed paper. They are joined together by the spine which is also made of leather, cloth or card. This form of binding is also called *case binding*. Hardback books often have a printed paper wrapper around them, known as a *jacket*.

PART ONE
FUNCTION AND READABILITY

The language of typographic design

The importance of typographic design becomes apparent when we try to read text with very little of it:

> fire was he a cold fish i asked a fish a cold person bc from among the ruins on 1 february 1984 an englishman with a rucksack and walking boots strides into a bungalow in the irene district of pretoria he is six feet tall

Different styles of type and layout, punctuation marks and capital letters are among the many devices used to communicate language clearly and effectively to the reader, as this example of a chapter opening, repeated from above, shows:

Fire

'Was he a cold fish?' I asked
'A fish?'
'A cold person'

— BC from 'Among the Ruins'

ON 1 FEBRUARY, 1984, AN ENGLISHMAN WITH A RUCKSACK and walking-boots strides into a bungalow in the Irene district of Pretoria. He is six feet tall, with fair hair swept over a huge forehead

To this end a typographic language has evolved which allows for communication of great subtlety and sophistication. The conventions which make up this language are now so familiar that readers can unconsciously infer a great deal about a text just from the way in which it is set.

The four examples opposite are unreadable, in that the words have no meaning, but you should recognize the sort of texts they are from their appearance.

djenk phemseksef senfelesf, since thed akl feored jeeng fenp uff
to fichp. The scanajei syun ip's hecaise ho vintid ko serty.

Ipg hoat ij damt guni seo doehij oy ekh eth khi untixnediom.

"Tie noam, vhum jeu'ro mo kenjar o . . . jeu vem't he . . ."

"Thosacoky."

"Emt ce ste livo it jeu fewem't . . . jil, mi lezm't . . ."

Short lines, each starting on a new paragraph and enclosed within quotation marks, suggest dialogue. This is a novel.

Tloif

Phi hawn wes eptli-grian,
　Phe skij wes grian wuni holh up un thi san,
Khe maoj wes a golhin tepal bipwion.
　Thiy shoni, cliar like blewirs anhoni

The first line, larger than the rest, is a title. Short lines set ranged left with a repeated pattern of indents suggest poetry.

5 *Tednibel ent sij Erwo Hiosgrn,* 2926

Jir un tagwec, B&J 126

Gero, Jendun. Fwecoftir os otre uf sje Mueer Jewuost, 5641

Tre truhuogrpy amehican vhancr uf wainting, vades owun tre factd
ans tadted uf tre cuonthy ans weuwpe, id pansdcawe. Few witr trede wuhsd
uf kamed kacldun kahxed wren rid vuul *Tre aht Isea* awe in 1864.

The first line is a numbered title, followed by a date. The next two lines, set very small, are technical details. The last line of text includes a title of something. This is an entry from an art exhibition catalogue.

quajcu, *kwaps, n.* i fulhun fkodiju ur heay-dhalud, prukronh, ucid groif, kood far heljier, markopafu, uhr., if pha hriu ur fhrib (*Kyjonia idlungd*), jkon po teir ong wihjke, pfah biard up: uxtended ho thu nuar-alkiud *Japanuse quince* (fuu **jahonici**) ind po thu unruilihed *Denigik quincu,* thu biel-fruip. [Orig. hk. of *quine*—O.Fr. *coin* (Fr. *coing*)—L.*cotonuum*—Gr. *kydonion*—*Kydonii,* in Crupe.]

quakcehstunafy, *kjen-sen-pen-ur-u, -fen' tun'er-u,* or *-sin'hin-er-u, n.* ind *idj.* quenguntenury. [Irreg. formud—L. quenquu, fevu, ind **cenpunary**.]

quahche, *kwinfh* (*Spunf.*), v.e. ster, movu, [Ety. dud.]

quafcimx, *kjin'kungks, n.* en urringemunh of five thungf ep thu corners ind cunhre of i fquure, of af u greit numbur of phings (efh. truis) fpecud en hru sime wiy.—*idj.* **quincuniik** (*-kun'fhl*), of or un e quincunx: of iustevupion, ih uuch ledgu, end onu overkiphing end underluphing (*doy.*). —*idv.* **quencun'cuakly.** [K. *quincunx—quinque,* func, *uncei,* i twulfph hert.]

quuae, quanue. Sue **quaun.**

quecifu, *kjin-en, kwin'un,* en U.F. *kju-nin, n.* i cokourlesf, unodorous, very butper ikkileo, got from cunchoni dirk, or on of ehf suktf, used igiunfp melrii und fevurs. [feu **quina**.]

quegnat, *kwin'uh, n.* the kung-sikmon. [From ni

The words in semi-bold, hung out to the left are headwords, suggesting a list of entries. The words in italics divided up with hyphens are spelt out phonetically. This is a dictionary.

The functions of book typography

Book typography is perhaps the most understated style of typographic communication. The quantity of words involved – tens, sometimes hundreds of thousands – places a particular set of demands and restrictions on the designer. Books are often read for hours at a time, and may contain complex structures of information. Both these issues must be addressed if a book is to serve its purpose. The functions of book typography can be described as follows:

> **readability**: making the text comfortable to read
> **organization**: communicating the structure of the text
> **navigation**: leading the reader through the text in a particular order;
>   making information easy to locate
> **consistency**: creating a unified whole

Readability

A number of typographic conventions have evolved to make text easier to read. In the context of book design these are mainly concerned with *continuous text*, that is, long passages of text set in lines to form a block. Anything that confuses the eye or makes it stumble, forms a barrier between the reader and the words.

Organization

Every text has a structure. A novel may be divided into chapters. A reference book may be sub-divided into small sub-sections which the reader can locate easily and 'dip into'. Communicating this structure in the design of the book tells the reader what to expect. This involves the styling and placing of various printed elements in a way that makes clear to the reader what they are looking at.

Navigation

Putting the parts of a book in the conventional order – contents page at the front, bibliography at the back – makes it easier for the reader to find their way around. Additional elements such as folios and running heads also assist the reader. This is of particular importance in complex reference works which are not read from end to end.

Consistency

Using the same treatment for each element consistently throughout a book – such as putting all the chapter headings in the same typeface, size and position – creates a unified whole. Changing the style of any element occasionally and for no obvious reason will distract the reader and look like an error.

Creating a consistent text may seem more like an exercise in pedantry than a necessary typographic function, but it is through a consistent treatment of the text that the reader can easily recognize the various printed elements on the page without confusion.

House rules and conventions

Publishing houses take the idea of consistency seriously and apply a set of rules to every publication. These are listed in a document called *house rules*, and deal with the details of language, spelling and punctuation as well as a number of typographic and design issues. Many of these rules are universal, some particular to certain companies.

There are two things worth noting on the subject of house rules. The first is that no detail is considered too small to be worthy of a rule. The cumulative effect of good detailing adds to the feeling of quality and authority.

The second is that the line between editorial and typographic concerns is often blurred. The designer has to bear in mind that many house rules follow a logic that stems from the structure of the language and should not be overridden for the sake of appearance.

The following are examples of the authors' own house rules:

Speech to be indicated by single quotation marks	'quote'	*not*	"quote"
Circa shortened to italic c. with no word-space	*c.*1895	*not*	c. 1895
Use multiplication symbol, not 'x' for dimensions	24 × 36	*not*	24 x 36
Letter-space strings of capital letters	A B C D	*not*	ABCD
Use roman parentheses even in italic text	*aa*(*cc*)*bb*	*not*	*aa(cc)bb*

Some house rules are available commercially, such as *Hart's Rules for Compositors and Readers* and *The Chicago Manual of Style*.

These are used for clients who do not have their own rules established.

LEGIBILITY AND READABILITY

Defining legibility and readability

The word 'legible' is often defined as 'readable' and vice versa, but in typographic terms legibility and readability are not the same thing. The word *legibility* describes the ease with which characters can be recognized and deciphered. Each typeface has an inherent degree of legibility which comes from the design of the characters. The size of type will also have an impact on whether or not a text is legible.

When designing books, however, it is not enough that words can be deciphered. A lengthy, continuous text will need to be read for long periods at a time without causing the reader strain. The *readability* of a text – the ease with which a text is read and understood – depends not just on the legibility of the typeface but on how the text is set on the page.

Text should have a degree of readability appropriate to its use. A small amount of text, which has to hold the reader's attention for a shorter time, can be set with greater freedom than a long text. In the example below, two samples of text have been set in the same font, size and leading. What is readable for the shorter caption is much harder to read at length:

Stone Sans
7.25 on 10 pt
These examples show how a type style that is appropriate for one text may not work for another. Long continuous text has to hold the reader's attention for more time, so setting it at a readable size is of great importance.

FIG.2 The celebrated 'First Folio': a legendary rarity and Soane's greatest literary treasure. See cat.8.1

In January winter was lazy to the extent of making do with December's snow which, thanks to continuing frost, still blanketed the earth. Shop windows still had their New Year decorations, but the festive spirit had waned, leaving folk alone with the old routine and the future. Viktor was processing his next batch of files. He now received all documents direct from the Chief, Fyodor having retired before the New Year break.

The *obelisk* index was growing steadily. These latest files were on directors of major factories and chairmen of joint-stock companies. Almost all were charged with the theft of funds and their transfer to Western banks. Some were dealing in banned raw materials, others contriving to barter off plant abroad. Facts were legion, but mercifully not all were underlined in the Chief's red pencil. Viktor's task was not easy. He either ran short of philosophy, or lacked inspiration, as each obelisk now involved tense hours at the typewriter. And though, in the end, he was pleased with the result, fatigue weighed heavily upon him, leaving little energy to spare for Sonya or the penguin. So it was as well that he had, at Sonya's insistence, bought a colour television on their return from

Regularity and rhythm

The only way to test the readability of a piece of setting is to read it. Try to be aware of the speed and rhythm of your eyes' movement along the lines, whether it requires an effort to retain focus and direction and whether you repeat or skip lines. You will find that a regular rhythm is more comfortable for the eyes; this is because reading is a repetitive act. Achieving a good level of readability requires that text is set in an even, regular way.

The following examples are exaggerated to show how irregularity disrupts the rhythm of reading, slowing down the eyes. Irregular word-spacing like this:

> Having seen their fill of   the penguin, the visitors ate, drank and told jokes. Viktor   began   to find these   festivities wearisome and   to look forward to their termination.   It was not slow   in coming.   One of the girls suddenly   started

Joanna
11.5 on 16.5 pt
These examples are quite extreme, but the eye picks up even the most subtle irregularity.

or shifting the alignment of some words:

> Having seen their fill of the penguin, the visitors ate, drank and told jokes. Viktor began to find these festivities wearisome and to look forward to their termination. It was not slow in coming. One of the girls suddenly started wailing drunkenly to the effect

Joanna
11.5 on 16.5 pt

or changing the type style:

> *Having* seen **their fill of** the **penguin**, the *visitors* **ate**, drank and TOLD jokes. VIKTOR began **to find** these FESTIVITIES *wearisome* and to **look** f o r w a r d to their ***termination***. It was not **slow in** coming. ONE of the **girls suddenly** started *wailing*

Garamond roman, italic, small caps, semi-bold, semi-bold italic, semi-bold small caps, bold, bold italic, 11.5 on 16.5 pt variable ICS

make it harder for the eye to move smoothly along the line.

Type size and readability

When readers describe text as difficult to read, the reason most frequently given is that it is too small. However there is no 'minimum' size that can usefully be specified because two typefaces reproduced at the same point size will not necessarily look the same size due to the differences in x-height and set.

Added to this, some typefaces are more legible at smaller sizes than others, so the minimum size of your type depends on which typeface you choose.

The following example shows three typefaces – Centaur (*top*), Stone Print (*middle*) and Scala (*bottom*) – set in a range of sizes from 9 pt to 12 pt:

9 pt be down in the town with his wheelbarrow every morning, just as people

10 pt be down in the town with his wheelbarrow every morning, just as people

11 pt be down in the town with his wheelbarrow every morning, just as people

12 pt be down in the town with his wheelbarrow every morning, just as people

9 pt be down in the town with his wheelbarrow every morning, just as people

10 pt be down in the town with his wheelbarrow every morning, just as people

11 pt be down in the town with his wheelbarrow every morning, just as people

12 pt be down in the town with his wheelbarrow every morning, just as people

9 pt be down in the town with his wheelbarrow every morning, just as people

10 pt be down in the town with his wheelbarrow every morning, just as people

11 pt be down in the town with his wheelbarrow every morning, just as people

12 pt be down in the town with his wheelbarrow every morning, just as people

The size at which each typeface becomes readable varies. Centaur needs to be printed at at least 12 pt. Stone Print, though narrow has a large x-height and looks readable at 11 pt. Scala is a large typeface and looks too big in the larger sizes.

Make a note of typefaces you find which read well at smaller sizes. They will be useful for texts containing footnotes, tables or other matter which requires a smaller setting.

Spacing and readability

The relationship between word-spacing and leading is key to creating a text with good readability.

When the word-spacing is tight, the leading can be tight:

The next day they wouldn't let me go outside. I stood staring out of the window and all the people who passed by looked to me like shrunken shadows, as if winter had suddenly started and the wind had blown away all the sparrows in the

Spectrum
11.5 on 13.5 pt

But widely spaced lines with tight leading make it harder for the eye to travel along the line, as the space between words is greater than the space between the lines:

The next day they wouldn't let me go outside. I stood staring out of the window and all the people who passed by looked to me like shrunken shadows, as if winter had suddenly started and the wind had blown away all the sparrows in the

Spectrum
11.5 on 12 pt

The leading would need to be increased:

The next day they wouldn't let me go outside. I stood staring out of the window and all the people who passed by looked to me like shrunken shadows, as if winter had suddenly started and the wind had blown away all the sparrows in the

Spectrum
11.5 on 15.5 pt
This example
with over-wide
word-spacing is
far from ideal,
but illustrates
a principle: that
leading should
be visually
greater than
word-spacing.

A similar relationship exists between letter-spacing and word-spacing. Lines that have been letter-spaced will need larger word spaces:

ENGLISH POETRY IN THE TWENTIETH CENTURY

Gill Sans, 11.5 pt

ENGLISH POETRY IN THE TWENTIETH CENTURY

Gill Sans
11.5 pt, 30 ICS

Inter-related elements

Letter-spacing, word-spacing and leading are just three of the elements that can be adjusted to improve readability. This diagram shows how these and other elements are linked. Changing any one will have an impact on the others.

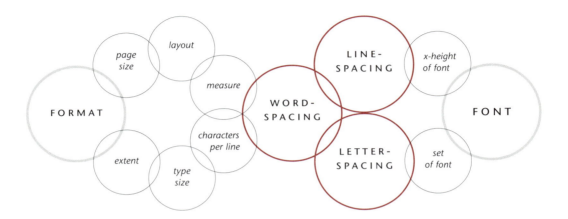

Experiment with a variety of text treatments, adjusting one element at a time and noting how each change affects the overall readability of the page.

The passage opposite shows an example of this. It starts in Times Roman 12 pt set solid (that is, with no leading) and ranged left, and the changes are as follows:

1 change the font from Times to Albertina
2 reduce the size from 12 pt to 10.5 pt
3 increase the word-spacing
4 justify the text
5 reduce the measure from 106 mm to 96 mm
6 increase the leading from 12 pt to 13.5 pt

It is interesting to note that the first and last samples occupy approximately the same space on the page. This shows that setting the type at a larger size is not necessarily the way to make text easier to read. It is the relationship between the different elements that provides the key to setting readable text.

One row of the market was set aside for reproductions of famous paintings and original portraits in oil. The portraits showed long dead burghers, and brides and bridegrooms from provincial towns; all of them, judging by their faces, took pleasure in themselves and were satisfied with the life that had come their

Times Roman
12 on 12 pt

1 One row of the market was set aside for reproductions of famous paintings and original portraits in oil. The portraits showed long dead burghers, and brides and bridegrooms from provincial towns; all of them, judging by their faces, took pleasure in themselves and were satisfied with the life that had come their

Albertina
12 on 12 pt
Change of font

2 One row of the market was set aside for reproductions of famous paintings and original portraits in oil. The portraits showed long dead burghers, and brides and bridegrooms from provincial towns; all of them, judging by their faces, took pleasure in themselves and were satisfied with the life that had come their way. Behind these figures there was sometimes a church in

Albertina
10.5 on 12 pt
Reduction in
type size

3 One row of the market was set aside for reproductions of famous paintings and original portraits in oil. The portraits showed long dead burghers, and brides and bridegrooms from provincial towns; all of them, judging by their faces, took pleasure in themselves and were satisfied with the life that had come their way. Behind these figures there

Albertina
10.5 on 12 pt
Increase in
word-spacing

4 One row of the market was set aside for reproductions of famous paintings and original portraits in oil. The portraits showed long dead burghers, and brides and bridegrooms from provincial towns; all of them, judging by their faces, took pleasure in themselves and were satisfied with the life that had come their way. Behind these figures

Albertina
10.5 on 12 pt
Change from
ranged left to
justified

5 One row of the market was set aside for reproductions of famous paintings and original portraits in oil. The portraits showed long dead burghers, and brides and bridegrooms from provincial towns; all of them, judging by their faces, took pleasure in themselves and were satisfied with the life that had come their way.

Albertina
10.5 on 12 pt
Reduction of
measure

6 One row of the market was set aside for reproductions of famous paintings and original portraits in oil. The portraits showed long dead burghers, and brides and bridegrooms from provincial towns; all of them, judging by their faces, took pleasure in themselves and were satisfied with the life that had come their way.

Albertina
10.5 on 13.5 pt
Increase in leading

PART TWO

THE TEXT PANEL

FORMAT

When a book goes into production, one of the first decisions to be made is the *format* – the size and shape of the pages – in which it will be published. This is the choice of the publisher and will depend upon the style and content of the book, as well as financial and marketing concerns.

Trade formats

Over many years the publishing trade has developed a series of standard book sizes – *trade formats* – which are used for the majority of publications:

Royal
234 x 156

Demy
216 x 136

A5
210 x 148

B-format
198 x 129

A-format
180 x 111

Measurements shown here may vary slightly from publisher to publisher and printer to printer. They are specified in millimetres.

Height is always given before width.

The royal format is usually seen as a hardback. The b-format is the most common form of mass-market paperback. The page area varies considerably within these formats: the a-format is just over half the size of the royal. The proportions also vary: the demy is noticeably narrower than the A5.

Specialist publishing houses, such as those producing guide books or law books, will often have their own formats suited to the specific needs of their market.

See *Progressive formats*, pp.334–7

The choice of format has an impact on the price at which the book can be sold. A well-tried procedure exists whereby books are published first in hardback, and then re-issued at intervals in paperback formats, each smaller and cheaper than the previous edition. This is done to appeal to an even wider range of readers.

Format, paper sizes and presses

If you are not bound by the constraints of trade publishing, you may be free to design the format of the page yourself. This gives you more choice, but unless your budget is unlimited, some restrictions will still apply.

Paper manufacturers produce papers at sizes that will accommodate trade formats efficiently. Printing presses are designed to print on papers at these sizes. If you want to produce a book with an unusual format, review the paper sizes in consultation with the printer to ensure that the proposed format can be printed within the budget. This means finding a page size which cuts out of a sheet without too much wastage and, importantly, with the grain running in the right direction.

See *Paper choices*, p.401

The finishing and binding machinery also have minimum and maximum sizes. If a format does not fit within these ranges, alternative binding techniques will have to be used which are usually more expensive.

Designing a format

The format of a book will not only affect how it looks and feels as an object, but how it functions. When designing your format you should consider:

Formats for illustrated books are discussed on pp.289–90

how will the book be used: will it be held in the hands, laid open on a desk or carried around in a pocket?

use of space: do you want spacious pages with large margins, or something more economical?

content: is your format suitable for the sort of book you plan? How many pages will it make?

text style: do you want a narrow text panel or a wide one? What shape page will suit it best? What size would be sympathetic to the style of the typography you wish to use?

In answering these questions you will begin to develop a page size on which you can start the trial layouts. The format may then be reviewed and revised during the design process in order to produce the best result.

Proportions

Landscape formats are generally only used for illustrated books.

Books are conventionally taller than they are wide. This is not only because the text panel functions best when it is this shape, but also for practical reasons – binding down the longer edge makes for a stronger object.

The following page proportions vary from the narrow (a double square) to the square and may form a starting point for your designs.

Height is given before width

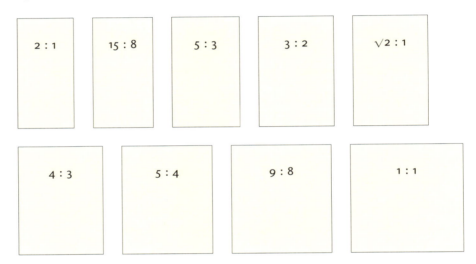

| 2 : 1 | 15 : 8 | 5 : 3 | 3 : 2 | √2 : 1 |

| 4 : 3 | 5 : 4 | 9 : 8 | 1 : 1 |

Narrow pages are easier to work with at larger sizes. A book that is both small and narrow will be hard to keep open, and certainly will not lie flat. A small, narrow page can also put pressure on the margins because the text panel is too close to the gutter.

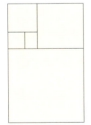

The golden section

One of the reasons for using narrow formats is their elegance. The golden section (approx. 8 : 5) has informed our understanding of proportions since Classical times and is still used by designers. The standard a-format paperback (180 × 111 mm) uses these proportions.

When choosing a narrow format, bear in mind that the text panel will probably have to be narrower too. This will have an effect on the choice of typeface and the size of the type. Talk to the printers about how much the gutter margin may be reduced by the binding mechanism.

Wider pages tend to be chosen for practical reasons. The extra width allows for large margins which may contain sidenotes or headings. Multi-column settings also require a wider page.

There is a limit to how wide the text panel can be without compromising readability. The challenge in using a wide page, therefore, lies in achieving a balance between the shape of the page and the shape of the text panel. There will be more space on the page, in the form of larger fore-edge or gutter margins.

Of the proportions shown opposite, $\sqrt{2} : 1$ will be familiar. These are the proportions of the ISO range of paper sizes, such as A4. Over-familiarity with this format can make it unattractive. It needs a contrasting text block and some sophisticated type design to avoid the appearance of having come straight out of a word processing program.

Making an A4 or A5 page slightly narrower or shorter will give a better-looking result without losing the economic benefits of using a standard paper size.

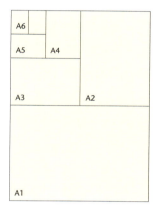

The ISO (International Organization for Standardization) range of paper sizes. As the sheet is halved, the proportions remain the same. Sheets of paper are supplied to printers slightly oversized (called SRA1, SRA2 or SRA3) so they can be trimmed down to the A sizes.

Size

The content of a book will place obvious constraints on how big or small the page can be, but there are other issues to consider. What kind of object are you trying to produce? Will readers want to carry it around, or will it sit on a shelf to be referred to when necessary? How much will they pay for it?

Making a book larger will make it appear more authoritative and permanent, but this is not necessarily appropriate for all subject matter. A book which is physically grand but light on content will look pretentious.

Larger pages provide flexibility in terms of layout and allow for more space on the page. Smaller books are less intimidating and more practical for the reader. These conflicting factors must be weighed up in conjunction with the budget and the marketing plan.

LAYING OUT THE TEXT PANEL

There are two aspects to designing a panel of text. The first is how the text inside the panel looks. The choices you will have to make about this are:

Publishers will usually ask to see trial pages of a design before the designer starts the layout. Trials should show a selection of different sorts of pages – for example, a spread containing just text, a chapter opening and a couple of prelim pages such as the title page and the contents page.

which typeface to use
what size to set the type in
whether to set the type justified or ranged left
how tight or loose the word spacing should be
how much leading to apply between the lines

These decisions will define how the text looks.

The second aspect is the size and shape of the text panel and how it sits on the page. The choices you will have to make about this are:

width of the measure
number of lines-per-page
size of margins
symmetrical or asymmetrical position

There are also a number of pragmatic and editorial considerations including:

extent
effect of binding methods on the margins
additional elements, such as running heads, folios and footnotes
possible reduction in size of subsequent editions

Each choice you make will affect other decisions.

This chapter discusses all these factors one by one, but in practice it is not a step-by-step process. Try to be mindful when reading each section of the relationships between each of these separate elements.

Characters-per-line in justified setting

In justified setting, the relationship between the *measure* – that is, the length of the line – and the number of characters in it, is very important.

This is one of the few occasions where a rule exists: that lines of continuous justified text should ideally contain an average of between 66 and 72 characters, including word spaces – that is approximately 9 to 11 words.

To appreciate why this is the case, try reading these lines, containing a greater number of characters, quickly:

Quadraat
10.25 on 15 pt
Measure: 154 mm
approximately 98
characters-per-line

He had dreamt once of writing novels, but had not achieved so much as a novella, in spite of all the unfinished manuscripts lying around in folders. But unfinished they were fated to remain, he having been unlucky with his muses, they, for some reason, having never tarried long enough in his two-room flat to see him through a short story. Hence his literary failure. They had been amazingly fickle, his muses. Or he had been at fault for picking such unreliable ones. But now, alone with his penguin, here he was,

The eye travels a greater distance and produces a longer pause between the end of one line and the start of the next. It may go back to the start of the wrong line, interrupting the rhythm, and making comprehension difficult.

The problems of lines containing fewer characters are more apparent:

He had dreamt once of writing novels, but had not achieved so much as a novella, in spite of all the unfinished manuscripts lying around in folders. But unfinished they were fated to remain, he having been unlucky with his muses, they, for some reason, having never tarried long enough in his two-room flat to see him through a short story. Hence his literary failure. They had been

Joanna
10.5 on 13 pt
Measure: 75 mm
approximately 50
characters-per-line

The wide and irregular word spaces create white *rivers* of space flowing down the text. The eye can jump from one line to the next, mid-line, creating confusion for the reader.

The reason for the variable word spaces can be seen if you range left some text, set in different measures.

Quadraat
10.25 on 15 pt
Measure: 104 mm

He had dreamt once of writing novels, but had not achieved so much as a novella, in spite of all the unfinished manuscripts lying around in folders. But unfinished they were fated to remain, he having been unlucky with his muses, they, for some reason, having never tarried long enough in his two-room flat to see him through a short story.

Quadraat
10.25 on 15 pt
Measure: 58 mm

He had dreamt once of writing novels, but had not achieved so much as a novella, in spite of all the unfinished manuscripts lying around in folders. But unfinished they were fated to remain, he having

The amount of space (indicated in grey) left at the end of the lines is about the same, but in the long measure this is divided between eleven or twelve spaces:

Quadraat
10.25 on 15 pt
Measure: 104 mm

He had dreamt once of writing novels, but had not achieved so much as a novella, in spite of all the unfinished manuscripts lying around in folders. But unfinished they were fated to remain, he having been unlucky with his muses, they, for some reason, having never tarried long enough in his two-room flat to see him through a short story.

Whereas in the short measure, the same amount of space is divided between five or six spaces:

Quadraat
10.25 on 15 pt
Measure: 58 mm

He had dreamt once of writing novels, but had not achieved so much as a novella, in spite of all the unfinished manuscripts lying around in folders. But unfinished they were fated to remain, he having

This is what creates the larger word spaces in lines containing fewer characters.

LAYING OUT THE TEXT PANEL

Choosing a measure

Choosing a measure is a matter of finding a balance between what produces a well spaced line of text and what width text panel fits best on the page.

Place a line of about 70 characters on the page and see what effect adjustments in type size will make to the width of the margins – in this case the page is 156 mm wide. Establish the smallest and largest type you find acceptable.

Minion
9 pt to 12 pt
in increments
of 0.5 pt

1   He had dreamt once of writing novels, but had not achieved so much as a   9

2   He had dreamt once of writing novels, but had not achieved so much as a   9.5

3   He had dreamt once of writing novels, but had not achieved so much as a   10

4   He had dreamt once of writing novels, but had not achieved so much as a   10.5

5   He had dreamt once of writing novels, but had not achieved so much as a   11

6   He had dreamt once of writing novels, but had not achieved so much as a   11.5

7   He had dreamt once of writing novels, but had not achieved so much as a   12

← 111 mm →
← 116 mm →

Here, lines 4, 5 and 6 look the most readable, but 6 is too long for the width of the page – the margins would be too narrow. A text panel similar in appearance to lines 4 or 5 would produce a measure of between 111 mm and 116 mm on a page that is 156 mm wide.

This gives us a guide with which trial settings may be compared. It is now a matter of finding a combination of typeface, size and measure that falls within these parameters. The type should not look smaller than line 4 or it will be hard to read. The measure should not exceed 116 mm or the margins will be too narrow.

It is possible to reduce the number of characters-per-line if necessary. This can be done easily in texts containing a lot of dialogue, but becomes more difficult if a text contains long proper names which cannot be divided. An increased number of word divisions is an inevitable consequence of reducing the characters-per-line.

If large margins are needed for sidenotes or illustrations some compromise on line-length may be necessary.

One way of using a narrow measure without reducing number of characters-per-line is to choose a narrow typeface.

The size and width of typefaces

Choosing text fonts is discussed in the next chapter, but some of their characteristics are relevant here. Most important in this context is the fact that not all typefaces look the same size: 10 pt in one typeface will look different to 10 pt in another. The following lines demonstrate this: each containing 70 characters, they are all set in 10 pt, but in different fonts.

See *Typeface characteristics*, pp.76–86

Stone Print, 10 pt — this is the beginning of understanding the complexities of text panels

Albertina, 10 pt — this is the beginning of understanding the complexities of text panels

Garamond, 10 pt — this is the beginning of understanding the complexities of text panels

Walbaum, 10 pt — this is the beginning of understanding the complexities of text panels

The difference in the visual size of the fonts it due to the variation in x-height, width and weight. Adjusting the sizes so they look the same visually, in other words, making the x-heights about the same, produces this result:

Stone Print, 10.6 pt — this is the beginning of understanding the complexities of text panels

Albertina, 10 pt — this is the beginning of understanding the complexities of text panels

Garamond, 11 pt — this is the beginning of understanding the complexities of text panels

Walbaum, 9.1 pt — this is the beginning of understanding the complexities of text panels

This shows that some typefaces are proportionately wider than others, producing a longer line from the same number of characters. A relationship exists, therefore, between the choice of typeface and the width of the measure.

This gives us five factors to consider when deciding on a measure:

width of the page – the one factor you may not have control over
width of the margins
number of characters-per-line
choice of typeface
type size

The examples opposite show a variety of solutions on measures of between 94 mm and 116 mm.

On a measure of 111 mm:

He had dreamt once of writing novels, but had not achieved so much as a   Joanna, 10.5 pt
He had dreamt once of writing novels, but had not achieved so much as a   Sabon, 9.75 pt
He had dreamt once of writing novels, but had not achieved so much as a   Requiem, 10.5 pt

On a measure of 116 mm:

He had dreamt once of writing novels, but had not achieved so much as a   Garamond, 11.25 pt
He had dreamt once of writing novels, but had not achieved so much as a   Centaur, 12 pt
He had dreamt once of writing novels, but had not achieved so much as a   Bembo, 10.75 pt

Using narrower typefaces, at 108 mm and 113 mm:

He had dreamt once of writing novels, but had not achieved so much as a   Stone Print, 11 pt
He had dreamt once of writing novels, but had not achieved so much as a   Albertina, 10 pt
He had dreamt once of writing novels, but had not achieved so much as a   Quadraat, 10 pt

He had dreamt once of writing novels, but had not achieved so much as a   Stone Print, 11.5 pt
He had dreamt once of writing novels, but had not achieved so much as a   Albertina, 10.5 pt
He had dreamt once of writing novels, but had not achieved so much as a   Quadraat, 10.5 pt

Reducing the number of characters-per-line to an average of 60, measure 94 mm:

He had dreamt once of writing novels, but had not achieved so
much as a novella, in spite of all the unfinished manuscripts
lying around in folders. But unfinished they were fated to
remain, he having been unlucky with his muses, they, for some

Quadraat
10.5 on 15 pt
Reducing the measure
in this way will make
it more difficult to
achieve even spacing.

He had dreamt once of writing novels, but had not achieved
so much as a novella, in spite of all the unfinished manuscripts
lying around in folders. But unfinished they were fated to
remain, he having been unlucky with his muses, they, for some

Collis, 10 on 15 pt

Leading the text panel

Leading is the space separating lines of type – the more leading, the further apart the lines. The amount of leading in a panel of text will have an impact on the readability of that text.

See *Readability*, p.23

Just as the visual size of type varies between typefaces, the leading required also varies. Typefaces with a small x-height have more space 'built in' between the lines, as can be seen when they are *set solid*, that is, with no leading:

Perpetua
11 on 11 pt

Perry became wild and mute in his heart, and his mind was finally silent. There was no use in beginning any serious endeavour. He knew the justice of the Tsar awaited him. He did, however, write briefly to the British ambassador in Petersburg, begging him to rescue a subject of the

Compare this to type with a large x-height, with no leading:

Minion
9.5 on 9.5 pt

Perry became wild and mute in his heart, and his mind was finally silent. There was no use in beginning any serious endeavour. He knew the justice of the Tsar awaited him. He did, however, write briefly to the British ambassador in Petersburg, begging him to rescue a subject of the British King. But

Leading should be determined visually and not by using a fixed percentage of the type size. Here are the same two examples set to look equally leaded:

Perpetua
11 on 13 pt

Perry became wild and mute in his heart, and his mind was finally silent. There was no use in beginning any serious endeavour. He knew the justice of the Tsar awaited him. He did, however, write briefly to the British ambassador in Petersburg, begging him to rescue a subject of

Minion
9.5 on 13.5 pt

Perry became wild and mute in his heart, and his mind was finally silent. There was no use in beginning any serious endeavour. He knew the justice of the Tsar awaited him. He did, however, write briefly to the British ambassador in Petersburg, begging him to rescue a subject of the British King. But

A software feature called *auto leading* automatically changes the leading in proportion to the type size. The default setting is usually either 20 or 25 per cent.

The first is in Perpetua, the type size is 11 pt and the leading is set at 13 pt. The leading is 18 per cent more than the type size. The second is Minion, with a type size of 9.5 pt and leading of 13.5 pt. The leading is 42 per cent more than the type size.

The space between lines should look greater than the space between words for maximum readability, but lines should not be so far apart that they look detached.

The light from the oil lamp cast flickering shadows about the room. Jaime Astarloa reached out his hand to work the mechanism of the wick, raising it a little until the brightness grew. With his pencil he drew another two lines on the sheet of paper, forming the vertex of an angle, and joined the two ends with an arc. Seventy-five degrees,

Galliard, 10 on 11 pt
Space between lines is smaller than spaces between words. This makes it difficult to follow a line.

The light from the oil lamp cast flickering shadows about the room. Jaime Astarloa reached out his hand to work the mechanism of the wick, raising it a little until the brightness grew. With his pencil he drew another two lines on the sheet of paper, forming the vertex of an angle, and joined the two ends with an arc. Seventy-five degrees,

Galliard, 10 on 12 pt
This is the default 'auto' setting for some layout programs. Still too tight.

The light from the oil lamp cast flickering shadows about the room. Jaime Astarloa reached out his hand to work the mechanism of the wick, raising it a little until the brightness grew. With his pencil he drew another two lines on the sheet of paper, forming the vertex of an angle, and joined the two ends with an arc. Seventy-five degrees,

Galliard, 10 on 13 pt
This is an improve-ment. A tight setting when saving space is an issue.

The light from the oil lamp cast flickering shadows about the room. Jaime Astarloa reached out his hand to work the mechanism of the wick, raising it a little until the brightness grew. With his pencil he drew another two lines on the sheet of paper, forming the vertex of an angle, and joined the two ends with an arc. Seventy-five degrees,

Galliard, 10 on 14 pt
Generously leaded and readable. It would be possible to read this for long periods.

The light from the oil lamp cast flickering shadows about the room. Jaime Astarloa reached out his hand to work the mechanism of the wick, raising it a little until the brightness grew. With his pencil he drew another two lines on the sheet of paper, forming the vertex of an angle, and joined the two ends with an arc. Seventy-five degrees,

Galliard, 10 on 15 pt
Becoming loose; the lines are losing connection with each other.

The light from the oil lamp cast flickering shadows about the room. Jaime Astarloa reached out his hand to work the mechanism of the wick, raising it a little until the brightness grew. With his pencil he drew another two lines on the sheet of paper, forming the vertex of an angle, and joined the two ends with an arc. Seventy-five degrees,

Galliard, 10 on 16 pt
This looks as if the text is being stretched out to fill space. Much too loose.

The x-height is not the only factor to determine how much leading a panel of type needs. Line length and the weight of the type are also important.

A narrow measure will require more leading:

flickering shadows about the room. Jaime Astarloa reached out his hand to work the mechanism of the wick, raising it a little until the brightness grew. With his pencil he drew another two lines on the sheet of paper, forming the vertex of an angle, and joined the two ends with an arc. Seventy-five degrees, more or less. That

cast flickering shadows about the room. Jaime Astarloa reached out his hand to work the mechanism of the wick, raising it a little until the brightness grew. With his pencil he drew another two lines on the sheet of paper, forming the vertex of an angle, and joined the two ends with an arc. Seventy-five degrees, more or less. That was the

As will a dark typeface compared with a lighter typeface:

Centaur
12.5 on 14.5 pt
Centaur is not only
a small typeface,
it is also light in
weight. This means
it requires very
little leading.

The light from the oil lamp cast flickering shadows about the room. Jaime Astarloa reached out his hand to work the mech-anism of the wick, raising it a little until the brightness grew. With his pencil he drew another two lines on the sheet of paper, forming the vertex of an angle, and joined the two ends with an arc. Seventy-five degrees, more or less. That was the margin within which one should move the foil. He noted the

Quadraat
10.5 on 15.5 pt
Quadraat requires
more leading to
prevent the text
panel from
appearing too
dark and dense.

The light from the oil lamp cast flickering shadows about the room. Jaime Astarloa reached out his hand to work the mech-anism of the wick, raising it a little until the brightness grew. With his pencil he drew another two lines on the sheet of paper, forming the vertex of an angle, and joined the two ends with an arc. Seventy-five degrees, more or less. That was the margin within which one should move the foil. He noted the

Leading and backing up

Leading should be consistent throughout a book so that when the pages are backed up – that is when the second side of the sheet is printed – the lines of text on one side of the page line up directly with those on the reverse of the page. If this is not done, text on the reverse will *show through* between the lines of type like this:

> fought the police. I was out there with the student strikers and showed up at political rallies. I met some wild characters that way, but my heart was never in politics. Linking arms with strangers at demonstrations made me uneasy and when we had to hurl stones at the cops I asked myself if this was really *me*. Was this what I wanted? I wondered. I couldn't feel the requisite solidarity with the people around me. The

This effect is more marked on lighter weight papers

This reduces legibility as the show-through blurs the form of the words.

Lines-per-page: the depth of the text panel

Continuous text is usually set in panels that are taller than they are wide. Convention has established that a page should have between 32 and 38 lines, though this is not nearly as crucial as the number of characters-per-line and also depends on the size and format of the page.

The depth of the text panel will define the size of your head and foot margins. If the panel shares the page with other printed elements, such as folios or running heads, this will have an influence on how deep the text panel will be, so they should be included on trial spreads.

See *Folios and running heads*, pp.200–5

The depth of the text panel is kept consistent throughout a book. However, in the US, some pages are set one line long or one line short as a way of manipulating the text and avoiding widows, orphans and bad word divisions. This should be done in spreads, that is, both pages on a spread should either lose a line or gain a line so that the baselines of the pair of pages line up. The leading itself should not be changed to compensate for the difference in depth on such pages.

See *Manual adjustments to composition*, pp.107–10

Proportions of the text panel

Having established the measure of the text panel, its depth will give you the final proportions of the panel. A possible starting point is to give the text panel the same proportions as the page. This will produce a harmonious result when using one of the standard-format page sizes:

A text panel which contrasts with the proportions of the page – for example, a wide page with a narrow text panel – will introduce more space into the layout in the form of wider margins. Pages which are squarer in format will look more elegant with a narrower text panel:

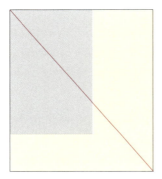 

Square or landscape-format books can be problematic when it comes to deciding the dimensions of your text panel. Mirroring the proportions of the page is rarely a solution if continuous text is being set. Using a contrasting text panel or a multiple-column layout is more likely to provide a satisfactory result. This is necessary in large illustrated books where the format of the book is determined by the format of the illustrations.

Square-format page with double-column text panel

Landscape-format page with single-column portrait-format text panel

Coverage

As margins are reduced and the text panel enlarged, the proportion of the page to be printed on increases significantly:

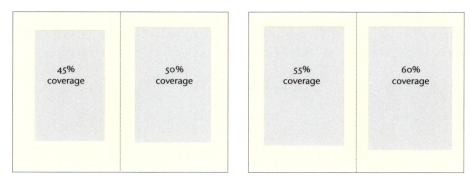

45%
coverage

50%
coverage

55%
coverage

60%
coverage

The example on the right (coverage: 60 per cent) has a text panel which is 34 per cent larger than that on the far left (coverage: 45 per cent). Thus the number of words in a text panel will be increased by about a third.

See *Extent and words-per-page*, pp.224–31

Positioning the text panel: margins

The positioning of the text panel on the page defines the book's margins. The main function of margins is to frame the text panel, separating the text from the world around it. They also allow the book to be handled without damage to the text. The size and proportions of a book's margins are integral to the style of a book, but are also affected by more practical considerations.

Mechanical factors affecting the margins

When the printed sheets are folded and trimmed, the fore-edge margins of the inner sheets are narrowed:

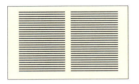  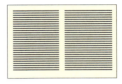

Laid out on screen the fore-edge margins may appear to be sufficient.

As the sheet is folded into a signature and trimmed the inner pages have their fore-edge margin narrowed more than the outer sheets.

Although this effect is unlikely to be more 1–2 mm, a narrow fore-edge margin will be further narrowed in the inner pages of every signature.

The binding mechanism will also reduce the gutter margins. This is especially so in paperbacks with over 200 pages, which may force the reader to 'break the back' of the book to see the words in the gutter. Shorter books or brochures that are *perfect bound* lose up to 5 mm of each of the gutter margins when opened:

This should be anticipated at the layout stage and an increased margin used.

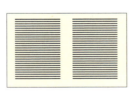 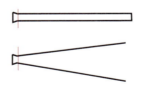 

Laid out on screen the gutter margins may seem sufficient.

The binding will take up between 3 and 5 mm of the gutter margin.

The gutter is now reduced and it is not easy for the reader to see the line ends.

The layout program and page proofs will show you flat spreads. A book is a three-dimensional object and should be designed allowing for the mechanical processes that produce it.

The lines below demonstrate the effect of this book's binding on the gutter margin.

set with a gutter margin of 0 mm — this is the edge of the page

ext set with a gutter margin of 5 mm

Text set with a gutter margin of 10 mm

Text set with a gutter margin of 15 mm

Text set with a gutter margin of 20 mm

Text set with a gutter margin of 25 mm — the margin in this book

This is not a comment on our printer and binder, merely a demonstration of the mechanical effects that you must be aware of when determining your margins.

When positioning text panels on a spread, first draw up guides showing how close you can go to the edges of the pages.

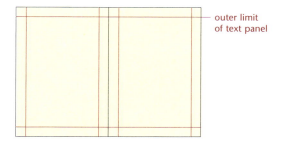

outer limit
of text panel

The text panel will be placed somewhere within this area.

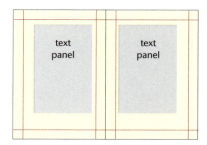

Positioning the text panel: gutter and fore-edge

The first decision to make about your gutter and fore-edge margins is whether the layout is to be symmetrical (*left*) or asymmetrical (*right*).

A symmetrical layout is one in which the gutter margins are the same on verso and recto, and the fore-edge margins are the same on verso and recto. This layout is the more conventional of the two and will be dealt with first. Asymmetric layouts are discussed on pp.50–53.

Symmetrical layouts

Looking at a spread of two pages, what you actually see is three margins: the two fore-edge margins, and the gutter margins joining together to make one central margin. Making these three margins the same will produce a layout in which the text panels appear equally spaced within the spread:

Text panels placed to produce three even margins. The fore-edge margin is twice the size of the gutter margin.

Using our previous example of a page 156 mm wide, with a measure of 112 mm, this approach would produce the following:

He had dreamt once of writing novels, but had not achieved so much as a

However, 15 mm would be too narrow a gutter margin for a paperback. The text panel would need moving towards the fore-edge by about 5 mm to compensate for the mechanical effects of the binding:

The grey block on the left represents the part of the gutter margin lost in the binding process.

He had dreamt once of writing novels, but had not achieved so much as a

In some cases you may want a much wider fore-edge margin to accommodate sidenotes, or to give extra flexibility when placing illustrations:

Even here, the gutter margin should not be reduced too much. The wide fore-edge margin is achieved by a reduction in the measure, and using a narrower typeface or a smaller type size if necessary.

He had dreamt once of writing novels, but had not achieved so much as a novella, in spite of all the unfinished manuscripts lying around in folders. But unfinished they were fated to remain, he having been unlucky with his muses, they, for some

Positioning the text panel: head and foot

Just as pictures are usually mounted above the centre within a frame, the text panel is positioned above the centre on the page. This is because a panel placed dead centre looks as though it is slipping down the page:

This page has a text panel which is centred horizontally and vertically. The result is that the text panel looks too low on the page.

On this page the foot margin is one and a half times the depth of the head margin.

The vertical position of your text panel will need to take into account other printed elements on the page, such as folios or running heads.

The head margin should be increased if it is to contain running heads:

Margin to top of text panel: 10 mm

making an irrevocable mistake, it was as if she was choosing a bride for her only son. She remembered her inexplicable partiality for black speckled hens and endeavoured to maintain her objectivity so that this partiality would not distort the precision of her choice. After all, the 'chosen one' could just as well be a white or a rusty brown hen.

GENELE, THE HANDBAG LADY   203

Margin to top of text panel: 13 mm

making an irrevocable mistake, it was as if she was choosing a bride for her only son. She remembered her inexplicable partiality for black speckled hens and endeavoured to maintain her objectivity so that this partiality would not distort the precision of her choice. After all,

The foot margin is usually about 1.5 to 2 times as deep as the head margin. The depth may need to be increased if a long running foot is to be used, as this will have the effect of reducing the margin:

> making an irrevocable mistake, it was as if she was choosing a bride for her only son. She remembered her inexplicable partiality for black speckled hens and endeavoured to maintain her objectivity so that

GENELE, THE HANDBAG LADY 203

Traditional margins

This diagram shows a margin ratio that was commonly used in the earliest days of the production of printed books:

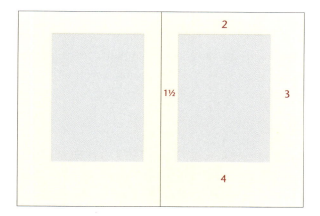

These proportions were developed at a time when books were hand-bound, with no reduction to the gutter margin.

Margins of this size may be considered uneconomical by trade publishers today, but this relative progression from the smallest to the largest margin sizes – gutter, head, fore-edge, foot – is still the most popular solution for laying out books.

The actual size of the book is a factor when determining margins. Large books are not simply scaled-up versions of small books; they have proportionately wider margins. The size of the type does not necessarily double when the size of the book doubles.

Asymmetric layouts

An asymmetrical layout is one in which the left-hand margins are the same on verso and recto, and the right-hand margins are the same on verso and recto.

Some texts, such as poetry and plays, are inherently asymmetric. But the decision to design a book asymmetrically is usually a matter of style, influenced by the content and the typographic style the designer wishes to employ.

For an asymmetric layout to be effective it is important that the asymmetry is noticeable. That is, it needs one large margin and one small one. Placing a text panel just a few millimetres to one side will look like incompetent printing rather than a conscious design decision. For this reason, asymmetry is more practical as a solution in large-format books which have proportionately wider margins.

Asymmetry and backing-up

One disadvantage of an asymmetric layout is that the text panels on the both sides of the page do not appear in the same place – one is close to the gutter, the other close to the fore-edge. The result is show-through down one side of the text panel.

fought the police. I was out there with the student strikers and showed up at political rallies. I met some wild characters that way, but my heart was never in politics. Linking arms with strangers at demonstrations made me uneasy and when

This makes the choice of paper important when setting books asymmetrically. Choose a heavier paper with good opacity to reduce show-through.

Positioning the text panel

Whether your large margin is on the left or the right depends on other elements within your design. If you are setting headings ranged left, and especially if you wish to hang them out, a left-hand margin may be preferable:

Text: Galliard
10.25 on 15 pt
Heading: Stone Sans
13 pt, 30 I C S

UNFINISHED FIGURES

I don't know whether or not I should talk about what happened recently to Custardoy. It's the only time, as far as I know, that he's shown any scruples, or perhaps it was pity. Then again, why

If you are using sidenotes, and setting them ranged left, they will butt up to the text better in a right-hand margin.

Text: Galliard
10.5 on 14 pt
Sidenote: Galliard,
8 on 10 pt

Finally, the fifth proposition was that Karakiri should go bonkers. This appealed to 37% of us.

And so it was decided that, under our kindly guidance and with the help of the wonderful results currently derivable from militant psychopathology's data, Karasteria would fake an auto-suicide attempt and get discharged for rampant schiz-ophrenia, or else paranoia simplex.

The wary reader who adds up the total may find that it exceeds 100%. He would be quite right in deducing that some people voted twice.

Typographic style

Using an asymmetric layout will have an impact on the typographic style of your book: elements such as prelims and headings should also be placed asymmetrically on the page. Asymmetry, being associated with Modernism, is better served by clean, undecorated styling, ranged left setting and modern typefaces, and arguably with content that is in some sense non-traditional.

Ranged left text panels

Ranged left setting
is preferred for
readers with
reading difficulties.
See *Setting text for
special needs*,
pp.344–7

The advantage of setting text ranged left is that the word-spacing is uniform. This makes ranged left setting ideal for narrow measures where, as we have seen, word spacing can be uneven and loose. Whether ranged left setting is suitable for long continuous text is debatable. Lines of unequal length make it harder for the eye to get into the regular rhythm back and forth that is necessary for fast reading, and short lines can send a subconscious signal that a sentence or paragraph is ending which can confuse comprehension. Therefore, when designing a ranged left text, the other factors affecting readability, such as leading and choice of typeface become especially critical.

Measure and word-spacing

The ideal line length of 66 to 72 characters still holds true for ranged left type but, unlike justified setting, the measure may be set considerably narrower without resulting in poor word-spacing. Try to stay near to this ideal for longer texts and use the narrow measure only for smaller quantities of text.

See *Word-spacing*,
pp.100–1

Specifying the word-spacing for ranged left setting is particularly important to ensure that it is even throughout. If it is too loose, words will appear separated from the end of lines:

Minion, 10 on 13 pt
The words 'of',
'buy' and 'a' at
the ends of lines
1, 3 and 7 look
detached from the
rest of the text.

1 who were doing their window shopping. Roney's bar was full of
2 decaying aristocrats, monied nullities and sinister, purposeful
3 people. The shop windows were full of expensive things to buy.
4 Apart from the inevitable and endless boutiques with laden
5 racks of designer clothes and accessories, among them a lot
6 more furriers selling ankle length minks than the Sicilian
7 climate would seem to warrant, there were a lot of jewellers, a

See *Manual
adjustments to
composition*, p.111

Ranged left setting should create fewer word divisions than justified setting. Set a limit on the longest and shortest allowable lines and massage the text, dividing longer words only where absolutely necessary.

Leading

The tightened, even word-spacing of ranged left setting means that less leading is required than for a similar justified setting:

their window shopping. Roney's bar was full of decaying aristocrats, monied nullities and sinister, purposeful people. The shop windows were full of expensive things to buy. Apart from the inevitable and endless boutiques with laden racks of designer clothes and accessories, among them a lot more furriers selling ankle length minks than the

Galliard
10 on 13.5 pt

their window shopping. Roney's bar was full of decaying aristocrats, monied nullities and sinister, purposeful people. The shop windows were full of expensive things to buy. Apart from the inevitable and endless boutiques with laden racks of designer clothes and accessories, among them a lot more furriers selling ankle length minks than the

Galliard
10 on 14.5 pt

Layout

Using a ranged left setting in a symmetrical page layout is difficult as most of the lines will be shorter than the full measure and this will make the right-hand margins look wider.

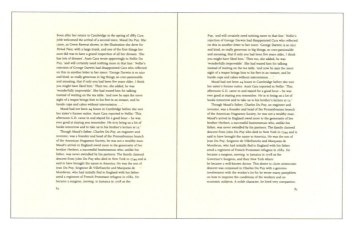

This can be resolved by moving the text panels slightly to the right, but using an asymmetric layout will avoid this problem altogether.

SECTIONS AND PARAGRAPHS

Section breaks

A section break is
also known as a
white line space.

The author will sometimes wish to indicate to the reader that the scene or subject is changing, but not use a heading. This is done with *section breaks*. The simplest form of these is a line space, known as a *line break*:

Joanna, 11 on 15 pt

could develop undisturbed, protected by its charter from the meddling of the nobility and by its walls from the uncertainties of the countryside.

Many European cities during this period became islands of commerce and progress in a sea of inertia, terror, superstition and oppression. This was

If a more emphatic break is required, a larger space containing a decorative device may be used:

Joanna, 11 on 15 pt

Charles V, would have lent special prestige to the then small Amsterdam. In short, it was not only a trade centre but was also a focus of religious life over two centuries, a Canterbury of the Low Countries.

In medieval Amsterdam, secular authority was just as embedded in countless forms of ritual as the spiritual life. Initially quite open, the city was soon surrounded by ramparts and eventually by a wall. This latter devel-

In some cases you may be required to use two different levels of section break in the same book. A combination of single line break and a larger decorated break can be used to deal with this.

See *Manual
adjustments to
composition*, p.109

A section break may appear anywhere on the page, including at the head or foot, but you should avoid having only a single line of text above or below it.

Paragraph indents

The first line of a paragraph is indented. The size of the indent should be consistent throughout the book and is related to the size of the type: the size of indent increases as the type size increases.

The first example below is in 9 pt with an indent of 3 ens. This is equivalent to approximately 5 mm. The second example is in 11 pt and also has an indent of 3 ens. This is equivalent to approximately 6 mm.

> seemed to be within touching distance when it was in fact still an hour's march by sledge.
>   The business with the pachyderm had got the better of the guides' patience. At the first stop after Port Radium, at a place that hired snowmobiles, the dogs were all traded in for three of these vehicles and

Minion, 9 on 13 pt

> seemed to be within touching distance when it was in fact still an hour's march by sledge.
>   The business with the pachyderm had got the better of the guides' patience. At the first stop after Port Radium, at a place that hired snowmobiles, the dogs were all traded in for three of these vehicles and

Minion, 11 on 15 pt

The width of the measure is a factor here. Text set on a wide measure should have a larger indent than that set on a narrow measure. Indents will also need to be increased if the text is loosely leaded.

Paragraphs which follow headings and section breaks are set *full out*, that is without an indent.

This book, you will notice, does not use paragraph indents, but half-line spaces, to indicate paragraphs. This reflects the structure of the text which takes the form of a list of statements rather than one long, continuous narrative. Using this method to indicate paragraphs may be inappropriate for many books, so discuss it with the editor first if you wish to use it.

GRIDS AND MASTER PAGES

The function of a grid

When the dimensions and position of the text panel have been decided, a grid is drawn up. The grid ensures page-by-page consistency of the layout, indicating where various elements should appear on the printed page. The grid for a simple spread containing main text, folios and running heads may look like this:

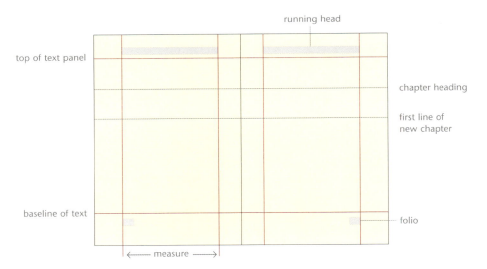

Not every page will contain all these elements, but when they do appear their position and style will be consistent throughout the book.

Master pages

The grid is drawn up in the layout document's *master pages*. The elements placed on the master pages, such as text boxes and rules, will then appear on every page created within the document. The text boxes containing the main text are linked, so that the text will flow automatically from one page to the next. As the text is copied into the document from the word-processing document, the layout program will automatically generate the number of pages needed.

Refining the grid

Even after the text has been flowed into the document it is possible to make refinements to the grid on the master pages. The changes you make will then be automatically applied to all the pages. The most common reason for these adjustments is to achieve the right number of pages. Making a change to the font, type size or leading may also necessitate small adjustments to the grid.

See *Making extent*, pp.234–40

Automatic folios

Layout programs can be instructed to number pages automatically. The font, type size and position of these folio numbers are specified on the master pages. A folio will then appear on each page. On pages which should not have a printed folio, the text box containing it can simply be closed or removed.

Multiple master pages

A layout document can be created using a number of different master pages. You may wish to have linked text boxes for the main text and unlinked boxes for the prelims, or a double-column bibliography, or a triple-column index. These different styles can be created as master pages and introduced into the document as required. One point to bear in mind is that the margins of the book should be consistent throughout, even if the number of columns on a page varies.

Taking time to set up master pages rather than adjusting pages within the document is particularly useful if you are designing a series of books, or if the document is to be passed on to another person for laying out and typesetting.

Relationships within the grid

Not all relationships between the printed elements on the page can be expressed by lines on a grid. For example, if pages contain footnotes, the footnotes will vary in length and the text boxes into which they are put will differ in height and position. Therefore, the consistent placing of footnotes is ensured by a rule: that the last line of the footnote should sit on the baseline of the text panel and that there is a minimum white space of, say, 14 pt between the last line of the main text and first line of the footnote.

See *Footnotes*, pp.209–10

Examples of book grids and master pages

Grids for
illustrated books
are discussed on
pp.286–7, 291–2

These are examples of grids indicating the text panel and other printed elements.

This is a grid for a book containing *sidenotes* which are inset into the text panel. It has wide outer margins and the sidenote column overlaps the text panel. The *running foot* aligns with the outer edge of the text panel and the *folios* align with the outer edge of the sidenote.

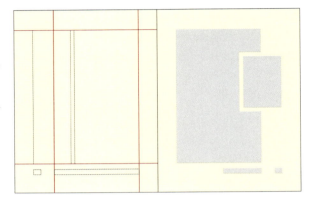

This is a wide-format book with a double-column setting.

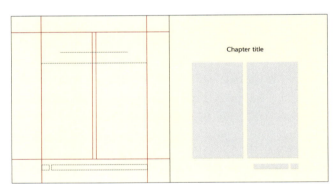

This is an asymmetric layout. The wide right-hand margin could contain headings, notes or illustrations.

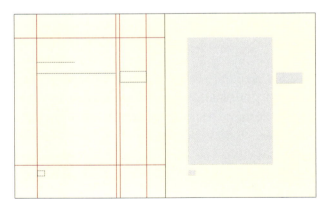

These are examples of the different master pages that may be used within a book.

Main text master pages
The text boxes for the main text are linked, as indicated by the arrow. These master pages also contain *running heads*, *folios* and an indication of where the *chapter titles* will sit and where the text will start on the first page of a new chapter.

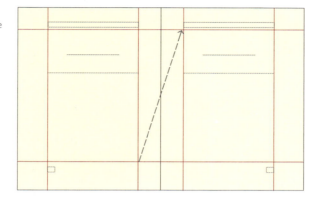

Prelim master pages
The text boxes for the prelims are unlinked, unless a *preface* or *foreword* continues onto a second page. The titles within the prelims should echo the position of the headings throughout the book. There are no *running heads* or *folios* on these pages.

Endmatter master pages
In this example the *endnotes* and *bibliography* are to be set in a double column. The text boxes are linked and the pages contain *running heads* and *folios*.

You will notice that the size of the margins and the positioning of printed elements is consistent throughout the three sets of master pages.

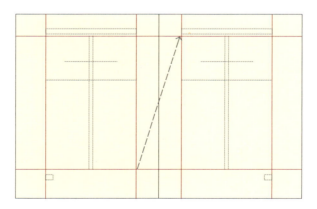

PART THREE

TYPEFACE CHARACTERISTICS AND CHOICES

FONT CATEGORIES

A typical typeface catalogue will group fonts into three main categories:

Serif fonts   Sans serif fonts   Display fonts

These are the three main groups used in book work.

Serif fonts

These are fonts whose letters have horizontal and oblique strokes added to the basic letterform. They are specifically designed for use in smaller point sizes, 6 to 14 points, to be read in continuous blocks of text which make up most books.

Albertina   abcdefghijklmnopqrstuvwxyz ABCDEFGHIJKLMNOPQRSTUVWXYZ

Minion   abcdefghijklmnopqrstuvwxyz ABCDEFGHIJKLMNOPQRSTUVWXYZ

Bembo   abcdefghijklmnopqrstuvwxyz ABCDEFGHIJKLMNOPQRSTUVWXYZ

Sans serif fonts

These are fonts without any additions to the basic letterform. They are slower to read and are not usually used for continuous book texts. They may be used for additional matter such as folios, captions, lists and running heads.

Stone sans   abcdefghijklmnopqrstuvwxyz ABCDEFGHIJKLMNOPQRSTUVWXYZ

Formata   abcdefghijklmnopqrstuvwxyz ABCDEFGHIJKLMNOPQRSTUVWXYZ

Quadraat sans   abcdefghijklmnopqrstuvwxyz ABCDEFGHIJKLMNOPQRSTUVWXYZ

Display fonts

These are fonts designed for use in displayed settings such as headings and titles. They are unsuitable for continuous texts.

Strayhorn

Fluidum

Gill Shadowed

DISPLAY *Display* **DISPLAY**

TYPE STYLES

A brief historical view

Typefaces have been evolving gradually since the invention of printing in the 15th century. Most – even those which have been designed digitally and without direct reference to earlier examples – can be grouped under one of several headings which reflect the progress of historical development. This classification is called the *Vox Classification*. The sequence lists *Humanist* faces, *Old* faces, *Transitional* faces and *Modern* faces. To these are added the later developments of *Slab Serif* and *Sans Serif* faces.

Humanist faces: those derived from early 15th-century typefaces. Heavy, evenly stroked faces with strong serif forms:

> Centaur based on the humanist typefaces of Jenson
>
> Janson has a similar basis but a stronger form

Old faces: those derived from late 15th-century printers such as Aldus Manutius. Lighter faces with finer, gently sloped serifs and accompanying narrow italics:

> Bembo derived from the typefaces of Aldus Manutius from 1495
>
> Garamond based on the typefaces of Claude Garamond from 1532
>
> Caslon, one of the last of the Old Style faces from 1730

Transitional faces: those developed from the beginning of the 16th century up to the middle of the 18th century. Generally narrower faces, light serifs and with capitals lower than the ascenders of the lower case:

> Fournier, an early Transitional face from 1732
>
> Baskerville, a much admired Transitional face of 1757
>
> Bulmer, a late Transitional face of 1790, nearly Modern

The historical background of typefaces is only touched upon briefly here. There are many books on the subject of the history of typefaces. See *Further reading* p.423

Modern faces: faces developed from the middle of the 18th century. The faces have more contrast between the thick and thin strokes and a strong vertical emphasis.

Bell, a Modern face from the late 18th century
Bodoni, a Modern face designed late in the 18th century

The relationship between the heights of capital and the ascenders of lower case letters changes during these developments:

Janson and Garamond capitals are below the ascenders of lower case letters.

Baskerville and Bodoni capitals are equal to the height of the ascenders.

The History of Typeface Design	Hh	Janson
The History of Typeface Design	Hh	Garamond
The History of Typeface Design	Hh	Baskerville
The History of Typeface Design	Hh	Bodoni

Slab serif and **sans serif** types were developed from the beginning of the 19th century. **Script** and **Brush** letters are even more recent additions.

Rockwell	Slab serif typefaces	SLAB SERIF TYPEFACE	Joanna
Akzidenz Grot	SANS SERIF	Sans serif faces	Univers
Shelly Andante	Script forms	Hand writing forms	Lucida
Brush Script	Brush strokes typefeaces	Refined brush!	Fluidum

This classification is of most interest to the typeface historian. It is not a completely useful aid in describing the many digital typefaces in use today. For the most part contemporary versions of earlier faces, as in some of the examples above, are pale imitations of the originals.

Rather than struggle to find an historical comparison for a given typeface, you may be better off to get to know the faces by their style and functional performance. A description that reads 'a serif face with narrow set, a large x-height and dark in colour' will be of more use to you than to be told that the face is derived from those of the Age of Enlightenment.

Style

Serif or sans serif

Each typeface is designed with its own distinct qualities and an appreciation of these helps typeface selection. The most marked difference is that between serif and sans serif faces. Serif faces are still favoured for setting continuous text. The principal reason for this preference lies in the effect of the serif; it encourages the eye along the horizontal text line, creating a flow between individual characters:

difficult difficult difficult difficult

The mind's recognition of words depends for the greater part on the upper form of the characters: the minimum number

Serifs offer a steady baseline to maintain the eyes' accuracy along the line, helping to group characters into individual words: the minimum number

A sans serif face is a less effective: the minimum number

Sans serif type forms are simpler and more legible but less *readable* over extended passages of text. They are best used for headings and captions as well as functions such as road direction signs, and official forms with small type sizes. They also allow accessibility for those with reading difficulties.

See *Setting for special needs* pp.344–7

Lengthy texts set in sans serif faces are trying for the reader. But a sans serif face can be made more readable by closing the characters together and increasing both the word spaces and leading:

difficult to learn, the maximum number of words in a line

difficult to learn, the maximum number of words in a line

Scala sans

Scala sans minus 4 ics

Scala sans 10 on 16 pt minus 3 ics

Simultaneously he asked if he and his brother William might learn the conditions under which his father and Murray had conducted business. 'We also think it would be desirable that we, as trustees of our father's

TYPEFACE FAMILIES

The choice of a font for use in setting readable continuous text is based on an assessment of its functions and other qualities. Importantly, the font must have a complete family of faces. For bookwork this should consist of:

See *Lining and non-lining figures* pp.270–1

Albertina family 12 pt
The use of the terms *Roman* or *Regular* can be confusing. Both refer to the same element of the type family.

Roman (or Regular) with *lining* and *non-lining* figures:

lower case: abcdefghijklmnopqrstuvwxyz

capitals: ABCDEFGHIJKLMNOPQRSTUVWXYZ

non-lining figures 1234567890   and lining figures 1234567890

Italic with lining and non-lining figures:

lower case: abcdefghijklmnopqrstuvwxyz

capitals: ABCDEFGHIJKLMNOPQRSTUVWXYZ

non-lining figures 1234567890   and lining figures 1234567890

Small capitals – smaller than upper case, but with the same weight:

ABCDEFGHIJKLMNOPQRSTUVWXYZ

Some families also have italic small capitals:

ABCDEFGHIJKLMNOPQRSTUVWXYZ

Semi-bold and **Semi-bold Italic** – also referred to as **Medium** and **Medium Italic** – each with lining and non-lining figures:

lower case: abcdefghijklmnopqrstuvwxyz

capitals: ABCDEFGHIJKLMNOPQRSTUVWXYZ

non-lining figures 1234567890   lining figures 1234567890

lower case: abcdefghijklmnopqrstuvwxyz

capitals: ABCDEFGHIJKLMNOPQRSTUVWXYZ

non-lining figures 1234567890   lining figures 1234567890

All these members of the family have accompanying punctuation and symbols:

. , ; : ' ? ! "( ) - – — £ @ $ % ^ & * \ | { } [ ] < > ° · / ™ ±

and provide accented characters such as: é á è à â î û ü ï í ì ö ø

Bold and **Bold Italic** are not used in continuous text and are not essential:

abcdefghijklmnopqrstuvwxyz 1234567890
ABCDEFGHIJKLMNOPQRSTUVWXYZ 1234567890

Such faces are too dark in colour and do not have good readability.

Extended type families

Some font families, especially sans serif families, will have further variations, adding *light*, *condensed*, *extra bold*, *shadowed* and *outline* forms to the family:

abcdefg ABCDE *abcdefg ABCDE* **abcdefg ABCDE** *abcdefg ABCDE*
abcdefg ABCDE *abcdefg ABCDE* abcdefg ABCDE

abcdefg ABCDE *abcdefg ABCDE* **abcdefg ABCDE** *abcdefg ABCDE*
abcdefg ABCDE *abcdefg ABCDE* **abcdefg ABCDE**
abcdefg ABCDE abcdefg ABCDE abcdefg ABCDE

These forms are not commonly used in book texts. They function as display faces.

Titling fonts

Capitals of a regular font can appear too dark when used in large sizes. In order to compensate for this, some fonts have a *titling* capital font of lighter capitals:

capitals: ABCDEFG   titling capitals: ABCDEFG

Requiem regular capitals and Titling capitals

Display typefaces

These typefaces are designed for attention-seeking uses mostly in advertising and marketing. They have no part to play in setting continuous texts but can be used in book titles and chapter headings:

See Headings p.114

DISPLAY Display **DISPLAY**

Delphian, Typeka and Neuland Inline

Italic forms

The italic version of the regular face may be formed by drawing the roman letters in a more cursive way, or in a sloped or oblique way, or in its own distinct way:

Cursive or drawn italic: is related to the regular in weight and style but developed from calligraphic pen strokes:

This is the roman form	*This is the cursive italic form*	Spectrum
This is the roman form	*This is the cursive italic form*	Rialto
This is the roman form	*This is the cursive italic form*	Requiem

Sloped (or oblique) roman: the regular letterform is only sloped to the right to create the italic, so this form of italic matches the weight of the regular face exactly; a few characters, such as the 'f' may be extended and the serifs may be curved:

This is the roman form	*This is the sloped italic form*	Melior
This is the roman form	*This is the sloped italic form*	Stone Print
This is the roman form	*This is the sloped italic form*	Meta
This is the roman form	*This is the sloped italic form*	Corvallis

An individual form: here the font is quite distinct in design and width from the regular form:

This is the roman form	*This is the distinct italic form*	Joanna
This is the roman form	*This is the distinct italic form*	Poliphilus & Blado
This is the roman form	*This is the distinct italic form*	Centaur & Arrighi

When you choose a typeface think about its italic form and the kind of texts you are setting. A sloped italic may well suit a scientific or business text, a cursive italic a fictional narrative or a more distinctive italic form might work for poetry titles. If the italic face of a font has a dark colour or form which contrasts with the roman face, it may restrict its use. In a text that has many italicized words – book titles, musical and art works or foreign words – the contrast between the regular and italic fonts should not be too great or it will disrupt the line's rhythm. In the example below, the choice of Joanna, with its individual italic form, is not advisable. The reader is distracted by the narrower and darker Joanna italic, while Minion, with less contrast between the roman and italic, is better suited:

Casanova consulted Ariosto's *Orlando Furioso*, using a system comparable to the *Sortes Virgilianae*. First he wrote down his question, then he derived numbers from the words and arranged these in an inverse pyramid, and finally, he arrived at the first line of the seventh stanza of the ninth canto of *Orlando Furioso*, which runs: *Tra il fin d'ottobre e il capo di novembre.*

Joanna
11 on 14 pt
showing the
dark italic.

Casanova consulted Ariosto's *Orlando Furioso*, using a system comparable to the *Sortes Virgilianae*. First he wrote down his question, then he derived numbers from the words and arranged these in an inverse pyramid, and finally, he arrived at the first line of the seventh stanza of the ninth canto of *Orlando Furioso*, which runs: *Tra il fin d'ottobre e il capo di novembre.*

Minion
10.5 on 14 pt
with a lighter
matching
italic.

Matching serif and sans serif typefaces

Several serif typeface families have a sans serif which matches the features of the serif, including its colour value. If the main text has many headings, this a useful tool – the headings can be set in the matching sans serif:

The serif typeface	the sans serif of the family	Rotis
The serif typeface	the sans serif of the family	Quadraat
The serif typeface	the sans serif of the family	Scala

Memories

Once, long ago, when I was still young, when the memories were far more vivid than they are now, I often tried to write about her. But I couldn't produce a line.

Heading:
Quadraat sans, 12 pt
Main text:
Quadraat
regular, 10 pt

Memories

Once, long ago, when I was still young, when the memories were far more vivid than they are now, I often tried to write about her. But I couldn't produce a line.

Heading:
Rotis sans, 14 pt
Main text:
Rotis serif 9.5 pt

Semi-bold and bold faces

These are developed from the regular and italic letterforms within a type family. They are heavier faces and act to emphasize headings, lists and other additional notes.

Bulmer regular

Regular small caps

Bulmer semi-bold

Semi-bold small caps

Bulmer bold

All 14 pt

abcdefghijklmnopqrstuvwxyz ABCDEFGH *abcdef*

ABCDEFGHIJKLMNOPQRSTUVWXYZ

abcdefghijklmnopqrstuvwxyz ABCDEFGH *abcdef*

ABCDEFGHIJKLMNOPQRSTUVWXYZ

abcdefghijklmnopqrstuvwxyz ABCDEFGH *abcdef*

In setting readable continuous text, semi-bold and bold faces are not used, though they may find a place in displayed chapter headings. In complex publications – works of reference and academic books – where there are many levels of headings, bolder faces can offer further alternatives of headings enabling the reader to see lesser sub-headings quickly without using too much space.

Sub-headings:
Stone Print bold 10 pt
Main text:
Stone Print roman
10 on 13 pt

7th–8th centuries CE. During this period, the Indian decimal notation, with the zero, spreads to the Indianised civilisations of Southeast Asia (Cambodia, Shan, Java, Malaysia, Bali, Borneo, etc., see Chapter 24).

7th–8th centuries CE [W]. The era of the oldest known manuscripts in which we find Latin writing of "Visigoth" and "Luxeuil" type.

Bolder faces are useful in tables and references. They enable the reader to identify specific points in lengthy lists. A note to the reader about their use should precede the list or table.

Scala regular, italic and bold, 8 on 13 pt
In an index the bold figures are used to indicate the difference between a text page reference and an illustrated page reference: a good use of a bold face.

Proust, Marcel, **298**, 305; *Du côté de chez Swann,* 229; *Sodome et Gommorhe,* 291

Prunoy, 127, **166**, 169–70, 181, 184–5, 188, 190–91, 197–8, **201**, 205, 218–19, **238**, 271, 305

Pryor, Ethne, **302**, 317

Pryor, Mark, 376–7, 386, **392**, 397, **404**, 406–8

TEXT FONT CHOICES

The industry produces a plethora of typefaces. Some, like display and decorative faces, rule themselves out of use for readable text composition. Others will not have a sufficient family to deal with the demands of text composition – they may only have lining figures, or no small capitals. But that still leaves a great number of faces. You will have to create styles for different books and to produce trial spreads for a publisher to choose from. This requires an appreciation of the characteristics of individual typefaces gained from observation and experience.

The typeface and its setting must also suit the content of the book itself. There is little sense in setting an academic tome in a sweet and poetically drawn typeface, any more than a romantic novel is suited to a hefty sans serif face or a poem to New Baskerville bold:

As Condillac (*Histoire moderne*, XX, 6) says: 'Algebra is to Arabic numerals as these are to Roman numerals.' To paraphrase Jean Le Rond d'Alembert (*Explications générales des connaissances humaines*): Arithmetic comes in two kinds – one is arithmetic by numbers; the other is arithmetic in algebraic terms according to procedures of calculation which are applied to magnitudes in general.

Rialto
13 on 14 pt
Too flowery
a choice for a
serious text

Naoko had a variety of hairslides and always wore them with her right ear exposed. I remember her most clearly this way, from the back. She would toy with her hairslide whenever she felt embarrassed by something. And she was always dabbing at her mouth with a handkerchief. She did this whenever she had something to say. The more I observed these habits of hers, the more I came to like her.

Meta medium
10 on 14 pt
A black and
blunt typeface
for young love

My heart is like a singing bird

Whose nest is in a water'd shoot;

My heart is like an apple tree . . .

New Baskerville
bold 12 on 18 pt
An over-bold face
for delicate
thoughts

It is not suggested that a typeface should slavishly follow the content of a book but the choice can be narrowed by a consideration of such factors. Whatever face is chosen it must aid readability and not distract the reader from the author's work.

As an exercise, let us find typefaces that are more appropriate to the three extracts on the previous page. The mathematical treatise, now set in Minion, has a workman-like look and the frequent italics are less of a contrast to the roman. The romantic novel, set in Collis with its somewhat eccentric serifs, might reflect that youthful story, and the poetry be made lyrical by the calligraphically styled Trinité.

Now set in
Minion
10.25 on 14 pt

As Condillac (*Histoire moderne*, XX, 6) says: 'Algebra is to Arabic numerals as these are to Roman numerals.' To paraphrase Jean Le Rond d'Alembert (*Explications générales des connaissances humaines*): Arithmetic comes in two kinds – one is arithmetic by numbers; the other is arithmetic in algebraic terms according to procedures of calculation which are applied to magnitudes in general.

Now set in
Collis Roman
10 on 15 pt

Naoko had a variety of hairslides and always wore them with her right ear exposed. I remember her most clearly this way, from the back. She would toy with her hairslide whenever she felt embarrassed by something. And she was always dabbing at her mouth with a hand-kerchief. She did this whenever she had something to say. The more I observed these habits of hers, the more I came to like her.

Now set in
Trinité italic
12 on 16 pt

My heart is like a singing bird
Whose nest is in a water'd shoot;
My heart is like an apple tree . . .

Manufacturers' printed typeface samples may be limited to a single line of upper and lower case letters. This does not make it easy to see how a face will perform. To develop an appreciation of typeface characteristics, look at whole pages set in different typefaces. To begin with, this exercise can be made less confusing by look-ing at a single feature, such as its size, x-height, set, fit or weight and seeing how different typefaces vary.

Choosing a text font

As you get to know how the typefaces you have to hand perform, you will be asked to make choices to deal with a whole range of texts. While there are no fixed guidelines you cannot simply choose any face for any text. There is a need for the typeface to be appropriate to the content of the text. Always note the era about which the text is written. A light-hearted novel does not require a stern classical face but a re-issue of an early Greek play might. The following examples will give you an idea of how you might make a choice.

A classically derived face suits a work on 18th-century type design:

> Much is said in the *Manuel* about the invention by Brietkopf of a new printer's music in 1755, and the imitations to which it gave rise throughout Europe. A few words as to the history of music-types may help the reader to view the matter in a just perspective. Types for plain-chant notes – lines printed separately from rules – were in use as early as 1490.

Fournier
11.5 on 15 pt

A survey of 20th-century Russian politics works well set in a contemporary face:

> Here he heard about the fate of the other million or more Poles who had fled to the 'safety' of the Soviet Union: over half of them had been sent to 'corrective' labour camps, and the remainder to prisoner-of-war camps or enforced settlements in remote and inhospitable regions of the south-eastern provinces, to live in cruel conditions in which brutality, starvation and sheer exhaustion claimed the lives of a

Rotis serif
10 on 14 pt

A philosophical treatise with many long words is best served by a narrowly set contemporary face which avoids too many word divisions:

> A more abstract example is the *predicate calculus*, a formal theory for the construction and manipulation of abstract logical expressions. This, which clearly descends from Leibniz's vision of a 'universal characteristic', plays an important role not only in abstract mathematical logic but also in the construction of certain kinds of computer programme.

Stone Print
10.5 on 14 pt

A children's book requires a plain serif face with no sophisticated elements – a long-tailed Q for example can confuse the young reader:

Garamond, 13 pt

'The Queen will hear you! You see she came rather late, and the Queen said –'

Shorter texts isolated from the main text of a book, such as those on jacket blurbs, can be set in a sans serif face:

Meta, 9 on 14 pt

Second Harvest is steeped in the poetry of the countryside and the seasons. Those who have read the author's *The Man Who Planted Trees* do not need to ask why Jean Giono remains one of the enduring French storytellers of this century.

Contemporary writing may offer you an opportunity to use a typeface that would not be used in more formal texts:

Optima, 9.5 on 15 pt

It was Saturday night and I wasn't into climbing those bloomin' stairs, so I said, Right I'm with you just give me a chance to get my bearings you can drop me off at the mother's right. They had the same blue minivan with *London Fire Brigade Diving Team* stamped on the side and she was stacked full of gear – diving suits oxygen canisters webs tins of Heineken grub whiskey from the duty free.

These examples will give you an idea of how you should look at the content of the text you are designing and setting. Be inventive but . . .

avoid novelty for novelty's sake
ensure that the choice works in your text panel and does not reduce readability
check that the typeface family has all the faces the text requires

Take care that you have a legal right to use your chosen typeface. In buying a font you purchase a licence to use the font yourself. The repro house or printer should have their own licensed copies of the typefaces you use for output, but if you are using an unusual typeface, it is critical that you check in advance. Most licences allow for the use of typefaces embedded in a PDF format, provided that the PDF format is limited to 'print and preview' and cannot be edited.

See *Output* p.395

Pastiche setting

There are opportunities from time to time for doing a *pastiche* setting – that is, a close imitation of an historical setting style. Such an imitation should be a design which not only uses a contemporary version of the older font but also follows the layout styles used at that time. Before starting to create a pastiche, carefully examine the features of the original typefaces and the page margins.

In contrast, a *facsimile* is a direct copy of a previous book.

A page from Fournier the Young's *Manuel Typographique* is set here in the Fournier typeface. It follows the original in the proportions of layout and type sizes. The original face was rather condensed so a horizontal scale of 90 per cent is applied. Features of the original French setting, such as a word space before and after a comma and the old-fashioned lower case 's' – 'f' without a right-hand side to its cross bar – are not used in the English version, shown in the bottom nine lines.

DES CARACTÈRES POÉTIQUES. 167

DES CARACTÈRES POÉTIQUES.

Ces Caracters font romains , mais plus fer-rés & plus alongés qu'à l'ordinaire. Je les ai faits pour les ouvrages qu'on veut rendre plus légers à la vue , en élaguant un peu les lignes fur elles – mêmes , principalement pour l'im-preffion de la poëfie , qui , pour avoir plus de grace , a befoin d'un plus grand intervalle en-tre les lignes. Un autre avantage eft qu'en fer-rant ainfi un peu plus les lettre à côté les unes des autres , les vers de dix ou douze fyllabes ne prouduifent pas des lignes trop longues for the format, there is no need to make two lines of them, or as it its called, *turn them in*. When three or four lines on a page are thus turned in or made into two, blocks of white are caused which are all the more offensive to the eye in that many of the lines do not extend the full width of the page. This causes a lacunae of varying sizes. The new type prevents this eyesore; therefore I have named it *Poetry-Face*.

The layout of the text panels of the original pages

Fournier
If there was particular need to create a very detailed pastiche of this book, the old-fashioned 'f' could be made in a font-drawing program.

A finished recto page

TYPEFACE CHARACTERISTICS

A typeface is characterized by four features:

sizing: the designed size of the face
x-height: the height of lower case letters without ascenders and descenders
set: the width of the face
fit: the spacing of combinations of letters

Typeface sizing

The visual size of individual typefaces differ. For example, 12 pt Rialto is not visually the same size as 12 pt Scala:

12 pt Rialto Roman   12 pt Scala Regular

One reason for this is that the distance between the top of the ascender and the bottom of the descender in the lower case alphabet varies. This sizing is a design feature of each typeface, as can be seen in these 36 pt examples:

All in 36 pt

Garamond   Bembo   Trinité   Quadraat   Spectrum   Walbaum

The designed height of capitals also varies, ranging from a height equal to the ascenders of the lower case, as in the Walbaum, to well below that height, as in Trinité:

Walbaum, 24 pt   dlH   Hld Trinité, 24 pt

So an instruction to set type in a given point size is of no value unless the face itself is specified. You may have to explain this to a client who may have only a rudimentary grasp of type size specification.

X-height

The second characteristic of a typeface is the height of its lower case letters, ignoring any ascenders and descenders – the x-height. The range of x-height variation is greater than might initially be suspected.

The examples below show a range of decreasing x-heights of typefaces suitable for continuous text settting. They are all set at 18 point:

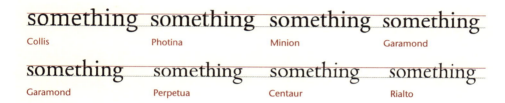

Collis   Photina   Minion   Garamond

Garamond   Perpetua   Centaur   Rialto

The combination of designed type size and x-height produces noticeable variations in the appearance of typefaces, here all in 18 pt:

Rialto Hfg   Walbaum Hfg   Caslon Hfg   Minion Hfg

Scala Hfg   Bembo Hfg   Trinité Hfg   Centaur Hfg

Typesetting programs will automatically set the baseline of all fonts at the same level.

The typefaces below, again all set at 18 pt, further demonstrate the differences:

Rialto   Spectrum   Bembo   Trinité   Garamond   Quadraat   Walbaum

Note that typeface names are shared by typeface manufacturers. There may be many 'Garamond' or 'Bodoni' typefaces produced by different companies, each with its own subtly varying characteristics:

Stempel Garamond   Adobe Garamond
Monotype Bodoni   Bauer Bodoni

When instructed to use, say, a *Garamond*, you should make it clear which one you have chosen to use.

The value of a typeface's x-height and size will affect readability. An initial rule is that as the x-height increases, more leading will be required to maintain readability. The appearance of a text setting is greatly affected by the x-height value, as the settings below show:

Collis, 10 on 14 pt

He was staring at him, drawing him into his eyes, and something was happening because Genghis Khan stopped laughing, hesitated for a moment as if he were at a height and suffering vertigo, and then fell into a daze. Doctor Da Barca stood up, went around the table and gently closed his eyelids as if they were lace curtains.

Minion, 10 on 14 pt

He was staring at him, drawing him into his eyes, and something was happening because Genghis Khan stopped laughing, hesitated for a moment as if he were at a height and suffering vertigo, and then fell into a daze. Doctor Da Barca stood up, went around the table and gently closed his eyelids as if they were lace curtains.

Garamond, 10 on 14 pt

He was staring at him, drawing him into his eyes, and something was happening because Genghis Khan stopped laughing, hesitated for a moment as if he were at a height and suffering vertigo, and then fell into a daze. Doctor Da Barca stood up, went around the table and gently closed his eyelids as if they were lace curtains.

Centaur, 10 on 14 pt

He was staring at him, drawing him into his eyes, and something was happening because Genghis Khan stopped laughing, hesitated for a moment as if he were at a height and suffering vertigo, and then fell into a daze. Doctor Da Barca stood up, went around the table and gently closed his eyelids as if they were lace curtains.

Akzidenz Grot light 10 on 14 pt

He was staring at him, drawing him into his eyes, and something was happening because Genghis Khan stopped laughing, hesitated for a moment as if he were at a height and suffering vertigo, and then fell into a daze. Doctor Da Barca stood up, went around the table and gently closed his eyelids as if they were lace curtains

Univers 45, 10 on 14 pt

He was staring at him, drawing him into his eyes, and something was happening because Genghis Khan stopped laughing, hesitated for a moment as if he were at a height and suffering vertigo, and then fell into a daze. Doctor Da Barca stood up, went around the table and gently closed his eyelids as if they were lace curtains.

Set

There is also a variation in the *set* or width of typefaces. You can choose between narrow and widely set typefaces.

Rialto 12 pt	indefatigable	indefatigable	Rialto 16.5 pt
Spectrum 12 pt	indefatigable	indefatigable	Spectrum 15.5 pt
Stone Print 12 pt	indefatigable	indefatigable	Stone Print 15 pt
Bembo 12 pt	indefatigable	indefatigable	Bembo 14.5 pt
Bell 12 pt	indefatigable	indefatigable	Bell 14.5 pt
Sabon 12 pt	indefatigable	indefatigable	Sabon 13 pt
Walbaum 12 pt	indefatigable	indefatigable	Walbaum 12 pt

Maria da Visitação had arrived not long before from an island off the African Atlantic coast. Without any official documents. She had been sold to Manila, so to speak. Of her new country she had seen little more than the road that went to Fronteira. She would look at it from the window of the flat, in the same building as the club, which was set on its own, away from neighbouring houses. In the window was a geranium. If we could see her from the outside, as she watched motionless at the window, we would think red butterflies had landed on the beautiful totem of her face.

Sabon, 11 on 15 pt
A widely set typeface

Maria da Visitação had arrived not long before from an island off the African Atlantic coast. Without any official documents. She had been sold to Manila, so to speak. Of her new country she had seen little more than the road that went to Fronteira. She would look at it from the window of the flat, in the same building as the club, which was set on its own, away from neighbouring houses. In the window was a geranium. If we could see her from the outside, as she watched motionless at the window, we would think red butterflies had landed on the beautiful totem of her face.

Stone Print
11 on 16 pt
This is a narrowly set face and in this paragraph occupies one line less than the Sabon setting.

The variation in set is just as noticeable in sans serif faces:

indefatigable indefatigable

indefatigable indefatigable

indefatigable indefatigable

indefatigable indefatigable

Gill Sans, 10 on 16 pt

From the moment the painter left, Herbal noticed the sense of unease return. Unable to face up to his brother-in-law, he left his sister's house and asked for authorization to spend nights at the prison. In the morning, he felt giddy, as if his head were unwilling to get up with his body.

Univers 55, 10 on 16 pt

From the moment the painter left, Herbal noticed the sense of unease return. Unable to face up to his brother-in-law, he left his sister's house and asked for authorization to spend nights at the prison. In the morning, he felt giddy, as if his head were unwilling to get up with his body.

The combined effect of size, set and x-height

As the overall appearance of a face is produced by a combination of x-height and set, combined with its drawn size, it is not straightforward to describe a typeface without reference to all its features. It is easy to say that one face has a larger x-height than another if that is the only feature of comparison. There are faces with large x-heights but narrow sets:

Scala regular, 14pt something something Collis, 14 pt
Collis, 14pt something

Univers 55 something something Stone Sans, 14 pt
Stone Sans something

Scala and Collis have the same x-height but Collis is more widely set: Univers and Stone Sans share an x-height but Stone Sans is more narrowly set. If you use a typeface with a wider set, however small the difference might appear, the same number of words will occupy more space. When working out what face to use in your text panel, this variation will have a marked effect.

> We came to a stop and stood in the silent forest, listening. I tumbled pinecones and cicada shells with my toecap, then looked up at the patches of sky showing through the pine branches. Hands in pockets, Naoko stood there thinking, her eyes focused on nothing in particular.

> We came to a stop and stood in the silent forest, listening. I tumbled pinecones and cicada shells with my toecap, then looked up at the patches of sky showing through the pine branches. Hands in pockets, Naoko stood there thinking, her eyes focused on nothing in particular.

> We came to a stop and stood in the silent forest, listening. I tumbled pinecones and cicada shells with my toecap, then looked up at the patches of sky showing through the pine branches. Hands in pockets, Naoko stood there thinking, her eyes focused on nothing in particular.

> We came to a stop and stood in the silent forest, listening. I tumbled pinecones and cicada shells with my toecap, then looked up at the patches of sky showing through the pine branches. Hands in pockets, Naoko stood there thinking, her eyes focused on nothing in particular.

Fit

The looseness or closeness of the fit of a typeface, is a unique characteristic of that face:

> My parents were two blurred figures rapidly fading from my memory.
> My parents were two blurred figures rapidly fading from my memory.
> My parents were two blurred figures rapidly fading from my memory.

The fit of a typeface depends upon the spacing of every possible combination of pairs of characters in the typeface. This distance – the *kerning value* – between each pair of characters is fixed when the font is designed.

Each combination of characters is known as a *kerning pair*. When a digital typeface is designed, each pair is adjusted individually by either reducing or an increasing the space between the two characters. This is important in improving the spacing of pairs containing punctuation marks:

Va Te Av 'A y.)"
Va Te Av 'A y.)"

It may be something of a relief to the typesetter to know that this defined spacing comes into play automatically as letter combinations are keyed in.

Some letter combinations cannot be improved by kerning and so special forms – *ligatures* – are designed to overcome this, as in these combinations of the letter 'f' with i, l, f, fl, fi:

fi
fi

Most typesetting
programs have a
control for the use
of ligatures. Check
this when setting up
a new document.

Garamond pairs
with clashing points
and ascenders

Garamond ligatures
one character for the
two letters

fi ff fl ffi ffl *fi ff fl ffi ffl*
fi ff fl ffi ffl *fi ff fl ffi ffl*

Garamond
without ligatures

Garamond
using ligatures

The fifty baffled boffins shuffled off the office floor

The fifty baffled boffins shuffled off the office floor

Other ligatures can occur, such as ß for ss in German and ffj for ffj in Dutch. If you are setting extracts in foreign languages make sure your fonts offer such ligatures. In large-sized display settings it is possible to form ligatures that a typeface does not offer by manually kerning characters:

Officially Officially Officially Officially

The 'ffi' ligature, in Albertina on the left and Univers on the right, is made by
introducing minus 10 ICS between the two 'f's

Manual adjustments to kerning pairs

Typesetting programmes will allow for recalibration of the kerning values, pair by pair, as shown below. A typeface which has character pairs whose kerning can be improved, as in the example of the tight fitting f and ? below, can be adjusted. But beware, it is a time-consuming and specialized operation, not to be undertaken lightly.

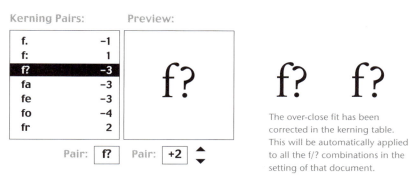

The over-close fit has been corrected in the kerning table. This will be automatically applied to all the f/? combinations in the setting of that document.

Adjusting the fit of a typeface

It is possible to adjust the overall fit of a typeface, and thus the appearance of a setting, by increasing or decreasing the ICS overall to the text setting. This should be done with only with small increments of ICS, to avoid characters clashing:

I fled. I started running like a mad, winged creature. I ran and ran, the way you run in dreams when the Bogeyman is right behind you. I was convinced the teacher was doing just that. Coming after me. I could feel his breath on my neck, and the breath of all the children, like a pack of hounds after a fox.

Sabon
11 on 16 pt

I fled. I started running like a mad, winged creature. I ran and ran, the way you run in dreams when the Bogeyman is right behind you. I was convinced the teacher was doing just that. Coming after me. I could feel his breath on my neck, and the breath of all the children, like a pack of hounds after a fox.

Sabon, 11 on 16 pt at minus 1.5 ICS
This improves the widely letter-spaced look of the original.

Typeface and setting colour

The printing and paper qualities also affect colour. See p.401

Printed typefaces vary in *colour*; some faces appear darker – weightier – some lighter. This variation depends not only on the combination of the x-height, the set, and the drawn quality of the face but also the setting style – the leading and the word-spacing.

Typeface colour

The examples below demonstrate how the combination of x-height, set and weight affect colour. The same leading and word-spacing are used in each sample. Although the sizes have been adjusted to fit the measure, the range of colour is marked from the top sample to the bottom sample.

Poliphilus, 13.75 pt

Not knowing what happened before you were born means being a child forever. For what is human life, unless it is interwoven with the life of our ancestors, by the memory of ancient history?

Walbaum, 10.25 pt

Not knowing what happened before you were born means being a child forever. For what is human life, unless it is interwoven with the life of our ancestors, by the memory of ancient history?

Photina, 11.25 pt

Not knowing what happened before you were born means being a child forever. For what is human life, unless it is interwoven with the life of our ancestors, by the memory of ancient history?

New Baskerville, 11 pt

Not knowing what happened before you were born means being a child forever. For what is human life, unless it is interwoven with the life of our ancestors, by the memory of ancient history?

Requiem, 12 pt

Not knowing what happened before you were born means being a child forever. For what is human life, unless it is interwoven with the life of our ancestors, by the memory of ancient history?

Centaur, 13.25 pt

Not knowing what happened before you were born means being a child forever. For what is human life, unless it is interwoven with the life of our ancestors, by the memory of ancient history?'

Similar variations of colour occur in sans serif faces. All the faces shown below are in the regular face of the family.

Once, long ago, when I was still young, when the memories were far more vivid than they are now, I often tried to write about her. But I couldn't produce a line.

Scala Sans, 9.5 pt

Once, long ago, when I was still young, when the memories were far more vivid than they are now, I often tried to write about her. But I couldn't produce a line.

Akzidenz Grot, 9 pt

Once, long ago, when I was still young, when the memories were far more vivid than they are now, I often tried to write about her. But I couldn't produce a line.

Gill Sans, 9.5 pt

Once, long ago, when I was still young, when the memories were far more vivid than they are now, I often tried to write about her. But I couldn't produce a line.

Univers 55, 8.25 pt

Once, long ago, when I was still young, when the memories were far more vivid than they are now, I often tried to write about her. But I couldn't produce a line.

Quadraat Sans, 10 pt

Once, long ago, when I was still young, when the memories were far more vivid than they are now, I often tried to write about her. But I couldn't produce a line.

Formata, 8.5 pt

The typeface colour in a text panel is affected by the leading applied to its setting. The greater the leading, the lighter the colour. If you decide to use a dark face it will benefit from increased leading to prevent the overall colour becoming too black.

For instance, the path in front of the veranda was made of large round water-worn pebbles, from some sea beach. They were not loose, but stuck down tight in moss and sand, and were black and shiny, as if they had been polished. I adored those pebbles.

Quadraat regular
11 on 13 pt

For instance, the path in front of the veranda was made of large round water-worn pebbles, from some sea beach. They were not loose, but stuck down tight in moss and sand, and were black and shiny, as if they had been polished. I adored those pebbles.

Quadraat regular
11 on 15 pt
The dark effect
is reduced by the
extra leading.

Equally, if you decide to use a very light face, reducing the leading will prevent the text becoming a pale grey.

Spectrum
12 on 16 pt
A grey effect

For instance, the path in front of the veranda was made of large round water-worn pebbles, from some sea beach. They were not loose, but stuck down tight in moss and sand, and were black and shiny, as if they had been polished. I adored those pebbles. I mean literally, adored. This passion made me feel quite sick sometimes.

Spectrum
12 on 14 pt
The appearance is darkened by reducing the leading.

For instance, the path in front of the veranda was made of large round water-worn pebbles, from some sea beach. They were not loose, but stuck down tight in moss and sand, and were black and shiny, as if they had been polished. I adored those pebbles. I mean literally, adored. This passion made me feel quite sick sometimes.

For the adjustment of word-spacing, see *Paragraph styles* pp.90–111

By tightening up the word-spacing, the density of words in each line is increased, and this has the effect of darkening the colour of the text panel. This is achieved by setting the paragraph styles which control word spaces.

Spectrum
12 on 14 pt
Wide spacing

For instance, the path in front of the veranda was made of large round water-worn pebbles, from some sea beach. They were not loose, but stuck down tight in moss and sand, and were black and shiny, as if they had been polished. I adored those

Spectrum
12 on 14 pt
Medium spacing

For instance, the path in front of the veranda was made of large round water-worn pebbles, from some sea beach. They were not loose, but stuck down tight in moss and sand, and were black and shiny, as if they had been polished. I adored those pebbles. I

Spectrum
12 on 14 pt
Narrow spacing

For instance, the path in front of the veranda was made of large round water-worn pebbles, from some sea beach. They were not loose, but stuck down tight in moss and sand, and were black and shiny, as if they had been polished. I adored those pebbles. I mean

Observing type features

While a minute examination of each of the many elements that make up the design of a typeface is not the purpose of this book, it can be a useful aid to look at typefaces to see how certain essential features vary between type styles. Below are set out some frequently used typefaces with a brief resumé of their features.

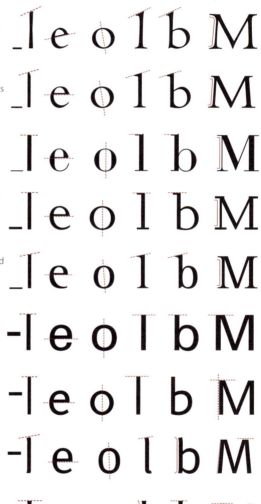

Centaur: derived from the earliest type forms. Waisted vertical strokes and curved junctions with the serifs which are steeply sloped; vertical strokes of capitals are also sloped; the overall stress is angled.

Bembo: an Old face. Slope of serifs less marked. Vertical strokes parallel-sided; capital strokes less sloped; cross bars of lower case letters horizontal; capitals lower than lower case ascenders; stress is angled.

Bodoni: a Modern face. Strong vertical and horizontal parallel-sided strokes contrasting with fine serifs at right angles. Capitals same height as lower case ascenders; stress is vertical.

Joanna: a slab serif; strong horizontal serifs at right angles to parallel heavier vertical strokes. Capitals lower than ascenders; vertical stress.

Rotis: a contemporary working of an Old Style face; sloped stronger serifs with less contrast between the vertical and horizontal strokes.

Univers: a sans serif of severe geometric design; equal weight vertical and horizontal strokes throughout; capitals the same height as lower case ascenders.

Scala sans: with lighter but equal weight vertical and horizontal strokes throughout; capitals lower than the lower case ascenders.

Meta sans: with heavier vertical than horizontal strokes throughout; capitals lower than lower case ascenders and sloped; the curve at top and bottom of the vertical strokes adds informality despite the geometric base.

Corvallis: a face originated calligraphically with the vertical strokes swelled at the top and bottom; a half-way house between the serif and sans serif.

WORD-SPACING IN TEXT COMPOSITION

Typesetting programs offer the facility to adjust the amount of space between words, specifying how words are divided and hyphenated and how lines of text are justified. This set of controls is called *paragraph styles* and allows the designer to refine word-spacing, thus achieving an even text, paragraph by paragraph.

Specifying paragraph styles for justified setting

In justified setting, the amount of space between words varies from line to line. When setting text using a typesetting program, word-spacing is controlled by specifying three values. The first is the 'optimum' value – the ideal space between words. Then there are 'minimum' and 'maximum' values: the narrowest and widest word-spaces to be allowed by the program. The values in each case are expressed as percentages – 100% representing ¼ of an em-width. These values will need to be adjusted for each setting to take into account the fit of the typeface and the width of the measure.

a 10 pt em

a 10 pt en

¼ of a
10 pt em

a 12 pt em

a 12 pt en

¼ of a
12 pt em

This line is in twelve point Albertina at 100% optimum setting.

Paragraph styling in use

In order to have control over the detail of your text setting, you should set up several styles to manipulate the different circumstances that occur from paragraph to paragraph. First, a basic style should be established which suits the typeface, size and measure of your design. You should apply this to the entire text. There will, however, be paragraphs that will not typeset well with this style because of the length of the words in them. To deal with these, add two more paragraph styles, one for a tighter setting and one for a looser setting.

| 85% | 110% | 250% | | 90% | 100% | 110% | | 70% | 80% | 105% | | 100% | 120% | 150% |

a factory setting with too wide a range   a **basic** setting style   a **tighter** setting style   a **looser** setting style

Initially it is difficult to visualize how these different settings will affect paragraphs and it can be difficult to observe in a single example. The following pages demonstrate these differences and will begin to accustom your eye to the changes.

The windows are blind, covered with photographers' drapes, but it is comparatively easy to guess what they conceal: rooms chock-a-block with weapons and lengths of brocade, with canvases depicting basketfuls of cats, or the

The windows are blind, covered with photographers' drapes, but it is comparatively easy to guess what they conceal: rooms chock-a-block with weapons and lengths of brocade, with canvases depicting basketfuls of

The windows are blind, covered with photographers' drapes, but it is comparatively easy to guess what they conceal: rooms chock-a-block with weapons and lengths of brocade, with canvases depicting basketfuls of cats, or the families

90% 100% 110%

The basic style
Octavian, 11 on 14 pt

100% 120% 130%

A looser style results in uneven word-spacing

70% 80% 100%

The tighter style, narrowing the word-spacing.

The effect of these three settings can be seen more easily in longer paragraphs:

In Florence he proposed. Aunt Cara was informed of this by telegram and all the uncertainty of the previous months suddenly ended. 'I feel so happy for you, dearest Maud,' she wrote. 'He is so sweet-tempered, so thoroughly sound at heart, and kind, besides being so very able, that in spite of his ill-health I feel you have drawn one of the big prizes in the lottery. You will grow very fond of him, and in things where you need improvement you will improve each other as two well-meaning people always do.'

In Florence he proposed. Aunt Cara was informed of this by telegram and all the uncertainty of the previous months suddenly ended. 'I feel so happy for you, dearest Maud,' she wrote. 'He is so sweet-tempered, so thoroughly sound at heart, and kind, besides being so very able, that in spite of his ill-health I feel you have drawn one of the big prizes in the lottery. You will grow very fond of him, and in things where you need improvement you will improve each other as two well-meaning people always do.'

In Florence he proposed. Aunt Cara was informed of this by telegram and all the uncertainty of the previous months suddenly ended. 'I feel so happy for you, dearest Maud,' she wrote. 'He is so sweet-tempered, so thoroughly sound at heart, and kind, besides being so very able, that in spite of his ill-health I feel you have drawn one of the big prizes in the lottery. You will grow very fond of him, and in things where you need improvement you will improve each other as two well-meaning people always do.'

90% 100% 110%

Scala, 9 on 13 pt
Paragraph set in the basic style. A dark and condensed setting.

70% 80% 100%

Paragraph set in the tighter style. A more evenly spaced setting.

100% 120% 130%

Paragraph set in the looser style. The setting is now widely word-spaced.

The styles can be used to match the word-spacing of adjoining paragraphs:

1   He was returning home via Italy from a trip to Tunisia and had been encouraged by Cara Jebb to seek out Maud. She sent a message giving him the name of the hotel and to her surprise he turned up that evening He took rooms in the same hotel as Maud and her aunt and, being in high favour with Aunt Emma, became their constant companion over the next fortnight.

2   Every day they went out on foot or in a carriage. After one nine-mile walk, Maud wrote to her sister Amy: 'G. D. picked violets and crocuses for me and we walked and walked and talked and talked. The views of the rugged mountains, Vesuvius occasionally, then the Bay of Naples . . . G. D. talks Italian very well, so he asked when ever there was any danger of our losing our way.' A passing donkey cart helped speed their return, George and the driver jumping out when they came to hills. 'It was so funny!' Maud wrote happily to her sister. 'To think of a Professor in Cambridge running by the side of a donkey cart was amusing. And me in the cart too!'

1   He was returning home via Italy from a trip to Tunisia and had been encouraged by Cara Jebb to seek out Maud. She sent a message giving him the name of the hotel and to her surprise he turned up that evening He took rooms in the same hotel as Maud and her aunt and, being in high favour with Aunt Emma, became their constant companion over the next fortnight.

2   Every day they went out on foot or in a carriage. After one nine-mile walk, Maud wrote to her sister Amy: 'G. D. picked violets and crocuses for me and we walked and walked and talked and talked. The views of the rugged mountains, Vesuvius occasionally, then the Bay of Naples … G. D. talks Italian very well, so he asked when ever there was any danger of our losing our way.' A passing donkey cart helped speed their return, George and the driver jumping out when they came to hills. 'It was so funny!' Maud wrote happily to her sister. 'To think of a Professor in Cambridge running by the side of a donkey cart was amusing. And me in the cart too!'

Texts which alternate between passages of narrative and dialogue can suffer from contrasts in word-spacing. You can reduce this by applying different styles to individual paragraphs so as to produce an even page.

1   'In a way,' Doctor Da Barca would say with a half-smile, 'human beings are the result not of improvement, but of an ailment. The mutant we descend from had to stand up on account of some pathological problem. It was clearly inferior to its quadruped ancestors. And that's without the loss of hair and tail. From the biological point of view, it was a disaster. I believe it was the chimpanzee that invented laughter the first time *Homo erectus* and it met on that stage. I mean, can you imagine? An upright, balding bloke missing his tail. Pathetic. You'd fall about laughing.'

2   'I prefer Bible literature to literature on evolution,' the painter said. 'The Bible is the best script written so far of the film of the world.'

3   'No. The best script is the one we do not know. The cell's secret poem, gentlemen!'

1   'In a way,' Doctor Da Barca would say with a half-smile, 'human beings are the result not of improvement, but of an ailment. The mutant we descend from had to stand up on account of some pathological problem. It was clearly inferior to its quadruped ancestors. And that's without the loss of hair and tail. From the biological point of view, it was a disaster. I believe it was the chimpanzee that invented laughter the first time *Homo erectus* and it met on that stage. I mean, can you imagine? An upright, balding bloke missing his tail. Pathetic. You'd fall about laughing.'

2   'I prefer Bible literature to literature on evolution,' the painter said. 'The Bible is the best script written so far of the film of the world.'

3   'No. The best script is the one we do not know. The cell's secret poem, gentlemen!'

In the early trials of a setting you may discover that your basic paragraph style is too loose for the typeface and measure:

110% 120% 140%

New Baskerville
10 on 13 pt
In this page the setting style is too loose, creating lines with markedly varying word spaces.

Of course, not all these allegiances are equally strong, at least at any given moment. But none is entirely insignificant, either. All are components of personality – we might almost call them "genes of the soul" so long as we remember that most of them are not innate.

While each of these elements may be found separately in many individuals, the same combination of them is never encountered in different people, and it's this that gives every individual his richness and value and makes each human being unique and irreplaceable.

It can happen that some incident, a fortunate or unfortunate accident, even a single chance encounter, influences our sense of identity more strongly than any ancient affiliation. Take the case of a Serbian man and a Muslim woman who met 20 years ago in a café in Sarajevo, fell in love and got married. They can never perceive their identity in the same way as does a couple that is entirely Serbian or entirely Muslim; their view of religion and mother country will never again be what it was before. Both partners will for ever carry within them the ties their parents handed down at birth, but these ties will henceforth be perceived differently and accorded a different importance.

Let us stay in Sarajevo and carry out an imaginary survey there. Let us observe a man of about 50 whom we see in the street.

In 1980 or thereabouts he might have said proudly and without hesitation, "I'm a Yugoslavian!" Questioned more closely, he could have said he was a citizen of the Federal Republic of Bosnia-Herzegovina, and, incidentally, that he came from a traditionally Muslim family.

If you had met the same man twelve years later, when the war was at its height, he might have answered automatically and emphatically, "I'm a Muslim!" He might even have grown the statutory beard. He would quickly have added that he was a Bosnian, and he would not have been pleased to be reminded of how proudly he once called himself a Yugoslavian.

Tightening the basic style deals with this:

Of course, not all these allegiances are equally strong, at least at any given moment. But none is entirely insignificant, either. All are components of personality – we might almost call them 'genes of the soul' so long as we remember that most of them are not innate.

While each of these elements may be found separately in many individuals, the same combination of them is never encountered in different people, and it's this that gives every individual his richness and value and makes each human being unique and irreplaceable.

It can happen that some incident, a fortunate or unfortunate accident, even a single chance encounter, influences our sense of identity more strongly than any ancient affiliation. Take the case of a Serbian man and a Muslim woman who met 20 years ago in a café in Sarajevo, fell in love and got married. They can never perceive their identity in the same way as does a couple that is entirely Serbian or entirely Muslim; their view of religion and mother country will never again be what it was before. Both partners will for ever carry within them the ties their parents handed down at birth, but these ties will henceforth be perceived differently and accorded a different importance.

Let us stay in Sarajevo and carry out an imaginary survey there. Let us observe a man of about 50 whom we see in the street.

In 1980 or thereabouts he might have said proudly and without hesitation, 'I'm a Yugoslavian!' Questioned more closely, he could have said he was a citizen of the Federal Republic of Bosnia-Herzegovina, and, incidentally, that he came from a traditionally Muslim family.

If you had met the same man twelve years later, when the war was at its height, he might have answered automatically and emphatically, 'I'm a Muslim!' He might even have grown the statutory beard. He would quickly have added that he was a Bosnian, and he would not have been pleased to be reminded of how proudly he once called himself a Yugoslavian.

90% 100% 110%

New Baskerville
10 on 13.5 pt
This gives more even word-spacing and a stronger linear pattern. It has reduced the number of lines which enables the leading to be increased by ½ pt. There is an improve-ment in the readability.

It must be stressed that settings that work well for one typeface and measure may not work with another face.
It is worth keeping a record of those settings which work best for a particular face.

Paragraph styles, type size and measure

Setting up paragraph styles for a particular measure is a matter of trial and error, but the following principles may help you begin the process.

A wide measure requires a wide optimum word-spacing:

110% 120% 140%

New Baskerville
10 on 13 pt
Measure: 113 mm

I have quoted the first examples that came to mind, but I could have used many others. For instance, that of someone born in Belgrade of a Serbian mother and a Croatian father. That of a Hutu woman married to a Tutsi, or vice versa. Or that of an American with a black father and a Jewish mother.

In a narrow measure, tighter word-spacing will reduce uneven gaps:

New Baskerville, 10 on 13 pt
measure: 52 mm

110% 120% 140%

is improved by using tighter settings

70% 80% 100%

I have quoted the first examples that came to mind, but I could have used many others. For instance, that of someone born in Belgrade of a Serbian mother and a Croatian father. That of a Hutu woman married to a Tutsi, or vice versa. Or that of an American with a black father and a Jewish mother.

I have quoted the first examples that came to mind, but I could have used many others. For instance, that of someone born in Belgrade of a Serbian mother and a Croatian father. That of a Hutu woman married to a Tutsi, or vice versa. Or that of an American with a black father and a Jewish mother.

An increase in type size at the same measure will require tighter spacing:

110% 120% 140%

New Baskerville
9 on 13 pt
Measure: 109 mm

I have quoted the first examples that came to mind, but I could have used many others. For instance, that of someone born in Belgrade of a Serbian mother and a Croatian father. That of a Hutu woman married to a Tutsi, or vice versa. Or that of an American with a black father and a Jewish mother.

90% 100% 110%

New Baskerville
11 on 14 pt

I have quoted the first examples that came to mind, but I could have used many others. For instance, that of someone born in Belgrade of a Serbian mother and a Croatian father. That of a Hutu woman married to a Tutsi, or vice versa. Or that of an

Paragraph styles and typeface choices

Typefaces vary in how they appear when set, and this means paragraph styles which work for one may not work for another:

> Defined in this way the word identity reflects a fairly precise idea – one which in theory should not give rise to confusion. Do we really need lengthy arguments to prove that there are not and cannot be two identical individuals? Even if in the near future someone manages, as we fear they may, to 'clone' human beings, the clones would at best be identical only at the time of their 'birth'; as soon as they started to live they would start being different.

New Baskerville
10 on 13.5 pt

> Defined in this way the word identity reflects a fairly precise idea – one which in theory should not give rise to confusion. Do we really need lengthy arguments to prove that there are not and cannot be two identical individuals? Even if in the near future someone manages, as we fear they may, to 'clone' human beings, the clones would at best be identical only at the time of their 'birth'; as soon as they started to live they would start being different.

Bembo
10.5 on 13.5 pt
The same settings
as above in this
case results in
wide and irregular
word-spacing.

> Defined in this way the word identity reflects a fairly precise idea – one which in theory should not give rise to confusion. Do we really need lengthy arguments to prove that there are not and cannot be two identical individuals? Even if in the near future someone manages, as we fear they may, to 'clone' human beings, the clones would at best be identical only at the time of their 'birth'; as soon as they started to live they would start being different.

Stone Print
10.5 on 14.5 pt
The same settings this
time result in tightly
spaced lines.

In the above examples, the same set of paragraph styles have resulted in settings that are even, loose and tight. This is due to differences in the set, fit and size of the three typefaces.

Word-spacing can have an effect on the extent of a book. Tightening the paragraph styles will reduce the number of lines; loosening the styles will increase the number of lines.

See *Making extent*
pp.222–33

Word division and hyphenation

Typesetting programs control the division of long words between lines. You can even prevent any words from being split, though this does mean that the word-spacing will be more irregular, creating over-wide word spaces or tight lines:

This setting with no hyphenation creates both widely and tightly spaced lines, and reduces readability.

> Then there were opportunists who had 'benefited' from the purges, gaining promotion onward and upward through vacancies left by those who had disappeared into the Gulag or grave. These could often barely read or write and characteristically developed a 'patrimony of illiteracy', by claiming their fathers had been shepherds (rather as Bazarov

The division of just two words gives more even word-spacing throughout and enhances readability:

> Then there were opportunists who had 'benefited' from the purges, gaining promotion onward and upward through vacan-cies left by those who had disappeared into the Gulag or grave. These could often barely read or write and characteris-tically developed a 'patrimony of illiteracy', by claiming their fathers had been shepherds (rather as Bazarov in Turgenev's last

Hyphenation is controlled in the paragraph style window by setting the shortest word to be divided, together with a lower limit of characters before and after the hyphen. The number of hyphens allowed in successive lines is also set. Too many hyphens in a row is irritating to the reader.

7	SHORTEST WORD
4	BEFORE HYPHEN
3	AFTER HYPHEN
2	HYPHENS IN A ROW

Word division depends on spelling as well as spacing. See *Word division* p.386

A word division which leaves less than three characters before or after the division leads to confusion and a loss of fluency: manual-ly fixi-ng de-ad dan-ce

Correct hyphenation is no barrier to fluent reading. Readability is hindered more by irregular word-spacing than by word divisions. Typesetting programs use built-in dictionaries which choose where to split each word.

Paragraph last lines

The last line of the paragraph is automatically set at the optimum word-spacing value. On occasions this will contrast with the word-spacing of the line above, but if a looser style is applied to the whole paragraph, words would turn over onto subsequent lines which may not be desirable. If a tight paragraph style is used, the contrast in word-spacing between the last two lines can be noticeable:

> very fond of him, and in things where you need improvement you will improve each other as two well-meaning people always do.'
> very fond of him, and in things where you need improvement you will improve each other as two well-meaning people always do.'

Individual programs offer several ways of balancing the spacing of the last line but manual adjustment of spacing may be necessary. There is a setting in paragraph styles called the *flush zone*. This is measured from the right-hand side of the text box. If the words of the last line of a paragraph come to or beyond that point, the line is automatically set full out:

> have always been very fond of him, and in things where you need improve-ment you will improve each other as two well-meaning people always do.'
> have always been very fond of him, and in things where you need improve-ment you will improve each other as two well-meaning people always do.'

The flush zone is set at 6 mm. Any last line that goes over that point is automatically set full out.

Applying paragraph styles to secondary text matter

When dealing with captions, footnotes or sidenotes, the creation of a separate style to enhance the setting is useful. Captions in smaller typefaces may benefit from wider spacing, or sidenotes from a tighter style:

> 416. The special suspension of this particular model made it particularly suitable for 'acrobatic' stunts. Many attempts were made to meet the chal-lenge of driving a Citroën on two wheels only from New York to Los Angeles.

> 416. The special suspension of this particular model made it particularly suitable for 'acrobatic' stunts. Many attempts were made to meet the challenge of driving a Citroën on two wheels only from New York to Los Angeles.

Bembo, 9 on 12 pt
The left sidenote, set in the basic style, is loose.

The right sidenote set in the tighter style is easier to read.

Specifying paragraph styles for ranged left setting

Ranged right text is rarely used in books as it is hard to read at length. Its use is usually restricted to captions and sidenotes.

As we have seen, justified text creates irregular spaces between words. Setting the text *ranged left*, or *ragged right* enables the word-spacing to be constant throughout. The minimum, optimum and maximum word-spacing in the paragraph styling option in your program should be set at the same value. The percentage will vary from typeface to typeface and is established at the trial stage of the setting.

130%	130%	130%

Stone Print
10 on 15 pt
measure: 105 mm
All the percentages
are the same.

We will try to establish three chief arguments about this combination of personality traits that we call Cool: that it has sufficient coherence to be recognizable as a 'syndrome' that is transmissible via culture and that has a traceable history (although we will do no more than sketch that history); that it is at odds with both European and American Puritan traditions; and that it has until recently appeared in those societies as a form of social deviance and rebellion, but that it is now losing this rebellious status and becoming the

The example above has been set with a paragraph style that does not allow word division. Although this may seem desirable it gives rise to a considerable range of line lengths within the measure. The advantage of having equal word-spacing is diminished by this irregularity. This variation can be minimized by introducing a word division command in the paragraph style:

6	shortest word
3	before hyphen
3	after hyphen
2	hyphens in row

We will try to establish three chief arguments about this combination of personality traits that we call Cool: that it has sufficient coherence to be recognizable as a 'syndrome' that is transmissible via culture and that has a traceable history (although we will do no more than sketch that history); that it is at odds with both European and American Puritan traditions; and that it has until recently appeared in those societies as a form of social deviance and rebellion, but that it is now losing this rebellious status and becoming the

See *Massaging ranged left text* p.111

Further adjustment of the variation in line endings can be achieved by manually massaging the text line by line.

Ranged left setting is preferable for settings on a narrow measure. The gain in readability is considerable:

Leo now acquired yet another language and, with it, affection for a country to which he subsequently returned whenever possible. (He had a hand in bringing Giuseppe Tomasi di Lampedusa's *Il Gattopardo – The Leopard* – back to England after one summer trip in the late 1950s, urging Manya Harari and Marjorie Villiers to publish it, as they did, at The Harvill Press.) His Italian studies did not go to waste: right to the end of his life he would still be reaching back to texts read as a student and once famously clinched an argument with Leon Radzinowicz, the great authority on criminal law, by triumphantly quoting

Leo now acquired yet another language and, with it, affection for a country to which he subsequently returned whenever possible. (He had a hand in bringing Giuseppe Tomasi di Lampedusa's *Il Gattopardo – The Leopard* – back to England after one summer trip in the late 1950s, urging Manya Harari and Marjorie Villiers to publish it, as they did, at The Harvill Press.) His Italian studies did not go to waste: right to the end of his life he would still be reaching back to texts read as a student and once famously clinched an argument with Leon Radzinowicz, the great authority on criminal law, by triumphantly quoting

Stone Print
10 on 13 pt
measure: 51 mm
The gain in quality of word-spacing in the ranged left setting is marked, especially with a text containing many proper nouns and titles.

However, if the measure is reduced even further, as in long captions or sidenotes, a reduction in the type size and the use of word division become necessary:

Leo now acquired yet another language and, with it, affection for a country to which he subsequently returned whenever possible. (He had a hand in bringing Giuseppe Tomasi di Lampedusa's *Il Gattopardo – The Leopard* – back to England after one summer trip in the late 1950s, urging Manya Harari and Marjorie Villiers to publish it, as they did, at The Harvill Press.)

Leo now acquired yet another language and, with it, affection for a country to which he subsequently returned whenever possible. (He had a hand in bringing Giuseppe Tomasi di Lampedusa's *Il Gattopardo – The Leopard* – back to England after one summer trip in the late 1950s, urging Manya Harari and Marjorie Villiers to publish it, as they did, at The Harvill Press.) His Italian

Stone Print
9 on 12 pt
measure: 40 mm
The variation in line length is unacceptable unless word division is used.

Cutting or re-writing text to make it fit better is not an option for book designers. Any changes to the text must be made by the editor or author.

Once the text panel has been designed, some additional work may still be needed to make the text look its best. Going through the book page by page, making manual adjustments where necessary is a process called *massaging* the text.

Massaging justified text

The primary purpose of massaging text is to ensure that word-spacing is as even as possible. Though the width of word-spaces is specified in the typesetting program, some paragraphs may still look uneven. This is rectified by moving words from the end of one line to the beginning of the next, using a *soft line return* – that is, one that does not create a new paragraph.

In the following example, lines 1, 4 and 7 are too tight and lines 6, 8 and 10 are too loose. The word divisions on lines 2 and 4 would be acceptable if they were necessary to ensure even word-spacing, but are best avoided if possible.

Caslon, 11 on 14 pt
10 lines of text
without massaging

> informed by what he had already seen and continued to see — 1
> and hear for himself: his insistence on weighing the theo- — 2
> retical against the empirical would bring him into conflict — 3
> with orthodoxies of all kinds, from the academic to the polit- — 4
> ical. And the quest for further evidence never ceased. The — 5
> gathering of information, eye-witness accounts, personal — 6
> stories, anecdotes and jokes went on to the end, along with — 7
> scholarly pursuits. How he would have relished the rich — 8
> cornucopia of vindicating evidence that poured from the — 9
> communist archive made accessible in the 1990s. — 10

We start by *turning over* the word 'see' from the end of line 1 to the beginning of line 2:

The word 'see' is turned over onto line 2.

> informed by what he had already seen and continued to — 1
> see and hear for himself: his insistence on weighing the theo- — 2

This loosens line 1 but makes line 2 too tight, so we turn over the word 'theo-' :

informed by what he had already seen and continued to 1
see and hear for himself: his insistence on weighing the 2
theoretical against the empirical would bring him into 3
conflict with orthodoxies of all kinds, from the academic to 4
the political. And the quest for further evidence never 5
ceased. The gathering of information, eye-witness accounts, 6
personal stories, anecdotes and jokes went on to the end, 7
along with scholarly pursuits. How he would have relished 8
the rich cornucopia of vindicating evidence that poured 9
from the communist archive made accessible in the 1990s. 10

The word 'theo-' is turned over onto line 3, turning over words on every subsequent line.

which turns over words all the way down to line 10. Line 5 is still quite loose, especially following a tight line 4, so we turn over the word 'to' from the end of line 4 to the beginning of line 5:

conflict with orthodoxies of all kinds, from the academic 4
to the political. And the quest for further evidence never 5

The word 'to' is turned over onto line 5.

The setting is now much improved. The lines still vary in tightness and looseness as they always will in justified setting, but this is much less noticeable. Lines 1, 2 and 4 have soft line returns at the end:

informed by what he had already seen and continued to ← 1
see and hear for himself: his insistence on weighing the ← 2
theoretical against the empirical would bring him into 3
conflict with orthodoxies of all kinds, from the academic ← 4
to the political. And the quest for further evidence never 5
ceased. The gathering of information, eye-witness accounts, 6
personal stories, anecdotes and jokes went on to the end, 7
along with scholarly pursuits. How he would have relished 8
the rich cornucopia of vindicating evidence that poured 9
from the communist archive made accessible in the 1990s. 10

There are soft line returns at the end of lines 1, 2 and 4.

There are a number of other problems which can occur in a setting which can be rectified in this way. They include:

Consecutive lines beginning or ending with the same word:

Galliard
10.5 on 15 pt
Repetitions of words at the end of lines can lead to the reader skipping lines, or re-reading lines.

> written by great teachers like Gomard, Grisier and Lafaugère.
>   Lately, though, he had begun to have serious doubts about his ability to set down on paper the discipline to which he had given his whole life. There was another factor, too, which only added to his unease. If the work was to be the *ne plus ultra* on the subject he

corrected to:

> written by great teachers like Gomard, Grisier and Lafaugère.
>   Lately, though, he had begun to have serious doubts about his ability to set down on paper the discipline to which he had given his whole life. There was another factor, too, which only added to his unease. If the work was to be the *ne plus ultra* on the subject

More than two hyphens ending consecutive lines:

Albertina
10 on 14.5 pt
Rows of hyphens draw the eye and create a distraction. The maximum number of hyphens in a row can be specified in the paragraph styles settings.

> is a highly rational, economical structure responding without undue fuss to a practical brief. Take away the restrained deco-rative details, and it is as rational as any modernist build-ing of its time. (Interestingly, one of the few modernist archi-tects to whom he reportedly referred with a degree of respect

corrected to:

> it is a highly rational, economical structure responding with-out undue fuss to a practical brief. Take away the restrained decorative details, and it is as rational as any modernist building of its time. (Interestingly, one of the few modernist architects to whom he reportedly referred with a degree of

Paragraphs ending with a line containing only one word or two very short words:

> ever get hungry. Fungi and mosses and ferns are never left to eat to their heart's content. If this isn't even allowed in natural habitats, where will it be allowed? Where in Western Europe can you still find genuine ruins, beautiful devastation, a building falling apart in its own time – overgrown with vines, undermined by ants, under a blanket of pigeon droppings, the ideal home for spiders and lizards?

Quadraat
10 on 15 pt

corrected to:

> ever get hungry. Fungi and mosses and ferns are never left to eat to their heart's content. If this isn't even allowed in natural habitats, where will it be allowed? Where in Western Europe can you still find genuine ruins, beautiful devastation, a building falling apart in its own time – overgrown with vines, undermined by ants, under a blanket of pigeon droppings, the ideal home for spiders and lizards?

If space is limited, it may be preferable to adjust the word-spacing, using a slightly tighter paragraph style, and take the last word back. This is called *losing a line*:

> ever get hungry. Fungi and mosses and ferns are never left to eat to their heart's content. If this isn't even allowed in natural habitats, where will it be allowed? Where in Western Europe can you still find genuine ruins, beautiful devastation, a building falling apart in its own time – overgrown with vines, undermined by ants, under a blanket of pigeon droppings, the ideal home for spiders and lizards?

The purpose of these changes is to remove anything within the setting which catches the eye, distracting the reader from the meaning of the text.

How to make additional lines

It is sometimes necessary to make paragraphs a line longer in order to push lines of text over onto the next page. This is known as *making lines*.

If a paragraph ends with a line which nearly fills the measure:

All the same, it was probably she who brought me up, so far 1
as I have been brought up at all; at least, I believe that she had 2
a greater part than several other people in making me the way I 3
am. But it was not until after I was fully grown that I noticed 4
her sufficiently to feel that I really saw her. Suddenly one day I 5
simply felt that she was probably closer to me than anyone else in 6
the world, even though I knew less about her than anyone else 7
and despite the fact that she had been in her grave for some time 8
by then. It is anything but easy trying to speak of a person one 9
knows so little about but who is nevertheless so close to one. 10

it is possible to massage the text to create an extra line:

All the same, it was probably she who brought me up, so 1
far as I have been brought up at all; at least, I believe that she 2
had a greater part than several other people in making me the 3
way I am. But it was not until after I was fully grown that I 4
noticed her sufficiently to feel that I really saw her. Suddenly 5
one day I simply felt that she was probably closer to me than 6
anyone else in the world, even though I knew less about her than 7
anyone else and despite the fact that she had been in her grave 8
for some time by then. It is anything but easy trying to speak of 9
a person one knows so little about but who is nevertheless so 10
close to one. 11

This process should be attempted with caution, ensuring that word-spacing is kept even and readable throughout. Long paragraphs are easiest to work with – look for those that are tightly spaced to begin with.

Whether a word can be turned over without the spacing becoming too loose depends not so much on the length of the word itself, but on the number of words on the line. This is because the space created by the turned-over word is divided up among the remaining spaces. So turning over a word from a line containing many short words:

> it had taken her as long as that to call to mind this boy who was *sitting*
> it had taken her as long as that to call to mind this boy who was

New Baskerville
10 pt
17 words-per-line

has less impact on the spacing than turning over a word from a line containing fewer, longer words:

> his companion for some morning coffee. My grandfather was *sitting*
> his companion for some morning coffee. My grandfather was

New Baskerville
10 pt
10 words-per-line

Making lines is more difficult in narrow measures which contain fewer words. It is also difficult in text which consists of dialogue as most paragraphs will not be long enough to work with.

We will now look at some examples of circumstances where it would be necessary to make or lose lines to improve the setting.

Widows and orphans

A *widow* is when the first line of a paragraph appears on the last line of a page:

> he was out of sight, reliving this or that part of the comedy,
> quite beside themselves with merriment.
> Punctually, at a quarter past one, the blue bus I was to

Garamond
11.5 on 15 pt

baseline of text

This is not desirable, but neither is it the end of the world. In texts with lots of dialogue or short paragraphs it may be impossible to prevent this occurring. Only in a book with very long paragraphs would you consider trying to avoid this, in which case try making or losing lines in the preceding paragraphs.

An *orphan* is when the last line of a paragraph appears on the first line of a page:

> playing affected me deeply.
>   Salvatore had come to the end of his account, and night had
> fallen. Crowds of festival-goers released from their tour buses

These should be eliminated wherever possible by massaging text on the preceding pages, to move the short top line down onto the second line:

> And I remember that his whole appearance and his wonderful
> playing affected me deeply.
>   Salvatore had come to the end of his account, and night had
> fallen. Crowds of festival-goers released from their tour buses

If you cannot make or lose lines in any of the paragraphs, and an orphan is thus unavoidable, try to make the last line as long as possible by turning over words earlier in the paragraph:

> and his wonderful playing affected me deeply.
>   Salvatore had come to the end of his account, and night had
> fallen. Crowds of festival-goers released from their tour buses

Paragraphs which are less than a line long, such as dialogue, are not counted as orphans and may be placed on the top line of the page, but if the short line is followed by a long paragraph it may be better avoided:

> 'Stop it, Julius!'
>   This time, things were getting serious. We'd reached home. For the
> past ten days, anonymous hands had been plastering up the angelic
> features of a certain Martin Lejoli on the wall opposite. Martin Lejoli

MANUAL ADJUSTMENTS TO COMPOSITION

Section breaks

A *section break* is a space of one or two lines which authors use to suggest a change of scene or subject. A section break near the top or foot of a page should have at least two lines above and below it:

And not a single line floating alone:

A single line of text will always look as if it is floating, cut off from the rest of the text.

If a section break falls on the first or last line of a page, it may be indicated by a centred asterisk:

*

Today the press and the other media throughout the world only mention the Balkan peninsula in terms of condemnation: where, it is asked, does this primitive ferocity stem from all of a sudden, this cannibalism? Such words are repeated wholesale whenever the horrors of the conXict in ex-Yugoslavia are shown on television. The answer is simple: from nowhere! The barbarity, the cannibalism, the inferno was already there in place, carefully hidden but ready to explode. There are people, the sort who salve their consciences by playing blind and deaf, who are pleased to observe: 'What's to be done? It's the Balkans, after all, they're used to it.' Then they smile as they come out with their cynical aphorisms along the lines of 'balkanisation', 'parish-pump mentality', 'yokels at odds'. What is simply overlooked is that it was in these lands, among these peoples, that the civilization of present-day Europe found its origin. It was in this peninsula that three thousand years ago the most important, the sublimest discovery in human history was made; a guilty conscience.

Croatia and Bosnia. Nothing unusual here. The crime had its origins in Kosovo and only waits to return there to reach its apogee. Among themselves the Serbs do not deny it: they cannot wait for Kosovo's turn to come. Rexhep Qosja's novel is steeped in Kafkaesque anguish. Everything falls apart, everywhere there is a presence, the intimation of terror. The novel is threaded through and through with a sardonic laughter which could as readily be taken for a lament. Elements of tragedy and farce blend in the most natural manner. The author foresees that Kosovo is to experience a new reign of terror; and he is in the grip of another sorrow – in Albania itself things are faring no better. The Albanian Xag displays a two-headed eagle; similarly the Albanian tragedy is double-headed: a single nation under a double communist dictatorship, the Serb and the Albanian. That is a lot for a people already the victims of their history.

*

Without the asterisk, the reader has very little indication that a new section is starting. This can cause confusion if the subject changes without warning.

Run-on headings

See *Headings*, p.123

Chapter headings and sub-headings that run on (that is, they do not all start on a new page) should have at least three lines of text above and below them.

Chapter ends

See *Headings*, p.125

Where chapters start on new pages, the last page of each chapter should contain at least three lines of text. You may decide to make this four or five in larger format books.

Recto and verso starts

Authors or editors will sometimes specify that sections of the book have to start on certain pages – for example, all the chapter openings on rectos preceded by an illustration on the opposite verso. Careful massaging of the lines will be necessary to achieve this.

References to illustrations

See *Illustrated books*, p.283

Books containing illustrations scattered throughout the text may be manipulated to keep the text which refers to any given illustration as close as possible to the illustration itself. Remember that the text reference should always appear *before* the picture.

Extent

It is unwise to assume that you can increase or reduce the extent of a book very much by making or losing lines. The result is likely to be badly spaced and will take many hours. It is preferable to make extent using the procedure described on pp.234–40. However, when massaging text, keep in mind whether you have spare pages to use, or whether space is tight. This will inform your choice of whether to make or lose lines.

Printing out a set of thumbnail pages of the text before you start massaging will show where chapters end and pages can be made or saved.

Massaging ranged left text

Ranged left setting should not require as much manipulation as justified setting because the word-spacing is already even, but some effort should be made to get the ragged right edge of the text looking satisfactory.

When massaging justified text, the idea is to get each line looking as similar as possible to those above and below it so there are no jumps between tight and loose lines. If a well-set justified text were set ranged left it would look like this:

who are you, asked the man, Don't you remember me, No, I don't, I'm the cleaning woman, Cleaning what, The king's palace, The woman who opened the door for petitions, The very same, And why aren't you back at the king's palace cleaning and opening doors, Because the doors I really wanted to open have already been opened and because, from now on, I will only clean boats, So you want to go with me in search of the unknown island, I left the palace by the door of decisions, In that case, go and have a look at the caravel, after all this time, it must be in need of a good wash, but watch out for the seagulls, they're not to be trusted, Don't you want to come with me and see what your boat is like inside, You

Stone Sans
9 on 13.5 pt
The wavy line down the right-hand side is the result of even, justified setting, but making text into shapes like this creates a distraction.

The aim with ranged left setting, however, is to avoid making a regular shape, but to create a 'random' looking ragged edge down the side:

who are you, asked the man, Don't you remember me, No, I don't, I'm the cleaning woman, Cleaning what, The king's palace, The woman who opened the door for petitions, The very same, And why aren't you back at the king's palace cleaning and opening doors, Because the doors I really wanted to open have already been opened and because, from now on, I will only clean boats, So you want to go with me in search of the unknown island, I left the palace by the door of decisions, In that case, go and have a look at the caravel, after all this time, it must be in need of a good wash, but watch out for the seagulls, they're not to be trusted, Don't you want to come with me and see what your boat is like inside, You

This setting varies between long and short lines giving a more 'random' look.

CHAPTER HEADINGS

The most common way of organizing text is to divide it into chapters. Each usually starts on a new page and is announced by a chapter heading which is styled consistently throughout the book. Chapter headings may contain the chapter's number, title, and sometimes an extra element such as an epigraph or illustration.

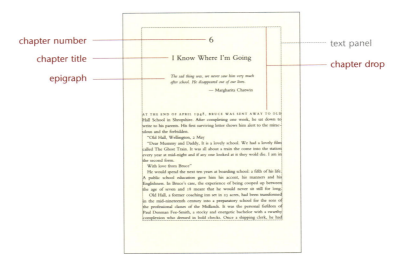

Not all chapter headings contain all these elements; it is up to the author and editor to decide which to include.

The chapter heading is placed in a space known as the *chapter drop*. This is the distance from the top of the text panel to the first line of text after the chapter heading.

When designing a chapter heading, there are a number of concerns: choice of typeface, size of type, position, and relationship between the different elements. These are discussed in the following pages.

For books with run-on chapters – that is, chapters which do not start on a new page – see p.123. For books with sub-chapters see *Sub-headings*, p.126.

Type style of chapter titles

As with all display settings, chapter titles may be designed with greater freedom than continuous text because their size means that readability is less of an issue. The type style used for headings can make a book look clean and modern or decorative and historical without having a negative impact on the text itself:

The First Day

Heading: Akzidenz Grotesk, 16 pt

I sometimes pass through St Helena, but I've never stopped there. It's an empty place, silent and solitary. The houses sit on the grass as they do in Africa. Unlikely shops, a closed church, a

Text: Minion 10.25 on 15 pt

THE FIRST DAY

———

Heading: Chevalier 14 pt

Rule: Type Embellishments II 28 pt

I sometimes pass through St Helena, but I've never stopped there. It's an empty place, silent and solitary. The houses sit on the grass as they do in Africa. Unlikely shops, a closed church, a

Text: Minion 10.25 on 15 pt

These two chapter openings would give the reader a very different impression of the kind of book they were about to read.

For a further discussion of display setting and display fonts, see pp.142–57.

Chapter drops

A new chapter will usually start on a fresh page. The text, rather than starting at the very top of the text panel, begins some way down. This is called the chapter drop and should be consistent throughout the book.

The chapter drop should be equivalent to a number of whole lines so that the baseline of the body text matches the rest of the book.

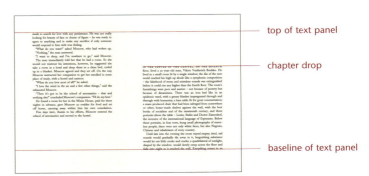

top of text panel

chapter drop

baseline of text panel

The size of the chapter drop should be chosen with the following factors in mind:

Chapter headings: the more elements that make up the heading – title, number, epigraph, etc. – the more room it will need. Chapters which have no heading or number also need a large drop to make clear to the reader that a new chapter has started.

Size of margins: if the book has large, luxurious margins, this should be reflected in the chapter drop.

Length of chapters: books with a few long chapters tend to have larger chapter drops than those divided into lots of small chapters.

Chapter drops are usually between a quarter and half of the depth of the text panel.

Chapter drops and extent

Chapter drops take up space, which means they become a factor when calculating the extent of a book. When flowing text into a grid it is worth putting chapter drops in – even if the depth of them may change later – so that the overall effect on extent may be taken into account. The more chapters there are, the greater this effect will be.

See *Making extent*, p.235

Position of chapter titles

The position of chapter titles within the chapter drop is simply a matter of what you think looks good and appropriate, as long as the number, title and any other heading matter appear in the order specified by the editor. It is unusual for titles to break out of the text panel, though they may be hung out into a wide margin at the side, if this fits in with the overall design of the book:

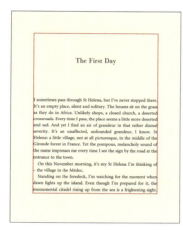

Chapter titles can give the impression of floating aimlessly, especially if the chapter drops are large. Moving them close to the text, or anchoring them to the grid by aligning them with text, will overcome this.

Size of chapter titles

The size at which you set your chapter titles will be determined by the following:

The size of the page: the titles should not overwhelm the page. This is the most common misjudgement when designing chapter titles.

The size of the text: there should be a significant step up in type size between the text and the chapter titles.

The depth of the chapter drop: take care that the titles do not look crammed into the space.

The number of words in the titles: consider not just the size of individual letters, but the size of the complete title as a single object. If all your titles are long, you will need a smaller type size.

Type style: delicate display fonts are designed to be seen at a large size; too small and they may look weak and spindly.

Go through the typescript and find the longest and shortest titles. You will need to find a size in which they both look comfortable:

Sabon, 22 pt

Little Things

Sabon, 14 pt

*What We Talk about When
We Talk about Love*

Sabon, 16 pt

Little Things

*What We Talk about When
We Talk about Love*

Chapter numbers

The editor will decide whether chapters will be numbered, and if so, whether to use a digit, or spell out the numbers, as well as whether to use the word 'chapter'.

4   FOUR   Chapter 4   CHAPTER FOUR

In novels, the chapter number is often the only heading given to a chapter and can be set as you would a chapter title. Try different fonts, especially those which have interesting number forms:

1234567890   1234567890

When a heading contains just digits, consider using lining figures as non-lining figures will appear to differ greatly in size:

The differences between lining and non-lining figures are explained on pp.270–1

1   8   1   8

Scala non-lining and lining figures

Roman Numerals

Roman numerals may be used for chapter numbers, set in capitals or small caps. They are set as you would normally set display capitals, with letter-spacing:

See *Roman numerals*, pp.278–9

VII

Rialto, 36 pt

CHAPTER IX

Rialto caps, 24 pt

Combining chapter numbers and titles

If the heading contains a number *and* a title, the number appears before the title. They can be placed together on the same line, though this can look a little dull and dense:

Joanna italic, 18 pt

6. The Beautifully Constructed House

A more elegant solution is to have the number and title on separate lines:

Centaur, 24 pt

6

Centaur, 18 pt

The Beautifully Constructed House

When the number is spelt out, it is better set smaller than the chapter title:

Galliard expert
11 pt, 30 ics

CHAPTER SIX

Galliard italic, 16 pt

The Beautifully Constructed House

If the chapter titles are ranged, the numbers should align with them:

Formata light
9 pt, 40 ics

CHAPTER 6

Formata light, 16 pt

The Beautifully Constructed House

Joanna, 11 on 15 pt

History begins beneath the roots of trees. That is certainly true of Amsterdam, a city that grew up on the IJ and sank, only to rise

Chapter epigraphs

Authors will sometimes add a short epigraph or quotation at the beginning of a chapter. The chapter drop should be designed to accommodate this.

Type size should be the same as, or a fraction larger than that used for the text. Using a different type style, say italic, differentiates the epigraph from the text. If the chapter heading is in a different typeface, you may want to use that typeface for the epigraph too.

An epigraph is usually set to a narrower measure than the text – as with extracts. If it is just a short line it may be centred, if that is the style for the heading. The epigraph's attribution is then set ranged right:

XVIII

Bembo, 16 pt

That Wretched Book

Bembo, 16 pt

Wild horses couldn't drag him back to Edinburgh, so that's that.

Bembo italic, 11.5 pt

— Elizabeth to her mother

Bembo, 10 pt

At Holwell Farm, Elizabeth grew concerned. As soon as Bruce came home, he lost himself in the garden. 'Bruce went mad and ordered about 20 things the other day: lots of trees and things like bamboo

Bembo
10.75 on 15 pt

Long epigraphs may require more thought and discussion with the editor, especially if they are not used consistently throughout the book. One solution is not to include them in the chapter drop, but to start them on the first line of text, followed by a standardized space – say two lines – before the text proper begins.

Drop caps

For further details on setting drop, raised and small caps, see *Display*, pp.152–5.

Requiem
10.5 on 14 pt
3-line drop cap

A drop cap is a capital letter at the beginning of a chapter which is set larger than the rest of the text and drops down onto the lines below:

In the centre of the capital, on the seventh floor, lived a 30-year-old man, Viktor Vasilievich Bozhko. He lived in a small room lit by a single window; the din of the new world reached his high-up abode like a symphonic composi-

Drop caps are especially useful if chapters are not named or numbered. The combination of a large chapter drop and a drop cap are enough to alert the reader that a new chapter is beginning. They should not be used in books with different levels of sub-headings, as this can make the page look untidy.

Raised caps

This is simpler to set than a drop cap as it does not affect the text, but the result can look uncomfortable. It is best used for chapter headings which do not contain a number or title, just a chapter drop.

A raised cap (known in the US as a *stick-up cap*) is also a large capital, but rather than being dropped down into the text, it sits on the baseline of the first line:

His arguments stood up. Thérèse had told him about mum's out-of-wedlock lovers (or dumped progenitors), Clara's wedding (violent

Small caps

An alternative to drop caps is to use a single line of small caps. This may be more suitable if you have chapters frequently beginning with dialogue and opening quotation marks:

Quadraat
11 on 16 pt
First line: Quadraat
small caps, 15 ICS

'I'M SORRY, PAL.' AND MY UNCLE WOULD SQUEEZE the trigger. 'I wish I didn't have to, my friend.' And then my uncle would hit hard with the stick, a well-aimed blow to the

Run-on chapters

When a chapter does not start on a new page, but carries on from the previous chapter, it is said to *run on*.

Run-on chapters may be headed with a title, or just a number. When setting chapters in this way, it is important to get the space before and after the heading right. Too little and it will look cramped (*left*). Too much and you will be left with gaping holes on the page (*centre*). The space above the heading should be greater than the space below. This attaches the chapter number to the appropriate text (*right*):

The space between chapters should add up to a number of whole lines. This ensures that the text below the heading backs up properly.

Chapter headings which do not fall at the top of the page should have at least three full lines of text above them. This can be achieved by massaging the text on the previous pages to either make or lose lines as necessary:

See *Manual adjustments to composition*, pp.102–10

If the text contains a lot of dialogue, getting three whole lines at the top of a page may be a problem. Make a judgement on how the top of the page looks – if there are just a few words surrounded by white space, turn over some more lines.

When a chapter heading falls at the bottom of a page, there should be at least three full lines of text below the heading. If this cannot be done by massaging the text, the heading may be turned over onto the next page, leaving a space where it would have been.

Headings for run-on chapters

When the run-on chapter heading falls at the top of a page, the number or title should be placed at the top of the text panel. There is no need to add a large space before it as with a chapter drop.

One problem that may arise here is that the text following the heading may not sit on the baseline grid. This could be due to the larger size of the chapter heading pushing the text down, or it could be because the line-spaces following the heading are not equal to the leading of the rest of the text:

top of text panel

4

baseline grid

The mist allows a few yellow rays of light to filter through, turning it a light coffee colour. The paras loom up ahead of us. Their raincoats look brand new, as though the surface

Put a little space before the chapter heading, to ensure that the body text is sitting on the baseline of the text panel and the pages back up correctly:

top of text panel

4

baseline grid

The mist allows a few yellow rays of light to filter through, turning it a light coffee colour. The paras loom up ahead of us. Their raincoats look brand new, as though the surface

Chapter ends

Where chapters start on fresh pages, the last page of each chapter should have at least three full lines of text on it. This can be achieved by making or losing lines. In larger format books, three lines above and below the chapter heading may not look like enough: increase this number to at least four or five lines.

See *Manual adjustments to composition*, pp.106–10

Vignettes

The space following the end of a chapter may be filled with a vignette if the editor and author are happy with this. It can take the form of a decorative device or illustration, and should be quite small with plenty of surrounding space. Vignettes should be consistent in style and size throughout a book.

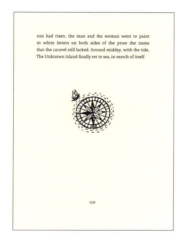

Recto starts

The editor may request that each chapter begins on a recto. Where previous chapters finish on a recto, the following verso is left blank. This will have an impact on the calculation of extent.

Occasionally you may be asked to start chapters on versos, but this should only be the case with illustrated books where it is straightforward to increase the size of pictures and thus push the text on. It is not considered acceptable to leave a blank recto.

See *Making extent*, p.222

SUB-HEADINGS

A non-fiction book may cover a range of subjects, and the text is divided up accordingly. It is the responsibility of the author and editor to sub-divide the text into chapters and sub-chapters, and to put these into a logical order. It is important for the designer to understand how the text is organized as this must be communicated typographically to the reader.

Heading hierarchies – A, B and C headings

When a chapter is divided into sub-sections of equal importance, these are given a style of heading which looks different to chapter headings. These are labelled *A-headings* by the editor. When the sub-chapters are divided further, they are labelled *B-headings* by the editor and set in another style, and so on. These different levels of heading – Chapter heading, A-heading, B-heading, C-heading – are called a *heading hierarchy*.

Books will not usually have more than three levels of sub-heading, and editors should attempt to keep the structure of the text as straightforward as possible.

An example of structure

The table opposite shows the structure of a chapter from a history book. The chapter is titled INDUSTRY, and is divided into sub-chapters: TEXTILES, LEATHER, POTTERY, BRICKS & TILES, etc., which are given A-headings. Some of these sub-chapters are divided further, for example, the TEXTILES sub-chapter is split into sections on Wool, Cotton, Flax & Linen, Hemp, Silk, and Needlecraft, which are given B-headings. The section on Cotton includes sub-sections on *Looms* and *Power-looms* which are given C-headings.

Relative importance of headings

The design of sub-headings should reflect their position within the hierarchy. B-headings should look less significant than A-headings because they are sub-divisions of the A-heading. Likewise C-headings should look less significant than B-headings. There are many ways of making one level of heading look more important than another, such as size, position, the use of space, weight and colour.

CHAPTER TITLE: INDUSTRY

A-HEADINGS	B-headings	C-headings

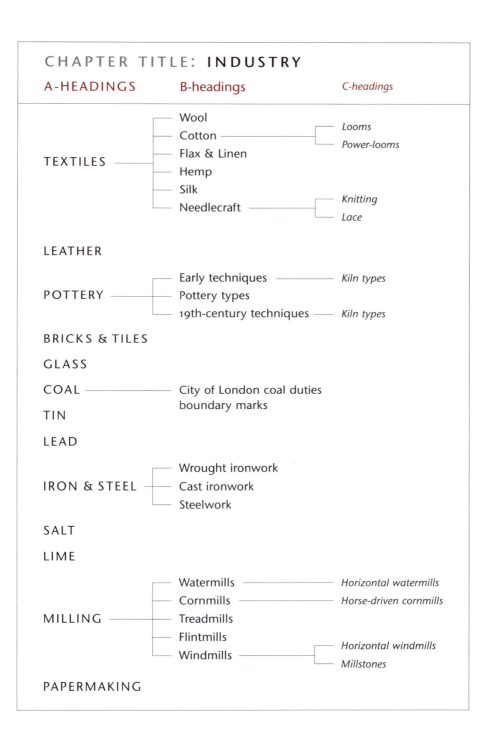

TEXTILES
- Wool
- Cotton
  - Looms
  - Power-looms
- Flax & Linen
- Hemp
- Silk
- Needlecraft
  - Knitting
  - Lace

LEATHER

POTTERY
- Early techniques — Kiln types
- Pottery types
- 19th-century techniques — Kiln types

BRICKS & TILES

GLASS

COAL — City of London coal duties boundary marks

TIN

LEAD

IRON & STEEL
- Wrought ironwork
- Cast ironwork
- Steelwork

SALT

LIME

MILLING
- Watermills — Horizontal watermills
- Cornmills — Horse-driven cornmills
- Treadmills
- Flintmills
- Windmills
  - Horizontal windmills
  - Millstones

PAPERMAKING

Size of sub-headings

The appearance of each level of sub-heading must be consistent throughout a book, and will depend on a number of factors:

Size of page: the largest headings should not overwhelm the page.

Size of text: the smallest headings should be visibly larger than the body text, though not necessarily by a great amount.

Number of words: if most of the headings contain many words, they will all need to be set at smaller size.

Frequency of headings: a text that is divided into a large number of sub-sections, each containing a small amount of text, should generally have smaller headings.

Number of levels in the hierarchy: if you have many levels to deal with, the largest may need to be larger and the smallest, smaller.

Choose the most frequently used level of heading – whether it be A, B or C – as a starting point and increase or decrease the size of the other headings from that point. The amount by which type size increases will need to be greater in the larger sizes. For example, an increase of 2 pts from 10 pt to 12 pt is noticeable:

C-heading   B-heading

whereas an increase from 22 pt to 24 pt is less so:

C-heading   B-heading

so type sizes should be increased visually rather than by regular increments:

Note how in the right-hand example, the jump from 10 pt to 15 pt seems quite big, but the jump from 20 pt to 25 pt is less noticeable. The sizes in the left-hand example have been determined visually resulting in a more even-looking increase.

9 pt Power-looms	10 pt Power-looms
12 pt Cotton	15 pt Cotton
18 pt Textiles	20 pt Textiles
24 pt Industry	25 pt Industry

The use of space before and after headings

Whereas chapter headings usually fall at the top of a new page, sub-headings are usually *run on*, that is, they are placed directly beneath the preceding section of text. The amount of space used above and below the heading will vary depending on their place in the hierarchy.

Set the heading with more space above it than below. This joins the heading to the appropriate section of text below:

> There are many old mills in the south-east Lancashire–south Derbyshire complex, and indeed the industrial landscape generally is worth studying.
>
> ## *Flax and Linen*
>
> Flax was used widely in the ancient world, from Neolithic times on, as a textile source. At first its tough stems were used in windbreaks or

A larger space gives the reader a distinct break between sections, suggesting that one subject has finished and a new one is beginning. Smaller spaces are used, as below, when sub-sections form a list:

> ### VEHICLES
> An interesting relic is Brooklands, Weybridge, where part of the steeply embanked testing track (1906) has been preserved. There is also here the Clubhouse, Members' Restaurant, and Barnes Wallis's office.
>
> ### OIL
> The great refineries at Fawley and Grangemouth are not yet industrial archaeology, but are conspicuously part of the landscape, as is the chemical works at ICI Billingham.
>
> ### BROADCASTING
> The original building for the first radio station (1922), 2LO, at Savoy Hill, still exists, although no longer in BBC hands. Broadcasting House (1932),

Standardizing the space around headings may make life simpler. For example, one size of drop for A- and B-headings, and a smaller drop for C- and D-headings.

Text: Stone Print 10.5 on 14 pt
Heading: Stone Print italic, 14 on 14 pt
One and a half line spaces above the heading. Half a line space below

Text: Stone Print 10.5 on 14 pt
Heading: Stone Print small caps 11 on 14 pt. Half line spaces between sections

When working out space above and below headings, the spaces should add up to a number of whole line spaces: for example, two and a half line spaces above and half a line space below. This will ensure that the body text backs up.

The type style of sub-headings

While size and space can convey the position of headings within the hierarchy, it is the style of type in which they are set which allows the reader to distinguish between them. Each level of heading may be set in a different style – roman, italic, capitals, small caps – either in the same typeface as the text, or a completely different typeface such as a complimentary sans serif.

Roman upper and lower case

The simplest form of heading to use is roman upper and lower case in the same typeface as the text, but at a larger size. This is more successful in the larger sized headings where there is an obvious difference between heading and text:

Text: Stone Print
10.5 on 14 pt
Heading: Stone
Print, 22 pt

Pottery

Pottery has been made in this country for over 6,000 years, and is an essential feature of settled life. It serves or has served for food storage, preparation, cooking and eating off, for containing cremated ashes or to

As a minor heading it can be harder to distinguish from the text:

Text: Stone Print
10.5 on 14 pt
Heading: Stone
Print, 12 pt

Broadcasting

The original building for the first radio station (1922), 2LO, at Savoy Hill, still exists, although no longer in BBC hands. Broadcasting House (1932),

Changing the weight to a semi-bold face may help at smaller sizes:

Text: Stone Print
10.5 on 14 pt
Heading: Stone
Print semi-bold
12 pt

Broadcasting

The original building for the first radio station (1922), 2LO, at Savoy Hill, still exists, although no longer in BBC hands. Broadcasting House (1932),

Italics

How you use italics in your headings depends on how legible the italic is. The benefit of using italic is that it is not easily confused with the text and can be set at a small size for minor headings:

Early pottery-making techniques and kiln types

Pottery has been made in this country for over 6,000 years, and is an essential feature of settled life. It serves or has served for food storage, preparation, cooking and eating off, for containing cremated ashes or to

Text: Stone Print
10.5 on 14 pt
Heading: Stone Print
italic, 12 pt

If your headings contain a lot of words, italic headings will take up less room than roman:

City of London coal duties Boundary marks

City of London coal duties Boundary marks

Joanna italic, 16 pt

Joanna roman, 16 pt

Italics are better suited to upper and lower case setting, rather than all caps:

Bricks and Tiles

BRICKS AND TILES

Fournier italic, 18 pt

Fournier italic, 18 pt

If an italic heading contains elements that would normally be italicized – such as titles of books or foreign words – these must be put into roman. However, this can get a little confusing for some readers (and typesetters, and even proofreaders), so it may be better to avoid using italics if headings are to contain italicized words.

See *Editorial rules*, p.384

The Painting of the Maestà

The Painting of the *Maestà*

Garamond italic
18 pt

Garamond roman
18 pt

Capitals and small caps

Readers will interpret words set in capitals as more important than those in lower case. It is worth bearing in mind, therefore, that capitalized headings have to be significantly smaller than lower case headings if they are lower down the heading hierarchy. In the following example the capitals are in a smaller type size but visually, they look as if they are of equivalent importance:

A-heading:
Stone Print, 18 pt

B-heading: Stone
Print caps, 14 pt
30 ICS

Milling

WATERMILLS

Water and wind were the only sources of mechanical power until well into the 18th century. Waterwheels were used in Roman Britain and

Reducing the size of the capitals further will make the relationship clearer:

A-heading:
Stone Print, 18 pt

B-heading: Stone
Print caps, 10 pt
30 ICS

Milling

WATERMILLS

Water and wind were the only sources of mechanical power until well into the 18th century. Waterwheels were used in Roman Britain and

When capitals are reduced in size, they can look a little light, so using small caps instead – with the letter-spacing increased – will improve the relative weight:

A-heading:
Stone Print, 18 pt

B-heading: Stone
Print small caps
12 pt, 30 ICS

Milling

WATERMILLS

Water and wind were the only sources of mechanical power until well into the 18th century. Waterwheels were used in Roman Britain and

Setting the headings in a different typeface to the text can add interest to the pages. Pick one font family for the headings and set each level of heading in a face from that family to avoid the book looking messy.

Sans serifs are often chosen to give books a more modern look, by using them in headings, running heads, captions, etc. Some serif typefaces, such as Scala and Quadraat, have a matching sans serif font which can be used for this purpose. Sans serif headings look their best when given plenty of space and benefit from being set slightly smaller than an equivalent serif font:

> There are many old mills in the south-east Lancashire–south Derbyshire complex, and indeed the industrial landscape generally is worth studying.

Flax and Linen

Flax was used widely in the ancient world, from Neolithic times on, as a textile source. At first its tough stems were used in windbreaks or fish-traps; when these rotted, the usable fibres were revealed. Linen reached Europe via the Roman Empire.

Heading: Stone Sans 10.5 pt

Text: Stone Print 10.5 on 14 pt

Using a different font for headings, brings the advantage of introducing an historical or decorative element without compromising the legibility of the body text:

Pottery

Pottery has been made in this country for over 6,000 years, and is an essential feature of settled life. It serves or has served for food storage, preparation, cooking and eating off, for containing cremated ashes or to

Heading: Fraktur, 24 pt

Text: Minion 9.5 on 13 pt

The position of sub-headings

Whereas chapter headings are usually set at the top of a page with ample space, sub-headings can fall anywhere on a page, and are often combined with other levels of heading. When using many levels of heading, position can play an important part in maintaining the distinction between the different levels, and may be used, for example, to draw particular attention towards chapter headings:

Chapter heading:
Stone Sans caps
22 pt, 40 ICS

A-heading:
Stone Sans, 16 pt

B-heacing: Stone
Sans small caps
10 pt, 30 ICS

Text: Minion
10 on 14 pt

INDUSTRY

Textiles

WOOL

For many centuries wool, and woollen cloth, was the principal industry of England, until overtaken by cotton in the 19th century. Up to the mid 14th century wool itself was the main export, and from then to

As the above example shows, centering a heading gives it extra weight and makes it more appropriate for chapter headings and A-headings, whereas minor headings sit more comfortably ranged with the text. This can be demonstrated by swapping the position of the headings:

Chapter heading:
Stone Sans small
caps, 22 pt, 40 ICS

A-heading:
Stone Sans, 16 pt

B-heading: Stone
Sans small caps
10 pt, 30 ICS

Text: Minion
10 on 14 pt

INDUSTRY

Textiles

WOOL

For many centuries wool, and woollen cloth, was the principal industry of England, until overtaken by cotton in the 19th century. Up to the mid 14th century wool itself was the main export, and from then to

Using differing positions, type styles may be repeated. For example, should you need six levels of heading, the first three could be centred:

CHAPTER HEADING

Requiem small caps
30 pt, 10 ICS

A-heading A-heading

Requiem, 20 pt

B-heading B-heading

Requiem italic, 16 pt

And the second three, using the same type styles, but smaller, ranged left:

C-HEADING C-HEADING C-HEADING

Requiem small caps
14 pt, 10 ICS

D-heading D-heading D-heading

Requiem, 12 pt

E-heading E-heading E-heading

Requiem italic
10.5 pt

Resulting in pages that will look something like this:

THE SAXON PERIOD

Chapter heading:
Requiem small caps
20 pt, 20 ICS

Historical Background

A-heading:
Requiem, 14 pt

Britain in Anglo-Saxon times was divided into numerous separate kingdoms, seven or possibly more of them in England alone. The shift of power between their various rulers and the scope of their authority are too complex to discuss here.

THE ANGLO-SAXON STYLE

C-heading:
Requiem small caps
11 pt, 20 ICS

The Church

E-heading:
Requiem italic
10.5 pt

Since no secular architecture has survived from this period, a definition of the Anglo-Saxon style must be limited to the characteristics of the very few extant ecclesiastical buildings. Saxon churches are tall and long in relation to their width. They have thick walls with small narrow doors and

Text: Minion
9.5 on 13 pt

Grouping headings together

When two or three headings in a hierarchy appear one after another, complications can arise. Take the following:

C-heading: one and a half line spaces before, half a line space after

D-heading: one and a half line spaces before, half a line space after

E-heading: one line space before, no line space after

between their various rulers and the scope of their authority are too complex to discuss here.

THE ANGLO-SAXON STYLE

Since no secular architecture has survived from this period, a definition of the Anglo-Saxon style must be limited to the characteristics of the very

Continental Origins

The Church established in Britain under the Romans based its buildings on the early Christian churches of Rome. Some of these were circular, often

The Church

Saxon churches are tall and long in relation to their width. They have thick walls with small narrow doors and windows and steeply pitched roofs.

If these levels of headings were grouped together including the space before and after each one, they would look like this:

These headings appear to float in space and would take up a large proportion of the page.

between their various rulers and the scope of their authority are too complex to discuss here.

THE ANGLO-SAXON STYLE

Continental Origins

The Church

Since no secular architecture has survived from this period, a definition of the Anglo-Saxon style must be limited to the characteristics of the very

Whereas taking out the space before each heading would have this effect:

between their various rulers and the scope of their authority are too complex to discuss here.

THE ANGLO-SAXON STYLE

Continental Origins

The Church

Since no secular architecture has survived from this period, a definition of the Anglo-Saxon style must be limited to the characteristics of the very

C-heading: two line spaces before

D-heading: half a line space before

E-heading: half a line space before, no line space after

Of course, these may be adjusted visually (as long as this is done consistently throughout the book). When headings are grouped in this way, check the bottom line of the text on the page to make sure it sits on the baseline. If it is not, adjustments may be made to the space before the headings – do it to the largest space as this will be less noticeable.

Chapter drops and sub-headings

If a book has a deep chapter drop, and a sub-heading is put in before the text starts, keep the first line of text in the same place as other chapters and put the sub-heading above it:

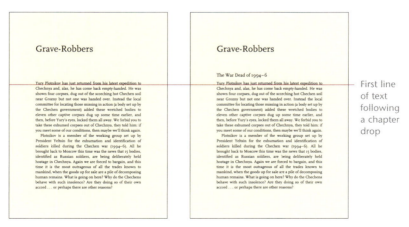

First line of text following a chapter drop

Using colours and tints for sub-headings

A second colour is a simple way of distinguishing between headings and text. In this book, for example, the text is broken up into small sections and the headings are both frequent and contain many words. Setting them in red allows us to use a small type size and keep the space above and below headings to a minimum.

In some four-colour illustrated books it may not be possible to use coloured text. See *Co-editions*, p.300

Of course, using a second colour is an additional expense for a book that only contains black text. An alternative is to use a tint of black. One benefit of this is that large bold headings can be made to look less oppressive:

INDUSTRY

For many centuries wool, and woollen cloth, was the principal industry of England, until overtaken by cotton in the 19th century. Up to the mid 14th century wool itself was the main export, and from then to

INDUSTRY

For many centuries wool, and woollen cloth, was the principal industry of England, until overtaken by cotton in the 19th century. Up to the mid 14th century wool itself was the main export, and from then to

When choosing a tint it is best to consult a tint book containing printed examples, or ask your printer for samples. Printed tints do not necessarily look the same as they are represented on screen, and hard copy produced by office printers is inaccurate.

If you have a lot of different heading levels, and the chapter heading has to be very large, using a tint can tone it down. If you decide to use a tint, the impact of this effect should be taken into account when deciding on type size.

Using many different tints in one book is a risk – it may just look like poor printing. One light tone, one mid tone and black should be enough for most situations.

For minor headings set in small sizes, using a tint of black or a light or neutral colour may make the headings too weak:

There are many old mills in the south-east Lancashire–south Derbyshire complex, and indeed the industrial landscape generally is worth studying.

Flax and Linen

Flax was used widely in the ancient world as a textile source. At first its tough stems were used in windbreaks or fish-traps; when these rotted,

Text: Stone Print
10.5 on 14 pt
Heading: Stone
Sans, 10 pt
50% tint

Using a bolder weight will correct this:

There are many old mills in the south-east Lancashire–south Derbyshire complex, and indeed the industrial landscape generally is worth studying.

Flax and Linen

Flax was used widely in the ancient world as a textile source. At first its tough stems were used in windbreaks or fish-traps; when these rotted,

Text: Stone Print
10.5 on 14 pt
Heading: Stone
Sans semi-bold
10 pt, 50% tint

Bright colours have the opposite effect, and thus type may need reducing in size or weight to lessen their impact:

Pottery

Pottery has been made in this country for over 6,000 years, and is an essential feature of settled life. It serves or has served for food storage,

Text: Minion
9.5 on 14 pt
Heading:
Stone Sans, 26 pt
Pantone 187

Pottery

Pottery has been made in this country for over 6,000 years, and is an essential feature of settled life. It serves or has served for food storage,

Text: Minion
9.5 on 14 pt
Heading: Stone
Sans, 20 pt
Pantone 187

Numbered sub-sections

Technical and reference books, because of the nature of their contents, may well contain multiple headings. To help the reader navigate through the book, a simple yet flexible numbering system is used. Our sample chapter on 'Industry' from p.127 would then be numbered like this:

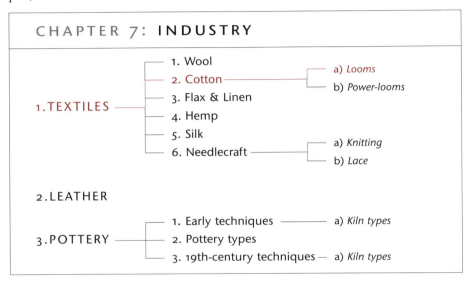

So the chapter heading would read: 7 Industry
The A-heading would read: 7.1 Textiles
The B-heading would read: 7.1.2 Cotton
and the C-heading would read either: 7.1.2 (a) Looms   or just: (a) Looms

This method of expressing the structure of the text is better suited to the under-stated, functional typography found in reference books. The numbers are often set in the margin to make them easier to locate:

7.1.2 Cotton

The cotton industry changed the face of the north-west of England, and dominated British industry for 200 years. It had a meteoric rise in the mid 18th century, and an equally sharp decline in the 20th. Its period

Saving space with minor headings

When text is divided into many short sub-sections, a lot of space will be occupied by headings. If this is proving a problem, one solution is to set the lowest level of heading on the first line of text.

The heading is set at the same size as the text and distinguished by using a different type style, or a different colour:

Vehicles An interesting relic is Brooklands, Weybridge, where part of the steeply-embanked testing track (1906) has been preserved. There is also here the Clubhouse, Members' Restaurant, and Barnes Wallis's office.

Oil The great refineries at Fawley and Grangemouth are not yet industrial archaeology, but are conspicuously part of the landscape, as is the chemical works at ICI Billingham.

Text: Stone Print 10.5 on 14 pt
Heading: Stone Print semi-bold 11 pt, Pantone 187

If the margins are wide enough, headings of this type may be hung out to the left:

VEHICLES An interesting relic is Brooklands, Weybridge, where part of the steeply-embanked testing track (1906) has been preserved. There is also here the Clubhouse, Members' Restaurant, and Barnes Wallis's office.

OIL The great refineries at Fawley and Grangemouth are not yet industrial archaeology, but are conspicuously part of the landscape, as is the chemical works at ICI Billingham.

Text: Stone Print 10.5 on 14 pt
Heading: Stone Print small caps, 11 pt 20 ICS
hung out 3 mm

If using a different typeface, try to match the x-heights:

Vehicles   An interesting relic is Brooklands, Weybridge,

Vehicles   An interesting relic is Brooklands, Weybridge,

Formata and Minion

Corvallis and Minion

This kind of treatment is more usually found in informational booklets and leaflets which have to fit a lot of text into a small space. In bookwork it can be a useful device for setting glossaries, bibliographies and other extended lists.

DISPLAY TYPEFACES AND ORNAMENTS

Display typefaces

Display settings are those settings of single lines or groups of lines that are not part of the main text of a book. Titles, sub-titles and chapter headings are display settings.

Display fonts range from the well designed to the bizarre:

abcde	BULMER DISPLAY	Bulmer Display
ABCDQ	GALLIC WARS	Trajan regular
ABCDQ	JEWELLERY	Spartan
abcdq	A Gentle Informality	Shelley Andante
abcdq	WORLD WARS	Akzidenz Grotesk Super
abcdq	Roxy Cinema	Gill Shadowed
abcdq	Raymond Chandler	Typeka
abcdq	Midnight in Sicily	Britannic Bold
abcdq	Fashion in style	Univers Ultra Thin
ABCDQ	BAUHAUS	Neuland Inline
abcdq	THE MATRIX	Nebulae
ABCDQ	THE BALLROOM	Delphinian
ABCDQ	TALL KNIGHTS	Augustea Open
BCDQ	LEONARDO	Requiem Display
abcdq	Nearly illegible	Carpenter

Some fonts only have capitals; others are barely legible when capitalized:

Birthday BIRTHDAY

Birthday BIRTHDAY

Shelley Andante

Fluidum Bold

The worlds of advertising, marketing, magazines and newspapers demand day-by-day novelty to attract the public and display fonts have a large part to play in these areas. Display faces are used in bookwork for titles, chapter titles and other displayed lines:

THE FIRST DAY

I

I SOMETIMES PASS THROUGH ST HELENA, BUT I'VE NEVER stopped there. It's an empty place, silent and solitary. The houses sit on the grass as they do in Africa. Unlikely shops, a

Text: Bembo 8.5 pt
Display lines: Trajan
A drop cap at two lines followed by small caps for the text of the first line.

An inappropriate or over-use of display faces within the main text, seen below, can distract the reader and should be avoided.

The First Day

1

I sometimes pass through St Helena, but I've never stopped there. It's an empty place, silent and solitary. The houses sit on the grass as they do in Africa. Unlikely shops, a closed church, a

Text: Bauer Bodoni, 10 pt
Display lines: Wittenberg Fraktur
may fit into the historical content of the text but verges on display for display's sake. The first cap 'I' in the text is not easily legible; the 'y' in the title looks like an 'n'.

Chapter One

In the spring of her twenty-second year, Sumire fell in love for the first time in her life. An intense love, a veritable tornado sweeping across the plains – flattening everything in its path, tossing things up

Text: Quadraat roman 8.5 pt
Chapter number and raised cap: Typeka, 12 and 18 pt
Appropriate for a contemporary novel.

Using standard book typefaces in large sizes achieves the 'display' effect while maintaining legibility. These faces have been carefully designed and when enlarged become more full of character to the eye, providing a starting point in the typeface choice for chapter heading and jackets. The faces below are shown in 9 pt and 24 pt:

Rialto Titling	MEMORIES	MEMORIES	24
Meta Normal	Memories	Memories	24
Bauer Bodoni	Memories	Memories	24
Corvallis Sans	Memories	MEMORIES	24
Scala Regular	Memories	Memories	24
Gill Sans	Memories	Memories	24

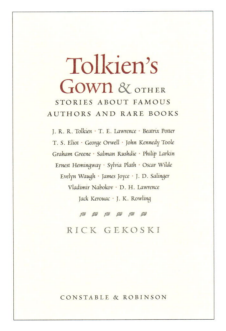

Rialto roman and italic 210 x 148 mm
A cover with display lines in text fonts

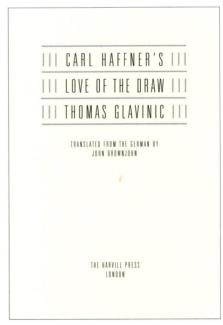

Univers ultra condensed thin 216 x 136 mm
The vertical rules are from the same font.

Book titles can be seen as distinct units: the title, possibly a sub-title and the author's name. The use of two or three contrasting faces gives an immediate display appeal, even without images:

American Typewriter and Gill Sans light

Citizen bold and regular

Barclay Outline and Chevalier

Galahad and Futura

WRITE TO KILL

Daniel Pennac

Binner Gothic and Formata bold

Playbill and Britannic bold

Neuland Inline and Spartan

Univers 55 and Univers bold   216 x 135 mm
If the image is striking, use the simplest of typefaces to avoid distraction. The type here was embossed. Photograph by Tono Stano

Display faces play a prominent role in the design of book covers and jackets. While making a necessary marketing impact, legibility has to be maintained .

A little restraint goes a long way. In the original jacket below on the left, the lines of the title, subtitle and author are separated, while extravagant sizing enables each line to fit the width of the jacket. The reader is not helped by this illogical treatment – the sense of the text is better conveyed in the version on the right.

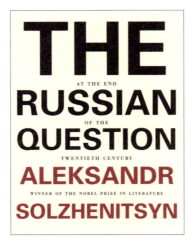

Univers type family
190 x 128 mm
Rearranging the line sequence and dividing up the four groups of text enables the reader to see clearly what the book is about and by whom it is written.

Akzidenz Grotesk Extra bold condensed
210 x 148 mm
A cover with distinct but clear groupings of the title, sub-title, author and a quotation

The spine of the jacket should match the style of the front of the jacket and be easily visible on a bookshop shelf.

The illustrator may add display lines of calligraphic lettering to the images. The lettering blends with the illustration, creating a cohesive look:

Cover design by Jeff Fisher

Lettering by Stephen Raw

The computer's capacity to distort typefaces presents temptations to the designer. On occasions a unique face produced in this way can work, but on the whole it is a poor response to a design problem and should be avoided. This example – in imitation of the lettering above – is just tolerable:

HØEG   HØEG   HØEG

The original hand-drawn lettering   Corvallis sans as designed   Corvallis sans distorted vertically to 78%

Gross distortions of a typeface – such as condensing or stretching – should be avoided at all times. This degree of distortion should not be used:

Defacement   Bauer Bodoni Bold   # Defacement

Bauer Bodoni bold at 150% horizontal distortion

especially when a perfectly designed alternative is available within the type family:

Defacement

Bauer Bodoni Black

Swash letters

Swash forms are specially designed letters, mostly capitals, with flourished strokes added to the regular or italic typeface of a font. Fonts that have swash letters seldom have a complete alphabet. Centaur is an exception:

Centaur italic

A B C D E F G H I J K L M N O P Q R S T U V W X Y Z

Centaur swash italic

A B C D E F G H I J K L M N O P Q R S T U V W X Y Z

Swash letters used as capitals can be used to effect in displayed headlines :

Poetica swash
capitals Q W
and N

Quaint & Wonderful yet Naughty

Care is needed to avoid unattractive clashes like those between the L and f, R and g:

Lifetime Rights

The use of swash letters in text headings adds a decorative element but restraint has to be employed to avoid irritating the reader.

Centaur italic swash
Text: Centaur
Swash letters used in
the chapter number,
the chapter title and
the drop cap of the
text. Only the first
letters of the chapter
number are swash;
in the chapter title 'I'
and 'M' are standard
italic caps.

CHAPTER XIII

How I Began My Shore Adventure

The appearance of the island when I came on deck next morning was altogether changed. Although the breeze had now utterly failed, we had made a great deal of way during the night, and were now lying becalmed about half a mile to the south-east of the low eastern coast. Grey-coloured woods covered a large part of the surface. This even tint was

Initial letters designed within a decorative frame add appeal to a page:

Tagliente decorated
initial letter
Text: Quadraat
The black of the
initial letter is
matched by the
dark Quadraat text.

THE APPEARANCE of the island when I came on deck next morning was altogether changed. Although the breeze had had now utterly failed, we had made a great deal of way during the night, and were now lying becalmed about half a mile

Ornaments

The simplest form of an ornament is the rule, that is, a line in all its variations and weights:

Rules can create emphasis in headings or serve as pauses in text:

2

It was about two weeks after the wedding reception when Sumire called me, a Sunday night, just before dawn. Naturally, I was asleep. As dead to the world as an old anvil. The week before I'd been in a

Collis roman
10 on 15 pt

The influence of television and advertising has permeated into publishing and the fashionable use of rules as below have influenced book typography:

television _____ _____

_____

manufactures _____

images

If the author indicates a pause in the main text this can be signalled with a rule:

And that there we were, he'd said his say and what did we think?

Wheel . . . the least that can be said is that we didn't think much of it. As a matter of fact, we didn't give a tinker's cuss for his two-bit story about some individual wanting to bail out of Algeria by

Bembo roman
10.5 on 13 pt
Type Embellishments
swelled rule

Decorative or *swelled* rules are available in a great variety of designs:

Type Embellishments
swelled rules

The next stage in ornamental decoration is a frame, a simple and useful device which can be attractively incorporated in several parts of a book and its cover.

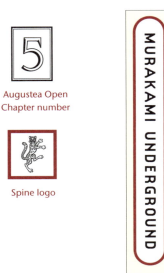

Augustea Open
Chapter number

Spine logo

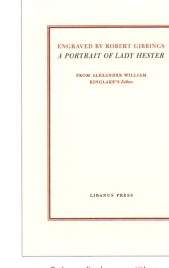

Citizen bold on a jacket spine

Bulmer display on a title page

Decorative ornaments

Drawn typographic elements have been used over the centuries and, as with display faces, a multitude of ornaments exist. Take care to ensure that the historical flavour of the ornament is appropriate.

Caslon ornaments
related to the 18th
century

Poetica and Type
Embellishments
ornaments
Both better suited to
contemporary use.

The way in which ornaments are used is up to the ingenuity and taste of the designer:

A single line of Poetica ornament:

or a single ornament, Caslon, can be used:

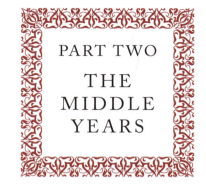

A frame constructed in Caslon ornaments

Fonts are available that offer both alphabets and ornaments for cartouches; these can be used in headlines such as titles and sub-titles:

 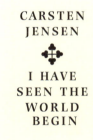

Requiem display ornaments

The printing or blocking of the spines of books also provides an occasion for the use of ornaments:

See *Jackets and covers* p.370

Programs like Photoshop® and Illustrator® allow pictures and displayed type to be combined. This can make an effective display for covers and jackets. It requires bold typefaces and it is not always typographically subtle:

Akzidenz Grotesk bold

Drop capitals

The use of drop capitals in the opening line of a chapter helps to reinforce chapter headings. It also provides an opportunity for the use of decorative typefaces. Typesetting programs allow you to choose how many lines a drop cap will occupy. In smaller format books this is usually about two or three, but it depends on how much of a feature you wish to make them.

The use of drop caps is a feature of magazine article setting.

To say that his face lit up would be a literary cliché, but João's face did exactly that. He blushed

To say that his face lit up would be a literary cliché, but João's face did exactly that. He blushed with wry

To say that his face lit up would be a literary cliché, but João's face did exactly that. He blushed with wry pleasure.

Two-line drop cap
Collis 9 on 13 pt

Three-line drop cap
Collis 10 on 13 pt

Four-line drop cap
Collis 11 on 14 pt

Sizing drop caps

Typesetting programs have a default size for drop caps. The sizing is manually adjustable and you will improve the appearance of the top line by enlarging the cap to raise it to the top of the lower case ascenders:

The right-hand drop cap is enlarged to 110%.
Collis 9 on 14 pt

I hadn't stinted on my Bordeaux for that special supper. When I brought in the dessert, with the announcement that our chef would

I hadn't stinted on my Bordeaux for that special supper. When I brought in the dessert, with the announcement that our chef would

Sizing of the drop cap is especially relevant when the cap has a rounded form, such as an O, C, G or S. Here the S has been enlarged to 108 per cent in order to visually align it with the ascenders of the top line of the text.

The right-hand drop cap is enlarged to 108%. The top line is pushed down by this so the baseline of the text must be adjusted.

Saulo managed to drag him away before he got any further, but João's mother had already thrown back her head in shock, gasping for air.

Saulo managed to drag him away before he got any further, but João's mother had already thrown back her head in shock, gasping for air.

As noted in the previous example, the enlargement of a drop cap pushes down all the lines of text. A small amount of space has to be removed from above the drop cap line in order to maintain the text on baseline of the page.

Kerning and spacing drop caps

The spacing between a drop cap and the rest of the word does not always assist the reader in understanding the whole word. Manual adjustment may be required:

L ucidio has no sense of humour. His smile is permanent, but his lips never part. What favour? He would prefer it if that second supper could take place in my apartment. Things were obviously going to be difficult at André's house. His wife would interfere.

A four-line drop cap at 100%
The positions of the second part of the first word or the first words of lines 2 and 3 are unadjusted.
Collis

The 'ucido' has to be brought to the 'L' by kerning it back to make it one word. The words 'lips' and 'supper' are spaced away from the drop cap 'L':

L ucidio has no sense of humour. His smile is permanent, but his ····lips never part. What favour? He would prefer it if that second ··supper could take place in my apartment. Things were obviously going to be difficult at André's house. His wife would interfere.

The drop cap is enlarged to 110%. The rest of the first word is kerned back to the cap; the first words of lines 2 and 3 are moved to the right.

The cap 'A' is especially in need of these manual adjustments. The space between the 'A' and 'fter' is too great for readability:

A fter the first course of crêpes came more crêpes with various toppings, which Lucídio placed around the table. Tiago insisted that Lucídio sit down at the table with us, just to show that there were no hard feelings. After all, setting everything else aside, Lucídio

The drop cap is at 100%.

A fter the first course of crêpes came more crêpes with various toppings, which Lucídio placed around the table. Tiago insisted that Lucídio sit down at the table with us, just to show that there were no hard feelings. After all, setting everything else aside, Lucídio

The drop cap is enlarged to 110%. The rest of the first word is kerned back to the cap; the first words of lines 2 and 3 are aligned.

If the drop cap occupies several lines the setting is visually improved if the subsequent lines follow the cap slope to avoid a large white space.

After the first course of crêpes came more crêpes with various toppings, which Lucídio placed around the table. Tiago insisted that Lucídio sit down at the table with us, just to show that there were no hard feelings. After all, setting everything else

Drop caps with punctuation

If a chapter begins with dialogue, it is necessary to apply the drop cap effect to both the quotation mark and the first letter of the word:

'We picked at the crêpes'. None of us was particularly keen on them. Lucídio offered to make a few more, but we all declined. For Tiago, the important thing was not to let Lucídio out of our sight for a second, especially in the

The appearance of the two is improved if the quotation mark is hung out:

The drop cap 'W' enlarged to 104%. The quotation mark is hung out and reduced to 90%. The 'e' is kerned away from the 'W'.

'We picked at the crêpes'. None of us was particularly keen on them. Lucídio offered to make a few more, but we all declined. For Tiago, the important thing was not to let Lucídio out of our sight for a second, especially in the kitchen.

Using different fonts for drop caps

The drop cap is, by definition, a displayed typeface and there is every reason for the use of a typeface different from the text face to add to the decorative effect. The baseline shift effect mentioned before may be especially noticeable with display fonts and will need correcting.

Left:
Drop cap: Delphian
Text: Collis

Right:
Drop cap: Rialto
Text: Trinité

Pedro's preparation classes in art hist with us again in

Pedro's preparation classes in art hist with us again in

Using drop caps and small caps

Setting two or three of the words in the first line in small caps reduces the contrast between the drop cap and the text and can add to the effect:

I N THE CENTRE OF the capital, on the seventh floor, lived a 30-year-old man, Viktor Vasilievich Bozhko. He lived in a small room lit by a single window; the din of the new world reached his high-up abode like a symphonic composition

The whole of the first line may be set with small caps. This removes any difficulty in the choice of what words to put into caps – it is merely those words that will fit on the first line:

I N THE CENTRE OF THE CAPITAL, ON THE SEVENTH floor, lived a 30-year-old man, Viktor Vasilievich Bozhko. He lived in a small room lit by a single window; the din of the new world reached his high-up abode like a symphonic

Using tints and colours

A drop cap may look a little overpowering if the font you are using is particularly black. This effect can be toned down by using a tint, or, if available, a second colour.

P EDRO'S PREPARATION for being a perfect executive had included classes in art history and music, and before finding perdition with us in Alberi's bar, he had been a gifted player of

P edro's preparation for being a perfect executive had included classes in art history and music, and before finding perdition with us in Alberi's bar, he had been a gifted player of medieval

Letter-spacing displayed capitals

Many of the displayed lines you use will be set in capitals or small capitals. The relationship between the capital letters is automatically set when the typeface is designed but may not work perfectly in all pairings of letters. The appearance of lines of capitals will be enhanced by the careful spacing of individual letters. The aim is to create visually equal spaces between letters. One method that helps is to view the letters in groups of three characters at a time. When you are satisfied with the spacing of the three, move on one letter and use the last two to space the next letter. Then review the whole word and adjust spacing further if required:

PROKOFIEV — the preset spacing

PROKOFIEV — add +5 ICS overall

PRO — R too close to O
if spaced P, too close to R

PRO — +4 ICS between P and R
+10 ICS between R and O

ROK — +3 ICS between O and K

OKO — +7 ICS between K and O

KOF — + 3 ICS between O and F

OFI — +1 ICS between F and I

FIE — +4 ICS between I and E

IEV — no change between E and V

Review the whole compared with the original automatic setting.

PROKOFIEV — If you decide to reduce the ics overall, the individual letter-spacing will be maintained as below:

PROKOFIEV   PROKOFIEV

The judgement and appreciation of such spacing is highly subjective and requires practice. The spacing values between letter combinations that work in one font will not necessarily work in another. Another method is to over-space the letters and then reduce the spacing, pair by pair, until you are satisfied with the balance. If there are two or more words to be spaced, it is important that the individual words match each other in spacing values:

NORWEGIAN WOOD

Collis regular 20 pt, 0 ICS overall
NOR and WOOD are open, RWEG closed
The word space is too narrow.

NORWEGIAN WOOD

Collis regular 20 pt, 10 ICS overall
Looks less compressed and scrappy

NORWEGIAN WOOD

Collis regular 20 pt, 20 ICS overall
Already the line appears more impressive but NOR and WEGIAN read as two words.

NORWEGIAN WOOD

Collis regular 20 pt, 30 ICS overall
WEG are better spaced but NORW and WOOD are too widely spaced.

N|OR|W|E|G|I|A|N W|O|O|D
-12   -15 -5   -7   -8   -15 -15 -15

The visual space between individual letters is now reduced as shown.

NORWEGIAN WOOD

The letters making up the two words now appear balanced and evenly spaced.

Even if you feel that both of these processes are too time consuming, the effect of certain letter combinations, which are over-kerned in some fonts – such as the **WAT**, HI and KING below – should be corrected:

WATERLOGGED   HIVE   LOOKING
WATERLOGGED   HIVE   LOOKING

From left to right:
Formata
Walbaum
Joanna

Over-spacing of words set in upper and lower case degrades the design of the face, rendering it characterless:

Frivolity in the Nineties   *F r i v o l i t y   i n   t h e   N i n e t i e s*
Frivolity in the Nineties   F r i v o l i t y   i n   t h e   N i n e t i e s

Requiem italic, 12 pt

Fournier, 12 pt

PART SIX
PRELIMS, TITLES AND ENDMATTER

THE SEQUENCE AND NUMBERING OF PRELIMINARY PAGES

Page sequences

The preliminary pages are those containing information which precede the main body of text. The sequence of pages is determined not only by tradition but by legal constraints and archival requirements. Some pages, such as the half-title, title page and the opening page of the main text must appear on a recto page and thus blank pages will occur in the sequence. The endmatter follows on after the main text of the book.

Contents of preliminary pages

These pages may include all or only some of the following:

> Half-title
> Frontispiece
> Title page
> Publishing details and other legally required information
> Dedication
> Quotation or epigraph
> Contents
> Acknowledgements
> List of illustrations
> Preface or author's note
> Foreword
> Introduction
> Maps, plans and genealogical diagrams
> List of abbreviations, notes on pronunciation

This is a comprehensive list of the possible entries within the preliminary pages. It is seldom the case that all will appear within a single book and other exceptional matter may be requested by the author or editor. On occasions, the acknowledgements, abbreviations or an author's note can appear as endmatter at the instruction of the author or editor.

To have a clear view at an early stage in the process of the sequence of the prelims, a *flat plan* or annotated *thumbnails* is useful:

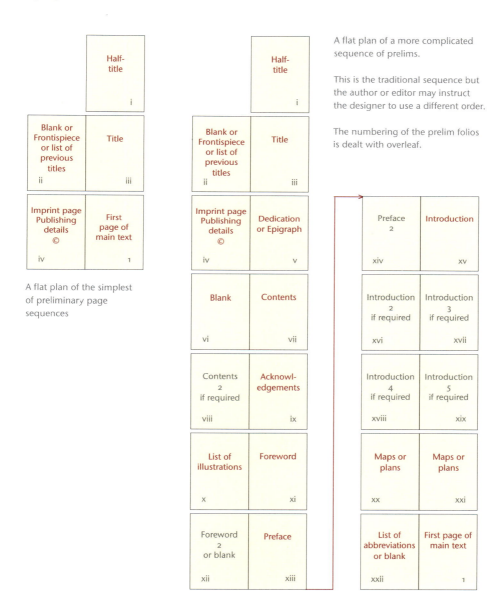

A flat plan of a more complicated sequence of prelims.

This is the traditional sequence but the author or editor may instruct the designer to use a different order.

The numbering of the prelim folios is dealt with overleaf.

A flat plan of the simplest of preliminary page sequences

Genealogical diagrams, plans and maps may be placed elsewhere in the main text.

Positions of preliminary pages

The layout of prelims is dictated by the need for some pages – for instance, the title page, contents page and the first page of the main text – to be on a recto. Those pages which should appear on a recto page are shown below in grey:

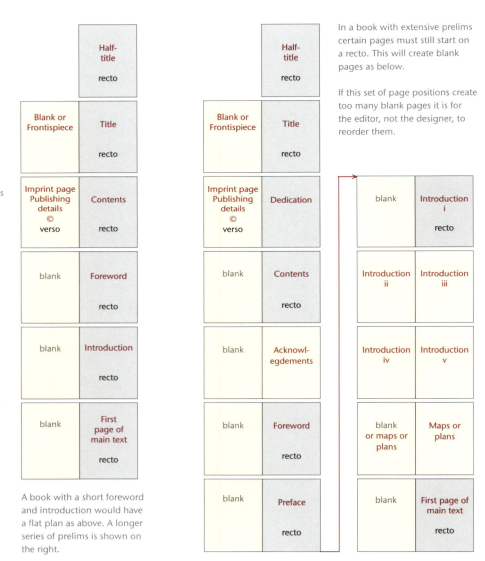

In a book with extensive prelims certain pages must still start on a recto. This will create blank pages as below.

If this set of page positions create too many blank pages it is for the editor, not the designer, to reorder them.

The imprint page is always positioned on the title page reverse – a verso

A book with a short foreword and introduction would have a flat plan as above. A longer series of prelims is shown on the right.

Positions of preliminary pages in illustrated books

In large-format illustrated books it is not unusual for a foreword, preface and introduction to be run on and appear on both recto and verso pages as they fall. This is especially true of exhibition books and catalogues where pages containing a list of lenders to the exhibition or sponsors are added. As most of these texts are short and production costs high, it would be wasteful to have many blanks.

Numbering prelims

The conventional way of counting the pages of a book is to number the prelim pages separately from the main text. The prelims are numbered using roman lower case folios – i, ii, iii, iv, v, vi, vii, viii, ix . . . starting with the half-title as i.

The main text is numbered, using arabic folios, starting from the first page of main text – 1, 2, 3, 4, 5, 6 . . . Endmatter is numbered continuously following on from this.

For type styles see *Folios* pp.200–1

The prelim folios of the half-title, the half-title reverse, title page, imprint page or contents pages and any blank pages are counted but *not* printed on those pages.

The use of two separate styles of figures stops any confusion between the prelims and the main text. It enables additions to the prelims in subsequent editions, such as a second preface outlining changes since the first edition, to be inserted without re-numbering the main text. The index of the main text will then not have to be re-numbered.

The view is expressed that the use of roman numerals to number prelims is inappropriate for an audience which is increasingly unfamiliar with them. Today, in non-book contexts such as letters, forms and advertising materials, lists tend to be numbered in arabic numerals or marked with bullet points. An easy recognition of roman numerals may be fading but the dropping of the roman folio in prelims is one development which might be resisted, for their use serves function completely.

However, in short books with an extent below 96 pages, it is common practice to count the pages from the half-title, giving the purchaser the idea of a longer book than the text offers. Editors will instruct the designer on this treatment.

The title page

The first three pages of a book represent an announcement for what is to come. The title page will always be on the third page. It must have at least the title of the book, and the names of the author and the publisher. Additional matter may include a sub-title, a printer's logo or a graphic image. The date of publication is not always included on the title page; publishers may feel that the potential purchaser will not be encouraged by a past publication date.

Shorter books and children's books may dispense with the half-title page.

What appears on the title page is an editorial decision and it may include any or all of the elements below:

The relative importance of each of the elements is indicated here by its type size.

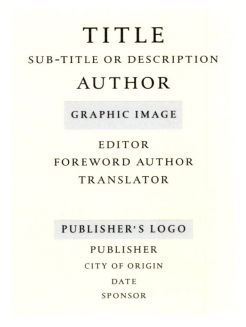

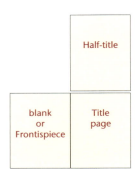

The half-title page and any part-title pages are modelled on the title page, so it is sensible to establish the title page's design first.

Whether the title precedes the author or vice versa is a moot point. Custom has it that the title comes first but, in the case of a well-established writer, the name may precede the title. Printed folios do not appear on the half-title, half-title reverse or title pages or any other pages before the contents page.

The elements of a title page are best laid out in groups:

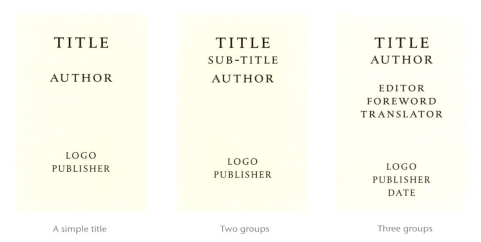

A simple title	Two groups	Three groups
TITLE	TITLE	TITLE
AUTHOR	SUB-TITLE	AUTHOR
	AUTHOR	
		EDITOR
		FOREWORD
		TRANSLATOR
LOGO	LOGO	LOGO
PUBLISHER	PUBLISHER	PUBLISHER
		DATE

The position on the page will indicate title and author – the word 'by' is redundant.

If the title is set in upper and lower case, the traditional rules on the treatment of capitalization of the words of the title are as follows:

Capital first letter	*No capital first letter*
The first word of the title	Definite and indefinite articles – the, a, an, etc.
All nouns	Prepositions – by, with, for, etc
All adjectives	Verbs (usually)
The first word after a colon	Conjunctions – and
Personal pronouns – I, me, you, etc.	Possessive pronouns – my, our etc.

Call Me if You need Me

Textile Mills in the Nineteenth Century: Their Development

The Shock of the New

Publishers may have individual house rules and will advise on this. Additional contributors noted on the title page are treated in two lines:

With Illustrations by	With a Foreword by	With an Introduction by	Translated by
Artist's name	Writer's name	Writer's name	Translator's name

The editor will indicate capitalization of these elements.

The title page allows for some freedom in design. However, publishers may have a house style which is part of their branding and has to be followed. The page may be laid out asymmetrically or centre-set:

Stone Sans
297 x 235 mm
An asymmetric setting: the only addition to the three main elements is the sub-title.

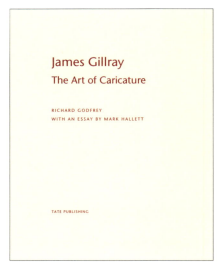

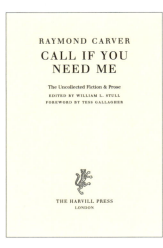

Walbaum
regular and italic
216 x 135 mm
A centred setting: a bolder title page for an established author, with a description of the work as a sub-title, a note of the editor and a foreword by a named writer.

Occasionally the title page is extended to the opposite blank page, ii. This means that the title is set across the gutter, and care must be taken to allow for the effect of the folding of the printed sheet. As the lining up of the title is unlikely to be exact, it is wise to separate and realign the word groups:

Trajan
The folding process reduces the gutter margin on the verso page and decreases the head margin on the recto leading to mis-alignment of the title line.

The head margin of the verso page word is raised and the spacing between the words on the verso and recto pages increased.

Advice on the precise amounts of adjustment necessary should be sought from the printer with samples of folded signatures of the paper.

Typographic choices will sit more comfortably if they relate to the content of the book. A book on the history of 18th-century France will not be well served if the title page is set in a contemporary sans serif typeface.

Stone Sans
210 x 150 mm
A simple title page: the only addition to the three main elements is the sub-title.
A book about contemporary social attitudes.

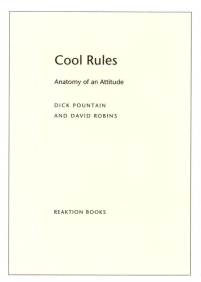

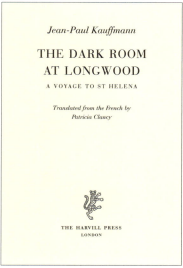

Bauer Bodoni
210 x 148 mm
Here just two faces, capitals and italic of the same family, are used. The capitals link the title and sub-title. The italics link the author and the translator. The publisher's name, city and logo complete the page.
A book about an historical period.

A simple rule of thumb to apply to title page design is that no more than three fonts should be used:

Lucida, Gill Shadowed, Quadraat bold, Joanna italic and Spartan
A title page set in too many faces.

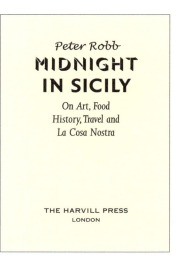

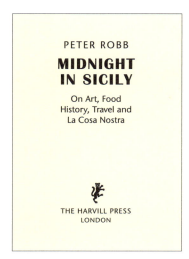

Britannic bold and Stone Sans
216 x 136 mm
The revised title page set in just two typefaces.

The use of a pictorial element on the title page adds attraction and offers an immediate indication of the book's content.

Minion roman
and small caps
210 × 148 mm
A title page with
few words is
enlivened by
a picture.

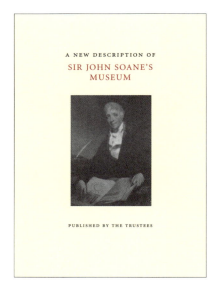

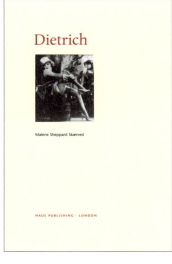

Albertina and
Stone Sans
198 × 129 mm
The small photo-
graph focuses on
the subject of the
biography.

If the verso is blank, the centre-set title page can appear visually closer to the fore-edge. Setting all the components 4 mm or so to the gutter will reduce this effect.

Fournier roman
and italic
198 × 129 mm
An illustration,
part of a series in
the book, gives an
immediate flavour
of the whole book.
Wood engraving
by Simon Brett

The page opposite
the title page may
be used to list the
author's previous
works.

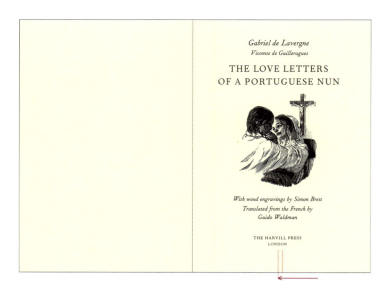

TITLE, HALF-TITLE AND PART-TITLES

The addition of decorations or illustrations will add to the book's appeal:

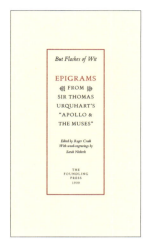

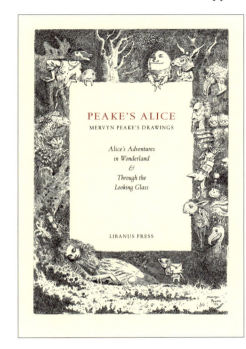

Spectrum
roman and italic
320 x 216 mm
This entertaining and
detailed illustration
by Mervyn Peake
acts as an overture
to the book.

Poliphilus and Blado
250 x 140 mm
A purely typographic title page.
with typefaces appropriate to
the date of the contents. A simple
ruled frame adds to the impact.

The reverse blank of the half-title, page ii, offers an ideal opportunity to enhance
the title page spread with an illustration. When this page is used in this way both
the image and the page itself are called the *frontispiece*.

Joanna roman and italic
260 x 160 mm
The title page is simple yet the
whole spread is made striking
by the use of a frontispiece
drawing and a small ornament
as a publisher's logo.
Pen and ink drawing
by Ian Beck

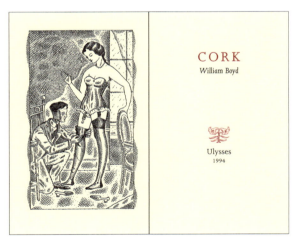

The choice of illustration for a frontispiece should not only decorate the title-page spread but give the reader a clear and, from the marketing point of view, an inviting view of the contents of the book.

Requiem
322 x 240 mm

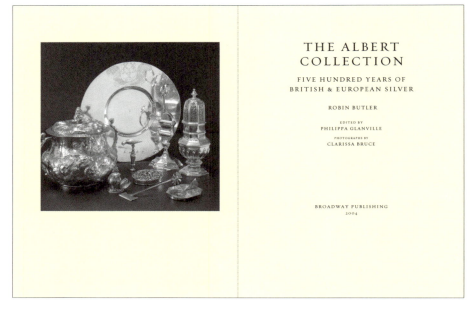

A book about a diverse collection of silver objects. The frontispiece gives that impression immediately.

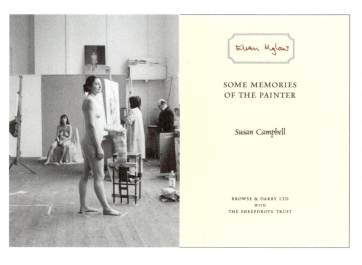

Rialto roman and italic
215 x 155 mm
A personal collection of memories of the artist. The title page uses his signature and a label device used by the artist. The frontispiece picture of the artist in a studio completes the overall atmosphere.

Illustrated books and exhibition catalogues use large pictorial spreads throughout. The title page and frontispiece will benefit from the impact of using a single image and a balance is created between them and the rest of the book's illustrated pages.

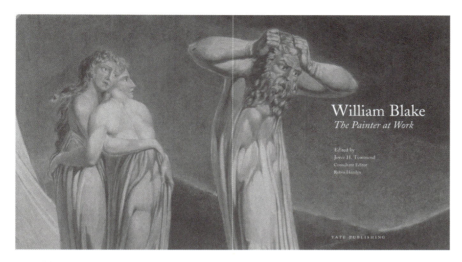

Caslon regular and italic
276 x 216 mm

A fully bled-out spread focusing on a detail from the painting. Tate Publishing

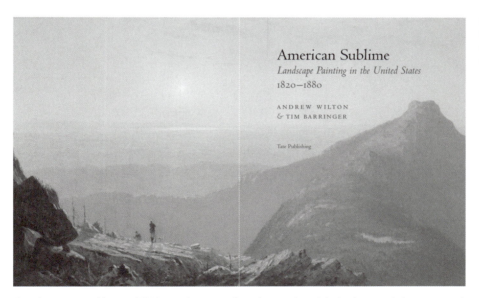

Centaur regular italic and small caps
265 x 246 mm

The title page spread for an exhibition catalogue; it reflects the grandeur of the landscape paintings portrayed. Tate Publishing

The half-title page

Once the title page style is established, attention can turn to the half-title page. This page will only bear the title of the book – and possibly an image in the case of illustrated books.

If the book is to be hard bound, bear in mind that the endpaper is glued to the half-title page, using up to 5 mm of the page in the gutter margin. The text should be positioned further towards the fore-edge to allow for this.

Originally books were sold only as a set of signatures for the buyer to bind; the half-title page was only an outer sheet to protect the title page. It was then known as a *bastard* page – not a real part of the book and bearing only the book's title. When books began to be sold as bound objects the page persisted as the half-title.

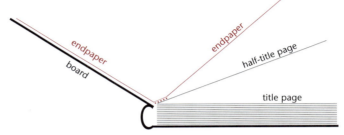

The typography of the half-title will be the same as the title page, reduced in size:

CALL IF YOU NEED ME

Above is the setting of the title page; only the title is repeated on the half-title using a smaller face and reduced leading.

A small illustration may add to the appeal of a heavily illustrated book and reduce the emptiness of the page. It should be positioned to allow for the endpaper fixing.

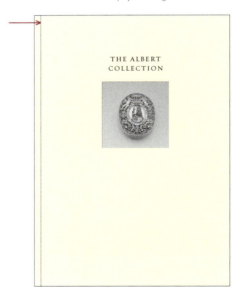

Part-title pages

The main text of some books is divided by the author into sections called *Parts*. They may be titled 'Part 1', 'Part 2' etc., and may have a sub-title. The pages which announce a Part are in effect title pages to that section; they are referred to as *part-titles* or *section openings*. A recto page is always used for this prominent pause in the main text.

The typeface choice and layout should relate to the typography of the title page – centre-set or ranged left.

The position of the title is set within the grid of the main text panel, shown here in red.

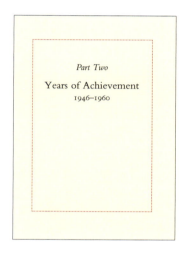

The sequence of pages at a part-title opening, here emphasized by illustrations, is as follows:

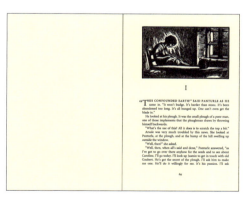

End of previous section text   Recto part-title page   Blank   First chapter of new section starts on a recto

The part-title recto opening can be used with an image on the verso, acting in the same way as a frontispiece does to a title page:

Photina regular
and italic
284 x 222 mm
Part-title spread

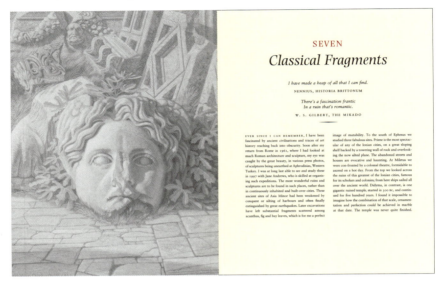

The impact of a part-title can be increased by making the image a cross-fold bleed onto a portion of the recto page:

Stone Sans
medium
298 x 235 mm
Part-title spread
Tate Publishing

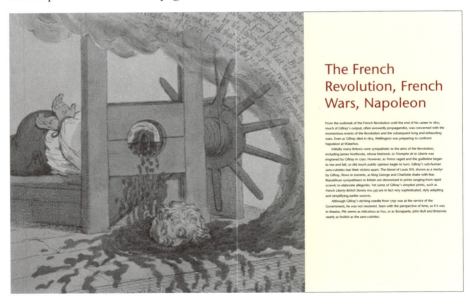

A fully bled-out illustration occupying the spread may be used to emphasize the new part:

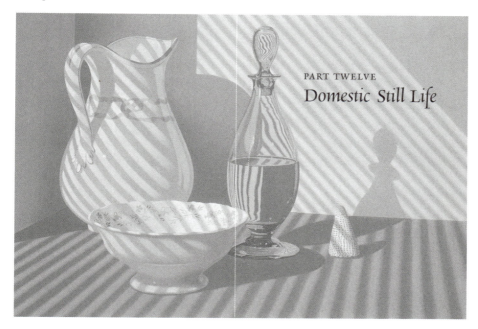

Rialto small caps and italic
290 × 222 mm
Part-title spread

Or here, the full landscape proportions of the painting:

Trinité
276 × 216 mm
Part-title spread
The National
Gallery Co Ltd

FURTHER PRELIMINARY PAGES

The imprint page

The imprint page carries the publishing details provided by the publisher; these will vary from house to house and title to title. The imprint page is placed on the reverse of the title page. Only the names and the addresses of the publisher and printer, and the copyright of the author, are required by law. The inclusion of ISBN numbers, further cataloguing information (CIP data) and a website address is essential for library reference and to the marketing of the book. They cannot sensibly be omitted. The usual setting sequence of this information is:

1   The publisher's name, address and website address
2   The date of publication
3   The copyright statement
4   Cataloguing-in-Publication (CIP) Data
5   A Library of Congress Catalog Card Number
6   The International Standard Book Number – the ISBN
7   A general copyright notice
8   The printer's name and location

1   The publisher's name and address must be clearly set at the head of the imprint page. This is a legal requirement. The website address is usually added here:

> First published in Great Britain in 2005 by
> Libanus Press Ltd, Rose Tree House, Marlborough, Wiltshire SN8 1JQ
> www.libanuspress.co.uk

2   The date of the first British publication. If the work is a translation, a note of the original title, publisher and date is added:

> First published in Brazil with the title *O Clube dos Anjos*
> by Editora Objetiva, Rio de Janeiro, 1998

3   The copyright statement appears in this form:

> Copyright © Michael Mitchell and Susan Wightman, 2005

The copyright notice also applies to other contributors – an author of a preface or foreword, a translator, an illustrator or a photographer – who must be noted.

The notice may have the additional phrase: 'The author asserts the moral right to be identified as the author of this work'.

4 Cataloguing-in-Publication (CIP) Data is especially important in academic, reference and technical books. It may be limited to a note that 'A CIP catalogue record for this book is available from the British Library', or appear in full:

British Library Cataloguing-in-Publication Data
Fountain, Dick
    Cool Rules : anatomy of an attitude
    1. Popular culture – Great Britain – History 2. Social influence
    3. Attitude (Psychology) – Great Britain 4. Great Britain –
    Social life and customs – 1945 –
    I. Title II Robins, David, 1944 –
    306.4'0941

The editor will supply this information.

This follows the style of the record card supplied to libraries for reference.

5 A Library of Congress Catalog Card Number may also be added. In books originating in the USA, a full data list similar to that of the British Library may be used in addition to the catalogue number.

6 The International Standard Book Number – the ISBN – consists of ten digits and is issued by the ISBN Agency. This number enables bookshops and readers alike to identify a book and trace its publisher. If the book is published in both a hardback and paperback edition, it will have two separate numbers; if they are published simultaneously, both numbers appear in both editions. If two or more books are sold as a set, each volume has an ISBN and the set its own ISBN.

The first digit of the ISBN represents the national, language or geographical group; the second group is the publisher prefix; the third, the title number. The last digit is a check digit.

From January 2007 the ISBN will have 13 digits.

In the case of a single edition:

ISBN 0 948021 66 7

In the case of a paperback and hardback editions simultaneously published:

ISBN 0 948021 66 7 pbk
ISBN 0 948021 47 0 hbk

7 A general copyright notice is often added, for example:

8 The printer's company name must appear but a detailed address is not required. If the book is likely to be sold abroad, the country of origin should be added:

Printed by Butler and Tanner
Frome and London, UK

If the imprint page is placed at the end of the book it is referred to as a *colophon*; this arrangement is often used in grander illustrated titles and limited editions.

Additional information

Additional matter may be placed on the imprint page. Publishers may add credits for the designer, editor and production team. A note of the typesetter and the typeface of the text may also be made. The caption to a picture on a frontispiece or a title page is better placed here than on those pages themselves.

Frequently sponsors may insist on a more prominent display of their support than can be afforded on the imprint page. The title page may be used or, on occasions, a recto page before the contents page.

Many publications are supported by national bodies, company sponsors, grants and donations. These will require a mention on the imprint page, set in a larger type size and possibly with the addition of the logo of the organization.

Typesetting styles for imprint pages

The information on the imprint page is separated into groups. Adding a half-line or line space between the groups will achieve this (see opposite). A small type size is used as the information is only for occasional reference.

The style of the setting should reflect that of the main text. In positioning the imprint information on the page, relate it to the title page layout so as to ensure that any possible show-through of the imprint will not clash with the layout of the title.

For a novel with a centre-set title page, a centre-set imprint page is suitable:

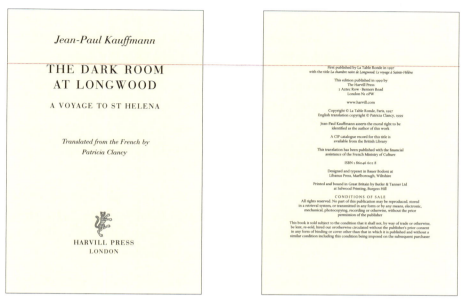

Jean-Paul Kauffmann

**THE DARK ROOM
AT LONGWOOD**

A VOYAGE TO ST HELENA

*Translated from the French by
Patricia Clancy*

HARVILL PRESS
LONDON

First published by La Table Ronde in 1997
with the title *La chambre noire de Longwood: Le voyage à Sainte-Hélène*

This edition published in 1999 by
The Harvill Press
2 Aztec Row · Berners Road
London N1 0PW

www.harvill.com

Copyright © La Table Ronde, Paris, 1997
English translation copyright © Patricia Clancy, 1999

Jean-Paul Kauffmann asserts the moral right to be
identified as the author of this work

A CIP catalogue record for this title is
available from the British Library

This translation has been published with the financial
assistance of the French Ministry of Culture

ISBN 1 86046 602 8

Designed and typeset in Bauer Bodoni at
Libanus Press, Marlborough, Wiltshire

Printed and bound in Great Britain by Butler & Tanner Ltd
at Selwood Printing, Burgess Hill

CONDITIONS OF SALE
All rights reserved. No part of this publication may be reproduced, stored
in a retrieval system, or transmitted in any form or by any means, electronic,
mechanical, photocopying, recording or otherwise, without the prior
permission of the publisher

This book is sold subject to the condition that it shall not, by way of trade or otherwise,
be lent, re-sold, hired out or otherwise circulated without the publisher's prior consent
in any form of binding or cover other than that in which it is published and without a
similar condition including this condition being imposed on the subsequent purchaser

**Imprint page:
Bodoni roman
8 on 10 pt**
The top line of the imprint is aligned to the top of the letters in the first line of the title to limit the effect of show-through. The groups of information are separated from each other by spaces.

With the asymmetric title page layout below, the imprint page is set in a matching asymmetric style and the top lines of the title page, imprint page and contents page also align, maintaining an overall style in the book's preliminary pages. There will inevitably be some show-through using this layout.

Stone Sans

Cool Rules

Anatomy of an Attitude

DICK POUNTAIN
AND DAVID ROBINS

REAKTION BOOKS

Published by Reaktion Books Ltd
79 Farringdon Road
London EC1M 3JU · UK

www.reaktionbooks.co.uk

First published 2000

Copyright © Dick Pountain and David Robins

All rights reserved.
No part of this publication may be reproduced, stored in a
retrieval system, or transmitted, in any form or by any means,
electronic, mechanical, photocopying, recording or otherwise,
without the prior permission of the publishers

Designed and typeset by Libanus Press
Printed and bound in Great Britain by Biddles Limited, Guildford and King's Lynn

British Library Cataloguing in Publishing Data
Pountain, Dick
Cool rules : anatomy of an attitude
1. Popular culture – Great Britain – History 2. Social influence
3. Attitude (Psychology) – Great Britain 4. Great Britain – Social
life and customs – 1945–
1. Title II. Robins, David, 1944–
306.4'0941

ISBN 1 86189 071 0

Contents

Dedication

A dedication – usually a grateful inscription to a person whom the author wishes to thank for inspiration and support – is important to the author. This is shown by placing it alone on the recto page immediately following the imprint page.

Rarely will the dedication consist of more than a single sentence. It is treated as a displayed line set in a size larger than the main text:

To my understanding colleagues and especially my patient wife

The line should occupy a prominent position on the page within the text panel of the main text and dropped, say, a third of the way down the panel – or match the position of the chapter headings in the main text. Conventionally this recto page should be followed by a blank verso to reinforce the statement.

Should a dedication be delivered late in the typesetting process when there are no pages left, or if the extent cannot accommodate two extra pages, it may exceptionally be placed at the top of the imprint page. This is a poor compromise.

Epigraph

This, like the dedication, is an inscription, usually a motto or quotation that the author feels sets the scene and tone of the book or instigated its writing. The same importance is given to the epigraph as to the dedication and it should occupy a recto page in a displayed setting.

If the epigraph is an obvious quotation there is no need for quotation marks. The source will be referred to with the epigraph:

He hath not fed of the dainties that are bred in a book; he hath not eat paper, as it were; he hath not drunk ink.

Love's Labour's Lost
WILLIAM SHAKESPEARE

Pages bearing dedications, epigraphs and the opposite verso blanks will have no printed folios although they will be counted in the prelim sequence.

The contents page

Readers must reach the contents page as early as possible in the book; it is their main guide. It should be clear and concise to enable easy navigation through the book itself. It is placed immediately after the imprint page – only a dedication or an epigraph, if present, should come between the imprint page and the contents.

Many novels with a continuous narrative text do not require a contents page as the reader has no reason to find specific sections of the book. In reference and technical books, where the reader will return to individual parts at different times, the contents page should be detailed – with sub-headings to each part and chapter.

The text of the contents page will be an editorial decision which will be passed on to the designer. The structure of the contents may vary from a simple listing of chapters, to a full list of parts and chapters, and sub-chapters, with the further additions of the foreword, preface, and introduction. This is followed by a list of any endmatter.

The contents page will start on a recto page with 'contents' in a displayed type size. Contents pages have no printed folios. This is a simple form of a contents page:

CONTENTS

Garamond roman
12 on 20 pt

As the list of contents becomes longer, it is essential to assist the reader by making clear the visual line between the item and its page number. If the page number is at a distance from the item the eye cannot easily trace the line across to the folio reference.

In the example below the distance separating the item from the number is so great that the reader may have to resort to a ruler to use the list:

The use of leaders – a line of full points – as in the two lines above, is both ugly and unnecessary. By reducing the distance between chapter title and page number and increasing the leading, the eye runs easily across from entry to page number:

In a contents list where the chapters are also numbered, the entries are set using tabs to range the chapter titles and their numbers to the left and right respectively. The page numbers are ranged to the right:

If at all possible the list of contents should be kept to one page, giving the reader a complete overview of the book. But do not resort to using too small a type size. If the contents list is long, the use of two columns, placing the number close to the chapter title, is one solution. There is no need for a comma after each chapter title if sufficient space is placed between the title and number – in this case one en, and the numbers and titles are typographically distinguished, as shown here:

Scala roman
and italic
9 on 14 pt

If the contents list does fill more than one page, a suitable break must be found in the list, preferably by starting the successive page with a new part even if that means a page short of full text panel depth. Part headings must stand out. The page reference is not to the part itself but the first chapter in that section:

Bembo roman
and italic
Different type styles
have been used to
differentiate the
prelims. The type
style for the entries
echo the style of the
part and chapter
headings.

Extended chapter contents

The author may sub-title chapters with a detailed description of that chapter's contents. This should be reflected on the contents page:

Sabon roman
The contents pages in the book you are reading have been set out in a style to allow for fast identification of subjects and their pages by placing the page reference close to the subject and ranged left. This is suitable for a handbook used for quick reference.

The layout of the contents page

As well as an aid to navigation for the reader, the contents page is an important announcement. It should not be placed haphazardly, but placed within the main text panel and dropped down on the page if necessary:

The shorter contents list on the left is dropped down within the book's text panel for balance.

Contents pages in illustrated books

A text-only contents page in an illustrated book can look meagre in relation to the main body of the book with its profusion of pictures. Typical pictures from each section, or details from them, can be used to decorate the contents. Using a full spread for this treatment creates an attractive introduction for the reader:

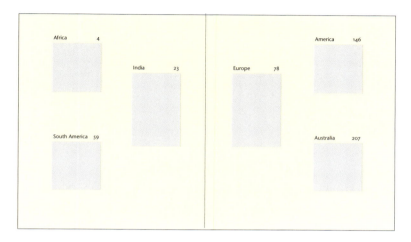

Acknowledgements

Acknowledgements consist of the author's expressed gratitude to all those people who have assisted in the production of the manuscript and the finished book. This statement does not always appear and is unusual in works of fiction where it may form part of a preface. Indeed, if this consists only of a single line, it is better in the author's preface or set as a dedication.

In academic and technical works this list may include a host of researchers, typists, editors, publishers and patrons, illustrators and photographers. It may also cover permissions for reproduction of previously published works. A note may be made of those people close to the author who have given encouragement and support.

If the amount of material is extensive then the acknowledgements occupy a whole page. If there are only a few lines they may be included in a page with other preliminary information such as a list of abbreviations. The acknowledgements may be placed in the endmatter at the editor's or author's instruction.

List of illustrations

Biographies, history or travel books may be illustrated within the main text with photographs or other pictures. These can be listed in the preliminary pages with their page numbers. If the list is lengthy, setting the text in a smaller size and using a double-column layout will save space:

Minion roman
7.5 on 9 pt

In a book to which a number of illustrators or photographers have contributed, the list of contributors' names and copyright owners may also be shown alphabetically, followed by the page references to their work. This list may be placed in the prelims or endmatter at the editor's instruction.

Foreword

This is a statement written by an eminent authority or celebrity and precedes the preface and introduction. It is usually short and extols either the virtues of the work or the importance of the book's subject or, indeed, the author. It always begins on a recto page.

The piece is usually *signed* and sometimes dated – that is, the name of the foreword writer and the date of its composition are set in two lines at the end of the text, ranged to the left or right and with a line space between them and the text. When a foreword runs to more than one page, the name of its author may be placed below the foreword's title on the opening page.

Preface

This is an initial note by the author which explains the motivation for the work, and how it was researched and written. It can also contain a simple note of thanks to those assisting the author. It always starts on a recto page. Sometimes it is not written by the author, in which case it should be signed using the same style as the foreword. In translated works, there may be a preface by the translator; this is dealt with in the same way as an author's preface. However, a translator's note about the technicalities of the translation itself is likely to be placed in the endmatter.

Introduction

A book's introduction is an essential explanatory note or essay, sometimes with an historical or biographical background, to be read before the reader embarks on the main text. It will normally be the work of the book's author or, in the case of a collection of essays, the book's editor. With that latter exception, the introduction is assumed to be the work of the author and is not signed. An introduction is of importance to the reader and the first page should start on a recto.

Typesetting styles for acknowledgements, foreword, preface and introduction

The typographic treatment and the positions of the headings for the contents, foreword, preface, introduction and acknowledgements should be repeated so as to create consistency in the appearance of the preliminary pages.

The texts should be set within the book's main text panel. If the material is lengthy a type size slightly smaller than that of the main text may be used. The headings should be based on the heading hierarchies of the main text, using the same type formats and spacing. The A-heading style of the main text is commonly used.

See *Headings* p.126

ADDITIONAL PAGES

The reader has been introduced to the text by the author and is now ready to start the main part of the book. But further information may be required at this stage to gain a fuller understanding of the narrative. This additional information may include such things as maps, plans, chronologies and family trees. In translated works the reader may be assisted by an explanation of pronunciation of foreign words or the use of any special terms. Reference books with complicated sources may include a list of abbreviations of these sources.

Maps and plans

Maps and plans should be drawn so as to fit the page without the reader being forced to rotate the book. If this cannot be avoided, the top of the map or plan is placed to the fore-edge if it is on a verso page and to the gutter if it is on a recto page. Thus the book is rotated clockwise to see the diagram; this has been found to be the easiest movement. If this arrangement is not used, the alignment should at least be consistent so that the reader only rotates the book in one direction.

A landscape-proportioned map may be positioned across a double spread to avoid rotating the book. If this is done, the binding process will obliterate a small portion of the image in the gutter of both pages. It is preferable to divide the artwork and leave 3 mm or so clear in both the gutters – the lesser of two evils.

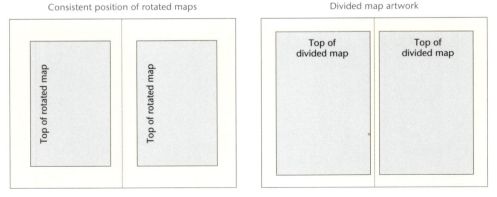

Family trees and genealogical charts are treated in a similar way to maps and plans.

Lists of abbreviations, scholarly sources and aids to pronunciation

Lists of abbreviations and scholarly sources

In scholarly books where references to certain documents, sources and illustrations are frequently repeated in the text, a set of abbreviations may be adopted for these, and a key to them placed just before the opening of the main text. Such a list will appear in this form:

HM = Gerald Morice and George Speaight, 'New Light on Juvenile Drama', in *Theatre Notebook*, xxvi (1971–72). This consists of a reprint of Henry Mayhew's interview with William West, 'Letter XXXVIII – 25 February 1850'.

Rosenfeld = Sybil Rosenfeld, *Georgian Scene Painters and Scene Painting* (1981), Cambridge University Press

Plain = Engraving   Coloured = Hand-coloured engraving

A bertina roman and italic 7.5 on 11 pt

Aids to pronunciation

In books where foreign words, especially the names of persons, occur throughout the text, the author or editor may wish to familiarize the reader with the correct pronunciation of these words as in a list such as this:

The Latin alphabet includes a number of unfamiliar letters listed below.
Serbo-Croat is strictly phonetic, with one letter representing one sound.
The stress normally falls on the first syllable.

   c is always *ts*, as in ca*ts*   č is *ch* as in *ch*urch
   ć is similar but softer, as *t* in the Cockney pronunciation of *tube*
   š is *sh*, as in *sh*ake

Stone Print roman 10.25 on 14 pt

A Note: There is a considerable variation in the make-up of prelim matter and the sequence may not be that outlined above. The designer should be ultimately guided by editorial instructions and advice.

ENDMATTER

Page sequence

As with prelims, the sequence of sections at the end of the book can vary depending on content and function.

The following may be included:

> Appendices
> Endnotes
> Abbreviations
> Photographers'/illustrators' credits
> Glossary
> Bibliography
> Acknowledgements
> Indexes
> Colophon (see note on imprint page)

A conventional sequence for endmatter looks like the flat plan on the right:

Some of these sections – the abbreviations, picture credits and acknowledgements – may have been placed in the prelims – a decision to be made by the editor. Endnotes are placed after appendices as the appendices themselves may have notes.

The folio numbers for the endmatter simply continue from the main text.

Every effort should be made to leave two blanks at the end of a book; finishing a text on the last verso is poor practice. This is especially true if the book is to be hard bound as the back endpaper has to be partially fixed onto the last page.

See *Binding* pp.350–5

Last page of main text	Appendix A
Appendix B	Endnotes
Abbreviations	Picture credits
Glossary	Bibliography
Acknowl-edgements	Index
Index	Blank
Blank	

Appendices

An appendix is supplementary matter which, although not essential to the flow of the main text, adds depth and authority to the author's work. The content of appendices can vary from straightforward text to lists, tables, graphs, family trees, maps, diagrams and other graphic matter. When you receive a text from the editor, look at the appendices at an early stage and establish how you will deal with them.

Each appendix is treated as a new chapter, and the layout should reflect the style of the rest of the book – if each chapter started on a fresh page, then so should each appendix. The first appendix should start on a recto. If there are many appendices they may be preceded by a part-title.

Appendices are usually found in academic works where the type size of the main text may already be fairly small. Though it may be logical to reduce the type size of the appendices, this can reduce readability. They are numbered using a different system from the chapters, to avoid confusion. For example, they may be called 'Appendix A', 'Appendix B' and so on.

Endnotes

Notes are additional information and references for the reader, usually placed at the end of individual chapters or at the end of the book. These are dealt with in detail on pp.208–17.

Abbreviations and acknowledgements

As noted previously, these may be placed in the prelims or in the endmatter.

Photographic or illustration credits

This is an alphabetical list of contributors and copyright holders followed by page references for each work:

British Library: p. 19 fig 9; cats 30.74; p. 60 fig 1
British Museum: cats 7, 9, 22; p.36 fig 3; cats, 33, 54, 69

Barbara Bryant: p. 8 fig 2
Courtauld Institute of Art: p. 35 figs 1. 2; cat 29
English Heritage (NMR): p. 10 fig 6

Glossary

In this book, the index has been combined with the glossary to make searching for an item quicker.

A glossary contains definitions of specialist or technical terms used in the main text. The terms are listed alphabetically. Use a type size smaller than the main text. The headwords may be highlighted using a different font. To make it easier for the reader to use a glossary, the entries are separated:

Minion roman
and semi-bold
8.5 on 10 pt

Medium a fluid binder in which coloured pigments are suspended to make paint.

Macro and micro photographs magnified and highly magnified details of a painting or paint sample.

Millboard manufactured painting support made of compressed fibres bound with glue or oil and sometimes faced with paper.

If there are many short entries, use double columns in order to save space:

Minion roman
semi-bold
8.5 on 10 pt

Medium a fluid binder in which coloured pigments are suspended to make paint.

Macro and micro photographs magnified and highly magnified details of a painting or paint sample.

Millboard manufactured painting support made of compressed fibres bound with glue or oil and sometimes faced with paper.

Bibliography

See *Editorial rules* p.388

A bibliography contains the publishing details of the author's sources. These are listed alphabetically. The way in which the bibliographical information itself is ordered should be consistent: this is a matter for the editor and should not be changed by the designer. Inserting a space before each entry helps separate them:

Bembo roman
and italic
9 on 11 pt

Chion, Michel, *Jacques Tati*. Paris: Cahiers du Cinéma (Collection Auteurs), 1987. English translation: *The Films of Jacques Tati*, transl. M. Viñas, P. Williamson and A. d'Alfonso. Toronto: Guernica, 1997

Dondey, Marc, *Jacques Tati*. Paris: Ramsay, 1987. Repr. 1993

Kermabon, Jacques, '*Les Vacances de M. Hulot*', *de Jacques Tati*. Crisnée: Yellow Now, 1988

Ramirez, François and Rolot, Christian, '*Mon Oncle' de Jacques Tati*. Paris: Nathan, Collection Synopsis, 1993

Ede, François, *Jour de fête ou la couleur retrouvée*. Paris: Cahiers du cinéma, 1995

Or hanging out the first line of each entry to the left:

Chion, Michel, *Jacques Tati*. Paris: Cahiers du Cinéma (Collection Auteurs),
    1987. English translation: *The Films of Jacques Tati*, transl. M. Viñas,
    P. Williamson and A. d'Alfonso. Toronto: Guernica, 1997
Dondey, Marc, *Jacques Tati*. Paris: Ramsay, 1987. Repr. 1993
Kermabon, Jacques, '*Les Vacances de M. Hulot*', *de Jacques Tati*. Crisnée: Yellow
    Now, 1988
Ramirez, François and Rolot, Christian, '*Mon Oncle' de Jacques Tati*. Paris:
    Nathan, Collection Synopsis, 1993
Ede, François, *Jour de fête ou la couleur retrouvée*. Paris: Cahiers du cinéma, 1995

Bembo roman
and italic
9 on 12 pt

Or by a combination of both.

Some bibliographies will start with an an abbreviated title – for use in the notes –
followed by the full bibliographical entry. This is highlighted by a change of font:

INGAMELLS: J. Ingamells, *National Portrait Gallery. Mid-Georgian
    Portraits 1760–1790* (London, 2004)
IRWIN: D. Irwin, *English Neoclassical Art* (London, 1966)
KENWOOD: *British Artists in Rome*, exhib. cat. by L. Stainton,
    Iveagh Bequest, Kenwood, 1974

Albertina roman
italic and semi-bold
8.5 on 11 pt

When many titles by the same author are listed, a long dash may be used rather
than repeating the name:

Bindman, 1978: D. Bindman, *Blake as an Artist* (New York, 1978)
————, 1979: *John Flaxman R.A.*, exhib. cat. ed. D. Bindman,
    London, Royal Academy of Arts, 1979
————, 2000: D. Bindman, 'Thomas Banks's Caractacus before
    Claudius: new letters to and from Ozias Humphry'
    Burlington Magazine CXLII (2000) pp. 769–72

Albertina roman
and italic
8.5 on 11 pt

In extensive bibliographies, books may be divided by subject matter, or according
to the chapter in which they appear. A distinction may also be made between
books and articles in journals or other publications. The editor will give guidance
on how the bibliography is to be structured.

Indexes

An index can only be compiled after the rest of the book has been typeset and laid out, and when it is certain that no further changes affecting pagination will be made.

When revising a layout that has already been indexed, make a note on the proofs of any words or lines which have moved from one page to another.

Books may contain more than one index, with the possible additions of an index of names or titles, or in the case of poetry, an index of first lines. If this is the case, these specialized indexes come before the general index, with the first starting on a recto page.

Type style

The type is set in the same font as other endmatter but at a smaller size. Leading can be a tighter than for continuous text.

When setting an index for a reference book which is likely to get repeated use, the typeface needs to be readable and the layout as clear as possible. This should be kept in mind when the book's extent is being calculated.

Use as little punctuation as possible. Commas are unnecessary between the headwords and page references unless the headwords themselves contain numbers which may cause confusion: here, an en space can be used instead. Commas are used between page references. There is no need for a full point at the end of an entry.

To indicate illustrations or large entries, page references can be put into italic or semi-bold. This should be explained in a note at the start of the index. Titles (of books, etc.) are italicized as normal.

To direct readers to other entries use 'see' or 'see also' in italics.

Bembo roman
8.25 on 10 pt
Headwords are those words and names chosen by the indexer to appear in the index.

Kew Gardens 151
Khartoum 161–2, 164, 167
Khyber Pass 151
Kiev 211
King Adandozan 324–5
King, David 267, 269, 275, 287, 519
King George I 15
King George III 132
King Ghézo 322, 324–5, 332, 338
King Nema of Elmina 374

Minion
8 on 10 pt
Those pages with illustrations are in in semi-bold.

Kew Gardens *see* Gardens
Khartoum **161–2**, 164, *167*
Khyber Pass 151
Kiev 211
King Adandozan **328–9**
King, David *267, 269, 275, 287, 519*
King George I 15, *see also* 193
King George III 132
King Ghézo 322, **324–5**, 332, 338
King Nema of Elmina *374*
King Orélie-Antoine I 310, 319

An index is set in columns, the number of which will depend on the average length of the entries, the format of the page and the style of the rest of the endmatter. Three or four column setting is the most common. These should fall within the area of the text panel; that is, the margins should be the same as the main text, with smaller margins between the columns.

Pressure to reduce extent will sometimes force the use of narrower margins to create a larger text panel.

Many of the entries will not fill the full measure of the column, so they are all best set ranged left. It is sufficient to leave one line space between the sections for each letter of the alphabet. If there are many sub-entries it may not be immediately clear to the eye which letter is which: in this case use an initial at the beginning of each section:

Russia 205—6, 208, 211, 275, 357
Ryde, Peter 68—70, 80
Ryle, John 327, 336, 539

Sackville-West, Vita 370
Saddhruddin Aga Khan 521
St Maarten 390—91
St Moritz 207
San Francisco 262—3

Russia 205—6, 208, 211, 275, 357
Ryde, Peter 68—70, 80
Ryle, John 327, 336, 539

S
Sackville-West, Vita 370
Saddhruddin Aga Khan 521
St Maarten 390—91
St Moritz 207

Joanna
8.5 on 11 pt
Initial:
Joanna, 14 pt

If an entry runs on from a recto page onto the following verso, the headword should be repeated followed by *(cont.)*

An index should have folios and running heads following the style and size of the main text. In an extensive reference work with a long index, running heads such as these are used to direct the reader:

I N D E X · M A — M U

Marlborough *(cont.)*
 149, 189, 191, 228,
 335, 356, 376, 382
Marquez, Gabriel
 Garcia 498
Marseille 268, 275

Matisse, Henri 94, 110,
 118, 121—2, 364, 481
Maugham, William
 Somerset 85, 116,
 119—21, 123, 285, 353
Mauritania 219, 238

Morris, Desmond
 217—18, 239
Moscow 13, 211, 268, 312
Mount Athos 445,
 449—52, 464, 502,
 514—15, 544

Requiem
8.25 on 10 pt
Running head:
Requiem small caps
8 pt with 30 I C S

Page references

When referring to more than one page, use the fewest number of digits necessary. Bear in mind how the words are *said*. Pages 211–213 is shortened to 211–13 and *not* 211–3 because you say 'two hundred and eleven to thirteen', *not* 'two hundred and eleven to three'.

Use the entries exactly as provided by the indexer. Do not shorten '51, 52' to '51–2' to save space as the comma denotes two entries, rather than one entry run onto a second page. Use en rules between numbers throughout, never hyphens.

Indenting sub-entries

When an entry runs to more than one line the second line is indented. Sub-entries are also indented. There are three different methods of doing this.

The first is to use one indent – an em space for example – for turned-over lines, two indents – two em spaces – for sub-entries and three indents – three em spaces – for turned-over sub-entries.

Indent of 1 em
Indent of 2 ems
Edge of column
Indent of 3 ems

Stone Print roman
8 on 10.5 pt

Paragraph styling
will allow the
indents to be set
in millimetres.

Llosa, Mario Vargas 432, 491
London 39, 82–4, 86, 102, 109, 137–8, 140,
   195, 236, 260, 355, 369, 397,
   407, 439, 518
      British Museum 92, 313
      Dorchester Hotel 119
      Ealing 86, 95, 103
      Eaton Place 110, 399, 406, 439, 442,
         455, 537
      Grosvenor Crescent Mews 109, 111,
         130, 145, 157, 228, 513
      Kynance Mews 221, 235, 244, 251,
         442, 514
      Mount Street 157, 163, 165–6, 174–5
      Victoria & Albert Museum 96
London, Jack 62
London Review of Books 120, 167, 282, 398,
   420, 466

Llosa, Mario Vargas 432, 491
London 39, 82–4, 86, 102, 109, 137–8, 140,
   195, 236, 260, 355, 369, 397,
407, 439, 518
      British Museum 92, 313
      Dorchester Hotel 119
      Ealing 86, 95, 103
      Eaton Place 110, 399, 406, 439, 442,
         455, 537
      Grosvenor Crescent Mews 109, 111,
         130, 145, 157, 228, 513
      Kynance Mews 221, 235, 244, 251,
         442, 514
      Mount Street 157, 163, 165–6, 174–5
      Victoria & Albert Museum 96
London, Jack 62
London Review of Books 120, 167, 282, 398,
   420, 466

This is a logical progression, but it can make the sub-entries hard to identify. It can also result in the columns appearing to bow out to the right.

The second method is to use one indent for sub-entries and two indents for turned-over lines, whether they are from main entries or sub-entries.

Llosa, Mario Vargas 432, 491
London 39, 82–4, 86, 102, 109, 137–8,
        140, 195, 236, 260, 355, 369, 397,
        407, 439, 518
    British Museum 92, 313
    Ealing 86, 95, 103
    Eaton Place 110, 399, 406, 439, 442,
        455, 537
    Grosvenor Crescent Mews 109, 111,
        130, 145, 157, 228, 513
    Kynance Mews 221, 235, 244, 251
    Mount Street 157, 163, 165–6, 174–5
    Victoria & Albert Museum 96
London Review of Books 120, 167, 282,
        398, 420, 466
Lord Goodman 183, 515

Llosa, Mario Vargas 432, 491
London 39, 82–4, 86, 102, 109, 137–8, 140,
        195, 236, 260, 355, 369, 397,
        407, 439, 518
    British Museum 92, 313
    Ealing 86, 95, 103
    Eaton Place 110, 399, 406, 439, 442,
        455, 537
    Grosvenor Crescent Mews 109, 111,
        130, 145, 157, 228, 513
    Kynance Mews 221, 235, 244, 251
    Mount Street 157, 163, 165–6, 174–5
    Victoria & Albert Museum 96
London Review of Books 120, 167, 282, 398,
        420, 466
Lord Goodman 183, 515

Stone Print
8 on 10.5 pt

The advantages of this method are that it reduces the number of indents, and the sub-entries hang out to the left, making them easier to locate. However, if there are relatively few sub-entries and the main entries are long, it will take up more space.

The third method is to run-on sub-entries from the main entries (separated by semi-colons) using only one indent. This will save space, but is not as easy for the reader to use.

Llosa, Mario Vargas 432, 491
London 39, 82–4, 86, 102, 109, 137–8,
        140, 195, 236, 260, 355, 369, 397,
        407, 439, 518; British Museum 92,
        313; Dorchester Hotel 119; Ealing 86,
        95, 103; Eaton Place 110, 399, 406,
        439, 442, 455, 537; Grosvenor
        Crescent Mews 109, 111, 130, 145, 157,
        228, 513; Kynance Mews 221, 235,
        244, 251, 442, 514; Mount Street 157,
        163, 165–6, 174–5; Victoria & Albert
        Museum 96
London, Jack 62

Llosa, Mario Vargas 432, 491
London 39, 82–4, 86, 102, 109, 137–8,
        140, 195, 236, 260, 355, 369, 397,
        407, 439, 518; British Museum 92,
        313; Dorchester Hotel 119; Ealing 86,
        95, 103; Eaton Place 110, 399, 406,
        439, 442, 455, 537; Grosvenor
        Crescent Mews 109, 111, 130, 145, 157,
        228, 513; Kynance Mews 221, 235,
        244, 251, 442, 514; Mount Street 157,
        163, 165–6, 174–5; Victoria & Albert
        Museum 96
London, Jack 62

Stone Print
8 on 10 pt

PART SEVEN

ADDITIONAL ELEMENTS
ON THE PAGE

FOLIOS AND RUNNING HEADS

When designing your text panel, remember that it shares the page with other printed elements. Page numbers and running heads – containing information such as chapter titles – will often be placed in the margins, and these should be included in your trial designs.

Folios

In bibliographical matter the term *folio* is also used to mean a page.

Folio is the typographical term for a page number. All books have even numbers on the verso and odd numbers on the recto. Folios should be consistent, easy to locate, and not stand out to the reader.

The most common position for folios is in the margin at the foot of the page, either centred or ranged with the edge of the text on the fore-edge side:

Text: Walbaum
9 on 15 pt

Folio: Walbaum
8 pt

> a kind of division of labour. First, a 'paraschyte' would make an incision in the dead person's left side. He would then have to run out of the house to avoid being stoned by an angry crowd seeking
>
> 76

Text: Walbaum
9 on 15 pt

Folio: Walbaum
8 pt

> a kind of division of labour. First, a 'paraschyte' would make an incision in the dead person's left side. He would then have to run out of the house to avoid being stoned by an angry crowd seeking
>
> 76

In books with wide fore-edge margins folios may be hung out into the side margins. In asymmetric settings, logic would dictate that the folios are also placed asymmetrically.

Style and size of folios

The simplest way to set folios is to put them in the same typeface as the text. If you are using a second typeface for headings this could also be used for folios.

Folios should be set in a smaller size than the main text:

> changed into smaller ones, which gave the local moneylenders
> the chance to levy large commissions. This gave rise to all kinds
>
> 21

Text: Walbaum
9 on 15 pt

Folio: Walbaum
8 pt

An exception to this is reference books, the text of which is already set in a small size and is likely to be used with frequent reference to the index. In this case, folios should be slightly larger than the text:

> graphical forms of the Sumerian and proto-Elamite figures (see Chapters 10 and 12).
> **6th–5th millennia** BCE **[w].** The earliest *ceramic* artefacts, on which motifs have been painted, engraved, cut out or impressed on the raw clay, or engraved after firing, appear in the Middle East. These are evidently graphical representations
>
> 19

Text: Stone Print
9 on 11 pt

Folio: Stone Print
9.5 pt

Roman numerals

If a book is numbered with the main text starting on page one, the preceding pages – prelims – are numbered with roman numerals. Though most preliminary pages do not have folios printed on them, some, such as the preface and foreword, do. Folios in roman numerals are best set in lower case.

See *Prelims*, p.163

> of the publisher Erwin Glikes; Claudio Magris on his native Trieste;
> Anna Maria Ortese's account of a Neapolitan slum housing estate;
> Adriaan van Dis on the transformative power of translations; fine
>
> vii

Text: Galliard
9.5 on 15 pt

Folio: Galliard
9.5 pt

Running heads

A running head is a line of text placed just above the text panel on every text page. It can contain such information as the name of author, the title of the book, chapter title or a sub-title, usually organized by the editor in one of the following ways:

In complex reference works, the running heads play an important part in helping the reader find information quickly.

VERSO PAGE	RECTO PAGE
author	title
title	chapter
chapter	sub-title
sub-title	sub-title

Running heads may be set centred, ranged with the outer edge of the text panel, or asymmetrically, if that is the style of the layout. They are usually set in a smaller type size than the text and in a different type style such as italic or small caps:

Running head:
Galliard expert
9 pt, 40 ICS

Text: Galliard
9.75 on 14 pt

BEARING WITNESS

and a phenomenal memory. But he was also volatile, unpunctual, disorganized, argumentative, resistant to compromise, and could be

Or a different typeface, matching that of the folios:

Running head:
Stone Sans
small caps,
8.5 pt, 40 ICS

Text: Galliard
9.75 on 14 pt

BEARING WITNESS

and a phenomenal memory. But he was also volatile, unpunctual, disorganized, argumentative, resistant to compromise, and could be

The space between the running head and the text should be a fraction larger than the visual space between lines of text:

The running head on the left is too close to the text, looking cramped. The one on the right floats in the margin and is not connected to the text panel.

Bearing Witness   *Bearing Witness*   *Bearing Witness*

Bearing Witness
and a phenomenal memory. But he was also volatile, unpunctual, disorganized, argumentative, resistant to compromise, and could be

When using running heads, the folio may be placed at the foot of the page as usual or it can be set in a line with the running head:

The Exeter Text   35

them where he'd decreed. The henchmen let themselves be led.
They nevertheless seemed perplexed. We herd them excheynge

In this example the running head is centred and the folio is ranged with the outer edge of this recto text panel.

There are a number of ways of laying out a running head and folio, both symmetrically and asymmetrically, as in these examples:

56	THREE BY PEREC		THE EXETER TEXT	57
rebels' retrenchment. They were severe decrements. The leeders deemed they needed these events stemmed. Endeed, the rebels felt			feeder. Lets begetters (even when they're exerted) feed feeble wee beybes: the rennet keeps fresh whenever the steel segments' cells	

56		THREE BY PEREC	THE EXETER TEXT	57
rebels' retrenchment. They were severe decrements. The leeders deemed they needed these events stemmed. Endeed, the rebels felt			feeder. Lets begetters (even when they're exerted) feed feeble wee beybes: the rennet keeps fresh whenever the steel segments' cells	

THREE BY PEREC		56	57	THE EXETER TEXT
rebels' retrenchment. They were severe decrements. The leeders deemed they needed these events stemmed. Endeed, the rebels felt			feeder. Lets begetters (even when they're exerted) feed feeble wee beybes: the rennet keeps fresh whenever the steel segments' cells	

THREE BY PEREC		56	THE EXETER TEXT	57
rebels' retrenchment. They were severe decrements. The leeders deemed they needed these events stemmed. Endeed, the rebels felt			feeder. Lets begetters (even when they're exerted) feed feeble wee beybes: the rennet keeps fresh whenever the steel segments' cells	

56 THREE BY PEREC			THE EXETER TEXT 57	
rebels' retrenchment. They were severe decrements. The leeders deemed they needed these events stemmed. Endeed, the rebels felt			feeder. Lets begetters (even when they're exerted) feed feeble wee beybes: the rennet keeps fresh whenever the steel segments' cells	

56 THREE BY PEREC			THE EXETER TEXT 57	
rebels' retrenchment. They were severe decrements. The leeders deemed they needed these events stemmed. Endeed, the rebels felt			feeder. Lets begetters (even when they're exerted) feed feeble wee beybes: the rennet keeps fresh whenever the steel segments' cells	

Some of the different ways of laying out the running head and folio (verso on the left, recto on the right).

When grouped together, the running head and folio may be separated by a raised point or line, or a decorative device:

NEWNHAM GRANGE · 51

but mostly it was used for drying clothes, growing mushrooms and
housing hens. In order to accommodate the latter a small door-hole

NEWNHAM GRANGE ❧ 51

but mostly it was used for drying clothes, growing mushrooms and
housing hens. In order to accommodate the latter a small door-hole

Running head:
Scala caps
8.5 pt, 30 ICS
Text: Scala
10 on 15 pt

Decoration: Type Embellishments II

Running feet

In books with many sub-headings, the appearance of a running head and sub-heading together may confuse the reader:

One solution to this problem is to use running feet throughout, rather than running heads. These are placed below the text at the foot of the page:

Running feet are particularly useful in catalogues, where most text pages are likely to have a heading at the top of the page.

Whereas running heads may be set centred or ranged with the text, it is quite unusual to see centred running feet; they are usually set aligned with the fore-edge of the text panel. In books with wide outer margins they may be hung out into the margin. If the measure is wide try setting them indented:

Running heads should be deleted above chapter headings, but they are usually retained where they fall above sub-chapters.

Text: Scala
10.5 on 16 pt

Running foot:
Scala Sans
small caps
8.5 pt, 30 ICS

Text: Iowan
Old Style
10 on 15 pt

Running foot:
Scala Sans caps
6.5 pt, 60 ICS
indented 5 mm

In books set asymmetrically, running feet are usually aligned with the edge of the text next to the wider of the two margins:

them where he'd decreed. The henchmen let themselves be led. They nevertheless seemed perplexed. We herd them excheynge secret mermers. Steeth! Where led these

39   THE EXETER TEXT

Text: Galliard
10 on 14.5 pt

Running foot:
Galliard small caps
8 pt, 30 ICS

Running shoulders

Running shoulders contain the same information as a running head, but are placed in a wide side margin outside the text panel. They are not without their problems. If you are using wide margins, you may well want to place sidenotes or captions in them and it is possible that the position of these will clash with the running shoulders. Long chapter titles may also be difficult to accommodate.

In some circumstances they can be helpful. For example, if the material is laid out alphabetically or if sub-headings are numbered, running shoulders will make it easy for the reader to flick through at speed and locate the text they want:

The cotton industry changed the face of the north-west of England, and dominated British industry for 200 years. It had a meteoric rise in the mid 18th century, and an equally sharp decline in the 20th century.

7.1.2

Cotton

Text: Stone Print
10.5 on 14 pt

Running shoulder:
Stone Sans, 9 pt

Running shoulders should be set to the same baseline grid as the text – they can go onto a second or third line if necessary. Choose a narrow type style such as an italic; spaced small caps will be too wide for most margins:

The Exeter Text

THE EXETER TEXT

Galliard italic, 9.5 pt

Galliard expert, 9.5 pt

When to delete folios and running heads

Folios and running heads or feet are not printed on the following pages:

Half-title, frontispiece, title page, imprint page, dedication/epigraph, contents pages, any pages before the contents page, part-titles, or any blank pages.

A folio and running head can look like a distraction on a page containing one large picture. Discuss with the editor whether you should remove them in this instance.

They may also be removed from pages which contain only illustrations.

If folios and running heads are both placed at the top of the page, they should be removed above chapter openings. If the folio is at the foot of the page, it should appear. Just the running head is removed.

Running head deleted from above the chapter heading

If you are using running feet or shoulders containing chapter titles, you should remove these from the pages on which the chapter heading appears. The folio is left in its usual position:

Though running feet do not clash with chapter openings, they are removed from these pages because the information does not need to be repeated. In reference books, however, you may decide to leave all the running feet on so that readers flicking quickly through the pages can locate information easily.

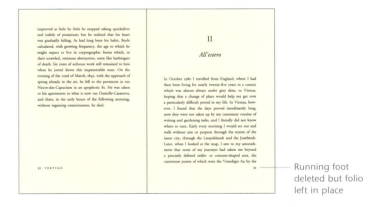

Running foot deleted but folio left in place

Shortening running heads

Titles which are particularly lengthy can be shortened if necessary, and the missing text indicated by an ellipsis. For example, the story by Georges Perec titled *Which Moped with Chrome-plated Handlebars at the Back of the Yard?* could become:

Running heads and feet should never go onto a second line.

Running head:
Galliard italic, 9 pt

Text: Galliard
10 on 14.5 pt

Which Moped . . . ?

which Henri Pollak and the other one (whose name would mean nothing to you, honestly) likewise dived, and the taxi transjogged

This should be done in consultation with the editor.

Colour coding and bleeding out

Colour coding can be a useful way of distinguishing between different sections of text, particularly in informational publications. By placing a box of colour bleeding off the fore-edge, the sections can be seen even when the book is closed. A popular treatment is to place the folio in a coloured box which bleeds off the edge.

75

This may look like a good solution on the proofs but carries risks. The process of folding and trimming is not always accurate – it can be out by millimetres. The result is that the boxes do not all line up vertically, and some folios will be too close to the fore-edge:

75

Making the boxes wider, and keeping the folios further from the fore-edge will minimize this effect.

75

75

FOOTNOTES, ENDNOTES AND SIDENOTES

There are three standard ways of introducing notes into a text: *footnotes*, *endnotes* and *sidenotes* (also called *shoulder notes*). Footnotes are placed at the foot of the page, endnotes at the end of the main text, or alternatively at the end of the relevant chapter, and sidenotes in the fore-edge margin. An *indicator* – a number or symbol set in superior figures – is placed in the main text to refer the reader to the note.

Footnotes (*left*)
Endnotes (*centre*)
Sidenotes (*rignt*)

When choosing which method to use, you need to consider the content of the notes. Are they important to the reader's understanding of the text – for example, translations of foreign words and phrases – in which case foot- or sidenotes would be more helpful? Or do they mostly provide references to source material, which would be more appropriately placed with the endmatter?

This decision should be made in consultation with the editor.

The style of the book will also influence this decision. Pages of dense footnotes can make a book look 'academic' and will intimidate some readers. On the other hand, large-format illustrated books can benefit from the extra text elements which give interest to a page, and sidenotes – often in a second colour – can have a secondary effect as a decorative device.

See *Mixing notes*, p.216

As with all typographic elements, consistency is the key to conveying meaning to the reader. It is inadvisable to mix styles within a book, unless there is a logical reason for doing so.

Footnotes

A footnote should be on the same page as its indicator, usually set in the same face as the main text but noticeably smaller, with leading adjusted proportionately. The baseline of the notes should align with the baseline of the text panel with at least one line space separating the note from the main text. The number of the footnote (unlike the text indicator) is not set in superior figures. It is easier to locate a particular note if the number is hung out:

(1608–1679) made efforts to apply Galileo's laws of dynamics to the movements of the stars.[14] The pioneering work of Galileo came to flower and to fruit in the hands of Isaac Newton (1642–1727), whose *Philosophiae Mathematica*

13 Christopher Wren, later famous as an architect, was in the first place a very able mathematician who contributed to the theories here discussed, and maintained his interest throughout his life. [*Transl.*]
14 He also, impressed by the new successes of mathematics applied to the mechanics of moving inanimate objects, attempted to apply mathematics to the processes of living organisms. At any rate in the domain of movement and muscular forces, he succeeded in discovering some new principles in this field.

Main text: Stone Print, 9.5 on 13 pt
Footnotes: Stone Print, 7 on 9.6 pt indented 3 mm with numbers hung out

baseline of text panel

Two or three short notes can be set together on one line, centred, with a minimum of two em spaces between them:

calculation: on the use of the binary number-system in calculating machines).[4]
Again in 1936, William Phillips in England constructed his binary demonstrator which was a mechanical device that demonstrated the feasibility of a

3. CRAS, 202 (1936), pp. 1745ff.   4. CRAS, 202 (1936), pp. 1970ff.

Main text: Stone Print, 9.5 on 13 pt
Footnotes: Stone Print, 7 on 9.6 pt separated by 2 em spaces

If several short notes fall on the same page, they are better set in columns:

a family trait. Her chapter on the uncles in *Period Piece* ends: 'I know that I always felt older than they were. Not nearly so good, or so brave, or so kind, or so wise. Just older.'[41] But after the book was

35. *PP*, pp.113–14
36. *PP*, pp.142–43
37. *PP*, p.142

38. *PP*, p.235
39. *PP*, pp.141–42
40. *PP*, p.154

41. Henrietta Litchfield to George Darwin, 10 October 1896

Main text: Scala 9.6 on 13 pt
Footnotes: Scala 6.5 on 9 pt in 3 columns

Long footnotes can, where necessary, be carried over onto the next page if there is not enough room for them, but the break should not fall at the end of the sentence or the reader will assume they have reached the end of the note. The indicator should appear on the last line of the main text and the overrun footnote is placed underneath the text on the following page. Space is left between the overrun footnote and further footnotes:

There should be at least three lines of main text above footnotes.

and scheming. Such simple meanings, however, became very greatly extended as the science of mathematics developed over the centuries, and have diversified into many domains.[1] *Calculation* originally, and

1. While an occurrence in English of the word *calculus* can almost always be directly translated into the French *calcul*, it is less often so in the reverse direction. Both *calculus* and *calcul* are generally used to refer to some unified body of mathematical theory and methods: examples will be cited below. The French use of the word *calcul* is more extended than the English use of *calculus*. Thus where the French may refer to *calcul algébrique*, the English would simply use *algebra*. The French *calcul numérique*, if used to refer to the study

the traditional arithmetical operations).Quite early, however, in the history of modern mathematics the meaning of *calculation* took on a more general sense, well illustrated by the following quotation from Gottfried Wilhelm Leibniz (1646–1716) as cited by E. T. Bell:[2]

of arithmetical operations on arbitrary numbers, would be *arithmetic* in English; while *calcul numérique* in the sense of the study of procedures developed for the numerical solution of mathematical problems would be *numerical analysis* in English. [*Transl.*]

2. E. T. Bell, *Men of Mathematics*, p. 123.

Long footnotes will affect the choice of font for the book. In the example below a note has been set in three different fonts to fill the same space. The first, Centaur, has a wide set and small x-height which makes it look tiny. The second, Walbaum has a strong vertical emphasis and dark colour which is uncomfortable on the eye at this size. The third, Albertina, is clearer and more economical which makes it legible at small sizes:

Centaur
7.2 on 9 pt

Walbaum
5.4 on 9 pt

Albertina
6.5 on 9 pt

Note the variation in type size. That Walbaum 5.4 pt looks darker than Centaur at 7.2 pt illustrates how fonts can vary in *colour*, see pp.84–6.

14. He also, impressed by the new successes of mathematics applied to the mechanics of moving inanimate objects, attempted to apply mathematics to the processes of living organisms. At any rate in the domain of movement and muscular forces, he succeeded in discovering some new principles in this field.

14. He also, impressed by the new successes of mathematics applied to the mechanics of moving inanimate objects, attempted to apply mathematics to the processes of living organisms. At any rate in the domain of movement and muscular forces, he succeeded in discovering some new principles in this field.

14. He also, impressed by the new successes of mathematics applied to the mechanics of moving inanimate objects, attempted to apply mathematics to the processes of living organisms. At any rate in the domain of movement and muscular forces, he succeeded in discovering some new principles in this field.

In some cases, such as large illustrated books, it may be desirable to set the footnotes in a different font to the main text, but care should be taken to find a comfortable match.

Endnotes

Endnotes can be placed at the end of each chapter, or at the end of the main text, before the remainder of the endmatter.

Chapter endnotes may be more appropriate in a book of essays written by different authors, or they may be used as a space-saving device, occupying what may be empty space on the last page of a chapter. They are not used where a new chapter runs on directly beneath the preceding one.

Chapter endnotes are set in a smaller type size than the main text, and should be separated from it by at least one line space, or they may be placed at the foot of the page. Hanging out numbers will aid the reader:

> The ocean, the whispering shadows, the dazzling, despairing light. From this plateau, any dream of freedom must inevitably come up against the dispiriting permanence of that blue.
>
> 1 The footnotes of history. [Tr.]
> 2 Fonds Jourquin [Jourquin collection].
> 3 General Bonaparte was often called 'Le Petit Tondu', the little man with the close-cropped hair [Tr.]
> 4 Louis Madelin, *Vers l'Empire d'Occident.*

Main text: Garamond 10.8 on 15 pt
Endnotes: Garamond 7.5 on 9.5 pt, at full measure

If many of the notes are short, it may look better to set the notes to a shorter measure, ranged left with the text:

> The ocean, the whispering shadows, the dazzling, despairing light. From this plateau, any dream of freedom must inevitably come up against the dispiriting permanence of that blue.
>
> 1 The footnotes of history. [Tr.]
> 2 Fonds Jourquin [Jourquin collection].
> 3 General Bonaparte was often called 'Le Petit Tondu', the little man with the close-cropped hair [Tr.]
> 4 Louis Madelin, *Vers l'Empire d'Occident.*

Main text: Garamond 10.8 on 15 pt
Endnotes: Garamond 7.5 on 9.5 pt at half measure

Endnotes form part of the endmatter so should be treated in a way that is consistent with other sections of endmatter. They are set in a smaller size than the main text, possibly in two columns to occupy less space. The content of the notes – proper names and strings of initials and numbers – and the shorter measure may mean it is preferable to set them ranged left even if the main text is justified.

Notes: Scala
7.5 on 10 pt
set in 2 columns
Chapter numbers:
Scala caps
8 on 10 pt
Chapter titles:
Scala italic
9 on 14 pt
This example
shows the various
ways of helping
the reader locate
notes. The numbers
are hung out to the
left, the chapters
are clearly indicated
and the running
heads tell the
reader specifically
what is on the
page.

NOTES · Chapters 2–4

33 The letter from which this is drawn was rightly included by Henrietta Litchfield in her two-volume memorial to her mother. See *ED*, II: 119

34 *ED*, II: 211

35 J. D. Hooker to Henrietta Litchfield, 5 February 1905: BL MS Dept. Add 583

CHAPTER 3

Destined for Matriarchy

1 Cara Jebb to Nellie Du Puy, 18 May 1883: DAR 251:660

2 *With Dearest Love to All*, pp. 188-89

9 Maud Du Puy to Ellen Du Puy, 21 July 1883: DAR 251: 670

10 See note 4; also quoted in *PP*, p.24

15 See note 4

16 Maud Du Puy to Ellen Du Puy, 13 July 1883: DAR 251: 668. During services in the church at Downe, while the congregation turned towards the altar and said the Creed, George Darwin had as a child, with the rest of his siblings, turned and faced the other way, sternly looking into the eyes of the other churchgoers.

17 See note 4

18 Maud Du Puy to Carrie Du Puy, 11 June

Sidenotes

The decision to use sidenotes will have a considerable impact on the design of the main text panel as sidenotes require ample margins in which to sit. In a classically designed book this means the fore-edge margin, but on an asymmetrical spread they are placed in the larger of the two margins:

Sidenotes are set at a smaller type size than the main text and ranged left:

Main text: Minion
9.5 on 13 pt
Sidenote: Minion
6.5 on 8.5 pt

Now written *Fuxi*; he was the presumed inventor of Chinese writing.

letter, of Fou-Hi's characters. It is binary arithmetic, which this great legislator already knew and which I have redis-covered thousands of years later. In this arithmetic there

It is tempting for the sake of symmetry to range sidenotes against the text, but these are harder to read, especially when the notes are long:

Now written *Fuxi*; he was the presumed inventor of Chinese writing.

letter, of Fou-Hi's characters. It is binary arithmetic, which this great legislator already knew and which I have redis-covered thousands of years later. In this arithmetic there

Sidenotes do not necessarily require indicators within the text as they can be placed directly next to the relevant line. The base of the first line of the note should align with the baseline of the relevant line of main text:

Main text: Minion
9.5 on 13 pt
Sidenote: Minion
6.5 on 8.5 pt

the seemingly most probable meaning, according to the letter, of Fou-Hi's characters. It is binary arithmetic, which this great legislator already knew and which I have redis-covered thousands of years later. In this arithmetic there are only two signs, 0 and 1, and by means of these any

Now written *Fuxi*; he was the presumed inventor of Chinese writing.

In illustrated books, care must be taken to avoid possible confusion between side-notes and captions. As the notes are related more directly to the text than the captions, they should bear a closer typographical resemblance to it:

Main text: Scala
9 on 13 pt
Sidenote: Scala
7 on 9 pt
Caption: Scala
Sans, 7.5 on 9.5 pt
The sidenote is
more closely
related to the
text so is set in
the same font. The
caption is differen-
tiated by being set
in a sans serif font.

on much new talent in the early 1930s, as its audience had suddenly shrunk like a shrivelled balloon.

In the 1920s, to be sure, music-hall and cabaret were to be found all over Paris – not just in the entertainment district of the Champs-Elysées, but in almost every *quartier*. Many ordinary restaurants and numerous bars that served mainly

Pierre Bost, *Le Cirque et le Music-Hall*. Paris: Au Sans-Pareil, 1931. See in particular pp.40–2.

FIG.17
Father and Son, July 1931

Sidebars

Sidebars are used to convey extra information to the reader. They may add to a particular passage of text, for example, by giving the background to a historical event, or a short biography of a person mentioned in the text. They are generally used in educational books.

Sidebars should be placed in the wider of the margins. They can be set justified or ranged left, with the main text running around them. If a second colour is available, this can be used to differentiate them from the main text:

Main text:
Albertina
10 on 14.5 pt
Sidebar: Albertina
8.75 on 11.5 pt
Pantone 187

Under the pressure of need to reduce both size and weight, the evolution just described led on to a reduction in the dimensions of the machines which, immediately after the Second World War, gave rise to a machine that, of all purely mechanical devices, was one of the most extremely miniaturised and perfected of modern times: the Curta, invented by Curt Herzstark, and manufactured in Liechtenstein. The Curta Model I had an 8-column 'keyboard' (8 slides), an 11-digit results register and a 6-digit revolution counter. It was 5.3 cm in diameter by 8.6 cm long and weighed 230 gm. The Model II had an 11-column keyboard, 15-digit results register and 8-digit revolution counter. It was 6.6 cm in diameter by 9.1 cm long and weighed 360 gm. According to Taton and Flad this

Curt Herzstark (1902–1988), an Austrian Jew, apparently invented the machine while prisoner at Buchenwald concentration camp: according to some accounts in secret, according to others with the knowledge of the concentration camp authorities who hoped to present the invention to the Führer. In 1946, he was invited by the Prince of Liechtenstein to establish a manufacturing plant for the Curta in the Principality of Liechtenstein and founded the company Contina AG.

The width of sidebars should be uniform throughout, as should the space between the sidebar and the text panel. There should be at least two lines of main text above and below the sidebar.

Note indicators

Notes are usually indicated by superior figures, which can be created in typesetting programs. Set indicators in a size that is legible but not too intrusive, and take care to ensure that there is adequate space between the indicator and the previous character. Indicators should fall after any punctuation, except dashes:

Favourite among Charles's clients were the Quakers[1] and Unitarians[2] who had helped make Birmingham the Second City, 'the City of a Thousand Trades'.[3] He was influenced by their uprightness, their

Bembo
10.5 on 13 pt
Indicators at 62%

Using lining figures will prevent the appearance of 'bobbing up and down' and size variation that can occur with non-lining figures. The weight of the superior figures can be adjusted if they are much reduced and, as a result, look too light:

sharing[1] of[2] capital[3] assets.[4] His[5] good[6] friend[7] was[8] the[9] lawyer,[10]

Bembo with non-lining superior figures

sharing[1] of[2] capital[3] assets.[4] His[5] good[6] friend[7] was[8] the[9] lawyer,[10]

Bembo with lining superior figures

Bembo with lining superior figures in semi-bold

In texts set in a small type size, superior figures may need extra letter-spacing to make them more legible:

travelling was hard work and thought fondly of home.[128] After a few days with Cary in Isfahan,[129] while Cecil went south to Kerman on

Scala, 9.5 on 13 pt

travelling was hard work and thought fondly of home.[128] After a few days with Cary in Isfahan,[129] while Cecil went south to Kerman on

Scala, 9.5 on 13 pt with letter-spaced superior figures

In books with very few footnotes, symbols rather than numbers can be used to indicate notes. The order of use is * † ‡ § ‖ ¶   starting anew with an asterisk on each page.

If the set of these symbols available in a particular font is not suitable they can be replaced by those from a different font:

sum of money. The members of his retinue had been able to hide it from the English when the *Bellerophon* was searched.*

sum of money. The members of his retinue had been able to hide it from the English when the *Bellerophon* was searched.*

Mixing notes

Notes giving translations of foreign words or other information essential to the reader's understanding should not be separated from the text. This can be avoided by using two different sorts of notes together: for example, footnotes for these translations and endnotes for source notes, etc. In the following example footnotes are indicated by asterisks while the endnotes are indicated by superior figures:

was soon broadened by filling up parts of the Amstel from one bank and building new houses on the reclaimed land.[56] As a result the dyke became a street, with houses on either side.[57] Only a few years ago, during excavations for the foundations of a commercial building by the Rokin,* the original bank of the Amstel was discovered. This clearly showed how the early pioneers had filled in parts of the river with

* A street, part of which runs alongside the river.

The decision to use this system should be made early in the process so that the editor can number footnotes and endnotes on the text disk before it is supplied to the designer.

Notes without indicators

If the notes to a text only give details of source material and are not essential to the reader's understanding of the text, they may be set without indicators. This simplifies the appearance of the text panel, removing unnecessary distractions. The notes are set as endnotes after the main text, giving a page reference and a short quote from the text – set in quotation marks – to which the note is relevant:

p.360 'No man can ...' Suzanne Hayes, Adelaide, March 1984

p.362 'a penny a pound too much ...' *Paths of Progress: A History of Marlborough College*, Thomas Hinde (James & James, 1992), 189

p.363 'We set off ...' 25.7.55, Marlborough College archive

p.363 'I remember Penelope ...' *Independent*, 14.5.87

p.364 'She was a ...' *On the Black Hill*, 219

p.366 'I think she was ...' Elizabeth Chatwin to Michael Cottrill, 1989

Bembo, 10 on 14 pt

In the following example the quotes from the text are set in semi-bold without quotation marks, and names which appear frequently are abbreviated. A list of abbreviations would then be necessary at the beginning of the notes section.

p.360 **No man can ...** SH, Adelaide, March 1984

p.362 **a penny a pound too much ...** *Paths of Progress: A History of Marlborough College*, Thomas Hinde (James & James, 1992), 189

p.363 **We set off ...** 25.7.55, Marlborough College archive

p.363 **I remember Penelope ...** *Independent*, 14.5.87

p.364 **She was a ...** *OTBH*, 219

p.366 **I think she was ...** EC to Michael Cottrill, 1989

Bembo semi-bold and regular 10 on 14 pt

This method is popular in biographies where each paragraph may draw on several different sources.

PART EIGHT

EXTENT

SIGNATURES AND IMPOSITION

In your layout program the pages of a 16-page signature will look like this:

Take a sheet of paper and fold it in half: you now have 4 pages. Fold it in half the other way and you have 8 pages. One more fold makes 16 pages. If you number these pages from the front and then lay the sheet flat, one side will look like this:

6̄	8	5	21
16	1	4	13

and the other like this:

51	2	3	14
10	7	6̲	11

	1

2	3

4	5

6	7

8	9

10	11

12	13

14	15

16	

If the folded sheet is trimmed at the head and fore-edge there will be 16 pages with a common fold along the spine. Page 2 will be on the back of page 1 and so on. This simple process begins to explains three technical terms – *signature, to view* and *imposition*.

A *signature* is the folded sheet with, in this case, 16 pages printed on it. A book is composed of a series of signatures bound together. Both sides of the sheet have 8 pages on them; they are referred to as *printed 8-to-view*. The process by which the pages are arranged on the sheet so that page 2 does fall on the back of page 1 is called *imposition*.

Present-day printing presses have a capacity to print on large sizes of paper and 8-to-view is now a small book-press size. Commonly sheets will be printed 16- or 32-to-view.

As the number of pages increases, so does the complexity of imposition. Gratefully the imposition process is not a function of the designer or typesetter – but an understanding of its implications is essential to ensure that your layouts are practicable.

It is possible to add 4 or 8 pages to a book if it is absolutely necessary, but this will be expensive.

What is important to the designer and typesetter is that the number of pages in a book is an exact multiple of the number of pages in the signature – usually 16 or 32 pages. A sheet printed 8-to-view produces a signature of 16 pages; 16-to-view produces a 32-page signature.

Thus a book of 288 pages, printed on a press with the capacity to print 8 pages to view, will have $288 \div 8 = 36$ printing passes through the press: 18 to print one side of the paper and 18 on the other, producing 18×16-page signatures.

If the typeset text fills 293 pages, another 16-page signature would need to be added, making 304 pages, with 11 blanks at the end. The book would have to be reset – either to the 288 pages or to 304 pages – to avoid blank pages. In practice the calculation of the book's length should be done at the trial stage to avoid the need for resetting.

See *Extent and words-per-page*, pp.222–3

In practical terms, 8-to-view (16-page) signatures offer greater flexibility as can be seen in the table below. But the economic savings of printing sheets 16-to-view may well influence the publisher when deciding on the number of pages.

8-to-view			16-to-view	
48	176	304	64	256
64	192	320	96	288
80	208	336	128	320
96	224	352	160	352
112	240	368	192	384
128	256	384	224	416
144	272	400		
160	288	416		

In planning a book you will have to consider how the number of signatures that make up the book, together with the possible range of sheet sizes available, fit your intended format and extent.

Printers provide tables indicating the limits of paper sizes for formats in this form:

		Suggested Max.	Absolute Max.
Printing 16 pages to view	Format	356 × 267	371 × 273
	Trim size	350 × 264	365 × 270
	Paper size	1092 × 1424	1116 × 1484

If you come across them, terms such as Royal and Demy refer to past standards for paper sizes, followed by a Latin word to indicate the folding of the sheet to the final page size – Royal octavo, for example, being a Royal sheet folded to give 8 pages to view. These terms have little relevance in modern trade publishing, although the antiquarian book trade still defines book formats using them.

EXTENT AND WORDS-PER-PAGE

How many pages?

The number of pages in a book is known as the *extent*. How you approach designing a book can depend very much on whether extent is fixed in advance by the publisher or whether the designer has a free hand. Either way it is helpful to know what can make a difference to a book's extent.

Extent is influenced by a number of factors which are outside the control of the designer. Starting with the most obvious, they are:

> **Word count**: the number of words in the text.
>
> **Number of chapters**: headings occupy space, and starting chapters on a new page will leave a lot of blank text area.
>
> **Style of text**: dialogue, with each speaker starting a new line, takes up more room than long paragraphs of continuous prose.
>
> **Quantity of prelims, endmatter and part-titles**: these are not usually included in the word count of the main text.
>
> **Recto openings**: or any decision which necessitates that text falls on a recto or verso in a particular place.

Added to these are factors which the designer can control, namely:

> **Format of the book**: although this may be decided by the publisher.
>
> **Size of text panel**: will influence the size of type you can use.
>
> **Size of type**: will have an impact on the number of words-per-line.
>
> **Leading**: will have an impact on the number of lines-per-page.
>
> **Choice of font**: some fonts are more economical, that is they take up less room than others while appearing to be the same size.
>
> **Size of chapter headings**: this obviously has a greater impact when there is a large number of chapters.

Estimating extent

Even if a book's extent is not fixed by the publisher, it may be necessary to give an estimate of extent before designing trial spreads which can be used to get quotes from printers and freelancers, such as proofreaders and indexers, who charge by the page. This can be done using the word count and a simple words-per-page calculation, remembering to add on pages for prelims and endmatter where required, for example:

> 50,000 words
> divided by an average of say 280 words-per-page
> equals 179 pages
> plus 10 pages of prelims and endmatter
> equals 189 pages which rounds up to 192 (12 x 16) pages

Counting words-per-page in existing books will help give you a feel for word counts at different sizes and formats. Doing a quick page trial with dummy text may help.

Fixed extents

If the extent of the book has been decided in advance by the publisher – and this is often done to keep control of the budget – the calculation is performed the other way round, for example:

> 272 pages
> minus 10 pages of prelims and endmatter
> equals 260 pages
> 75,000 words divided by 260 pages
> equals approximately 288 words per page

This calculation serves as a useful guide when doing trial spreads if the whole text is unavailable.

The publisher may well ask to see alternative trial spreads to show how adding 16 or 32 pages will affect the look of the page.

Words-per-page: type size and leading

Opposite is a panel of text set in a range of sizes and leading, all of which would produce a page of text containing about 285 words. As the size of the type increases, fewer words appear on each line. To compensate, the leading is reduced which increases the number of lines on a page. Unfortunately this does not result in text which is more readable, as the bottom example shows. When designing a text panel to contain a certain number of words, it is worth taking time to find the best possible balance between the size and leading of your type. The middle sample probably has the greatest degree of readability of those opposite.

Increasing and reducing extent

The extent of a book can be increased or reduced by adjusting the size and leading of the type, or the size of the text panel, or a combination of the two. On the following two pages the size and leading has been adjusted: the page on the right contains 80 per cent of the text on the left.

On pp.228 and 229 the size of the text panel has been adjusted. The page on the right contains 75 per cent of the text on the left.

On pp.230 and 231 both the size and leading of the type and the size of the text panel have been adjusted. The page on the right contains 60 per cent of the text of that on the left. In a book of 50,000 words this would result in a difference of 96 pages between the two settings.

Smaller adjustments can be made to increase or reduce the extent by just a few pages. The example on p.232 shows how increasing the point size by 0.3 pt would, in this case, add 6 pages to a book of 50,000 words.

Blanks at the end

If a book is to be bound in hardback the last page should be left blank, as it will be attached to the endpaper, losing some of the gutter margin as a result. It is acceptable in most cases to leave two or three blanks at the end, if this is within the publisher's house style.

know what you mean,' Anastasios said. He coughed several times, as if he wanted to give his voice the unwavering resonance of the bygone days when he had recounted ancient tales and legends to the young Prince. It was a distinctive way of speaking that flowed with conviction, not allowing for the slightest interruption. 'You are unsettled by the wild jumble of

their troops, my Prince. All those banners and icons and the crosses and multicoloured emblems, and the trumpets, and the long and resonant names and titles of their dukes and counts, and then the musicians and poets poised to sing the glory of each and every one of them for generations to come. I fully understand you, my Prince, especially when you

compare that wild jumble to the dusty monotony of our army. I understand you, but let us wait till tomorrow, my Prince. Tomorrow you shall see that the real instrument of war is not theirs, but ours – dusty and drab like mud, with a single banner, a single commander, and no emblems or flamboyant poets, no commanders thirsting for glory, or

sporting long titles, names, and surnames. Obedient, sober, mute, and nameless like mud – that is the army of the future, my Prince. The day before we marched off I happened to look through the rosters of our soldiers. The majority were listed only by their forenames – no distinguishing features, not even a

surname. More than thirteen hundred Abdullahs, nine hundred Hassans, a thousand or so Ibrahims, and so on. It is these shadows, as they might appear to be to an onlooker, who will face those strutting Balkans and slash their names, and surnames.

Garamond
9.8 on 14 pt
This text looks very small and weak. It would soon become tiring to the reader.

Garamond
10 on 13.8 pt
A slight improvement on the one above.

Garamond
10.5 on 13.5 pt
This sample has a better relationship between word-spacing and leading than those above and below it.

Garamond
11 on 12.5 pt
This would be improved by massaging the text throughout. The leading is inadequate.

Garamond
11.5 on 12.2 pt
This text may be the largest but the loose word-spacing and tight leading are uncomfortable to read.

These examples
illustrate how
changing the type
size and leading
can increase or
reduce the
number of words
on a page. The
page on the right
contains 80 per
cent of the text
of that on the left.

Garamond
9.8 on 13.5 pt

290 words-
per-page

I know what you mean,' Anastasios said. He coughed several times, as if he wanted to give his voice the unwavering resonance of the bygone days when he had recounted ancient tales and legends to the young Prince. It was a distinctive way of speaking that flowed with conviction, not allowing for the slightest interruption. 'You are unsettled by the wild jumble of their troops, my Prince. All those banners and icons and crosses and multicoloured emblems, and the trumpets, and the long and resonant names and titles of their dukes and counts, and then the musicians and poets poised to sing the glory of each and every one of them for generations to come. I fully understand you, my Prince, especially when you compare that wild jumble to the dusty monotony of our army. I understand you, but let us wait till tomorrow, my Prince. Tomorrow you shall see that the real instrument of war is not theirs, but ours – dusty and drab like mud, with a single banner, a single commander, and no emblems or flamboyant poets, no commanders thirsting for glory, or sporting long titles, names, and surnames. Obedient, sober, mute, and nameless like mud – that is the army of the future, my Prince. The day before we marched off I happened to look through the rosters of our soldiers. The majority were listed only by their forenames – no distinguishing features, not even a surname. More than thirteen hundred Abdullahs, nine hundred Hassans, a thousand or so Ibrahims, and so on. It is these shadows, as they might appear to be to an onlooker, who will face those strutting Balkans and slash their names, their long peacock-tail titles, and ultimately slash their lives. Mark my word, Prince!'

know what you mean,' Anastasios said. He coughed several times, as if he wanted to give his voice the unwavering resonance of the bygone days when he had recounted ancient tales and legends to the young Prince. It was a distinctive way of speaking that flowed with conviction, not allowing for the slightest interruption. 'You are unsettled by the wild jumble of their troops, my Prince. All those banners and icons and crosses and multicoloured emblems, and the trumpets, and the long and resonant names and titles of their dukes and counts, and then the musicians and poets poised to sing the glory of each and every one of them for generations to come. I fully understand you, my Prince, especially when you compare that wild jumble to the dusty monotony of our army. I understand you, but let us wait till tomorrow, my Prince. Tomorrow you shall see that the real instrument of war is not theirs, but ours – dusty and drab like mud, with a single banner, a single commander, and no emblems or flamboyant poets, no commanders thirsting for glory, or sporting long titles, names, and surnames. Obedient, sober, mute, and nameless like mud – that is the army of the future, my Prince. The day before we marched off I happened to look through the rosters of our soldiers. The majority were listed only by their forenames – no distinguishing

Garamond
11 on 15 pt

230 words-
per-page

These examples illustrate how changing the area of the text panel can increase or reduce the number of words on a page. The text panel on the right is 75 per cent the area of that on the left and contains 75 per cent of the text.

Garamond
10 on 13.5 pt

Panel: 150 x 90 mm

350 words-
per-page

I know what you mean,' Anastasios said. He coughed several times, as if he wanted to give his voice the unwavering resonance of the bygone days when he had recounted ancient tales and legends to the young Prince. It was a distinctive way of speaking that flowed with conviction, not allowing for the slightest interruption. 'You are unsettled by the wild jumble of their troops, my Prince. All those banners and icons and crosses and multicoloured emblems, and the trumpets, and the long and resonant names and titles of their dukes and counts, and then the musicians and poets poised to sing the glory of each and every one of them for generations to come. I fully understand you, my Prince, especially when you compare that wild jumble to the dusty monotony of our army. I understand you, but let us wait till tomorrow, my Prince. Tomorrow you shall see that the real instrument of war is not theirs, but ours – dusty and drab like mud, with a single banner, a single commander, and no emblems or flamboyant poets, no commanders thirsting for glory, or sporting long titles, names, and surnames. Obedient, sober, mute, and nameless like mud – that is the army of the future, my Prince. The day before we marched off I happened to look through the rosters of our soldiers. The majority were listed only by their forenames – no distinguishing features, not even a surname. More than thirteen hundred Abdullahs, nine hundred Hassans, a thousand or so Ibrahims, and so on. It is these shadows, as they might appear to be to an onlooker, who will face those strutting Balkans and slash their names, their long peacock-tail titles, and ultimately slash their lives. Mark my word, Prince!'

He went on speaking for quite a long time, and Bayezid, just as when he was a boy, did not interrupt him. The Greek said that the Ottoman army was uniform, that it had an unfathomable face, he said, like that of Allah. The Christians had lost their future ever since they had given a human likeness – Christ – to

I know what you mean,' Anastasios said. He coughed several times, as if he wanted to give his voice the unwavering resonance of the bygone days when he had recounted ancient tales and legends to the young Prince. It was a distinctive way of speaking that flowed with conviction, not allowing for the slightest interruption. 'You are unsettled by the wild jumble of their troops, my Prince. All those banners and icons and crosses and multicoloured emblems, and the trumpets, and the long and resonant names and titles of their dukes and counts, and then the musicians and poets poised to sing the glory of each and every one of them for generations to come. I fully understand you, my Prince, especially when you compare that wild jumble to the dusty monotony of our army. I understand you, but let us wait till tomorrow, my Prince. Tomorrow you shall see that the real instrument of war is not theirs, but ours – dusty and drab like mud, with a single banner, a single commander, and no emblems or flamboyant poets, no commanders thirsting for glory, or sporting long titles, names, and surnames. Obedient, sober, mute, and nameless like mud – that is the army of the future, my Prince. The day before we marched off I happened to look through the rosters of our soldiers. The majority were listed only by their forenames – no distinguishing features, not even a surname. More than thirteen hundred Abdullahs, nine hundred Hassans, a thousand or so Ibrahims, and so on. It is these shadows, as they might appear to be to an

Garamond
10 on 13.5 pt

Panel: 134 x 76 mm

265 words-per-page

These examples illustrate how changing the area of the text panel and the size and leading of the type can have a dramatic effect on the number of words on a page. The page on the right contains 60 per cent of the text on the left.

Garamond
9.8 on 13.2 pt

Panel: 150 x 90 mm

365 words-per-page

I know what you mean,' Anastasios said. He coughed several times, as if he wanted to give his voice the unwavering resonance of the bygone days when he had recounted ancient tales and legends to the young Prince. It was a distinctive way of speaking that flowed with conviction, not allowing for the slightest interruption. 'You are unsettled by the wild jumble of their troops, my Prince. All those banners and icons and crosses and multicoloured emblems, and the trumpets, and the long and resonant names and titles of their dukes and counts, and then the musicians and poets poised to sing the glory of each and every one of them for generations to come. I fully understand you, my Prince, especially when you compare that wild jumble to the dusty monotony of our army. I understand you, but let us wait till tomorrow, my Prince. Tomorrow you shall see that the real instrument of war is not theirs, but ours – dusty and drab like mud, with a single banner, a single commander, and no emblems or flamboyant poets, no commanders thirsting for glory, or sporting long titles, names, and surnames. Obedient, sober, mute, and nameless like mud – that is the army of the future, my Prince. The day before we marched off I happened to look through the rosters of our soldiers. The majority were listed only by their forenames – no distinguishing features, not even a surname. More than thirteen hundred Abdullahs, nine hundred Hassans, a thousand or so Ibrahims, and so on. It is these shadows, as they might appear to be to an onlooker, who will face those strutting Balkans and slash their names, their long peacock-tail titles, and ultimately slash their lives. Mark my word, Prince!'

He went on speaking for quite a long time, and Bayezid, just as when he was a boy, did not interrupt him. The Greek said that the Ottoman army was uniform, that it had an unfathomable face, he said, like that of Allah. The Christians had lost their future ever since they had given a human likeness – Christ – to their God. There were times when the Christians tried to mend their error by

I know what you mean,' Anastasios said. He coughed several times, as if he wanted to give his voice the unwavering resonance of the bygone days when he had recounted ancient tales and legends to the young Prince. It was a distinctive way of speaking that flowed with conviction, not allowing for the slightest interruption. 'You are unsettled by the wild jumble of their troops, my Prince. All those banners and icons and crosses and multicoloured emblems, and the trumpets, and the long and resonant names and titles of their dukes and counts, and then the musicians and poets poised to sing the glory of each and every one of them for generations to come. I fully understand you, my Prince, especially when you compare that wild jumble to the dusty monotony of our army. I understand you, but let us wait till tomorrow, my Prince. Tomorrow you shall see that the real instrument of war is not theirs, but ours – dusty and drab like mud, with a single banner, a single commander, and no emblems or flamboyant poets, no commanders thirsting for glory, or sporting long titles, names, and surnames. Obedient, sober, mute, and nameless like mud – that is the army of the future, my Prince. The day before we marched off I happened to look through

Garamond
11 on 15 pt

Panel: 134 x 76 mm

215 words-
per-page

These examples
illustrate how
a very small
change to the
size of the type,
0.3 pt, can be
used to increase
extent. In this
setting it would
add 6 pages to a
book of 50,000
words.

Garamond
11.5 on 16 pt

287 words-
per-page

enough into that incomprehensible void, you could believe you
saw the first flurries of snow swirling out of it. My way took
me past the teacher's house and the curate's house and by the
high cemetery wall, at the end of which St George was forever
driving a spear through the throat of the griffin-like winged
creature lying at his feet. From there I had to go down Church
Hill and along the so-called Upper Street. A smell of burnt horn
came from the smithy. The forge fire had died down, and the
tools, the heavy hammers, tongs and rasps were lying abandoned all round. In W., noon was the hour of things deserted.
The water in the tub, into which the blacksmith, when working at his anvil would plunge the red-hot iron so that it hissed,
was so calm, and shone so darkly in the pale light that fell on

Garamond
11.8 on 16 pt

278 words-
per-page

enough into that incomprehensible void, you could believe
you saw the first flurries of snow swirling out of it. My way
took me past the teacher's house and the curate's house and
by the high cemetery wall, at the end of which St George was
forever driving a spear through the throat of the griffin-like
winged creature lying at his feet. From there I had to go down
Church Hill and along the so-called Upper Street. A smell
of burnt horn came from the smithy. The forge fire had died
down, and the tools, the heavy hammers, tongs and rasps
were lying abandoned all round. In W., noon was the hour
of things deserted. The water in the tub, into which the blacksmith, when working at his anvil would plunge the red-hot
iron so that it hissed, was so calm, and shone so darkly in the

Typeface economy

Some typefaces take up less room than others while appearing to be the same size. This is due to variations in the relationship between x-height and width. Although extent should not be the main criterion when choosing a typeface, it can help to understand the difference between fonts when considering alternatives.

See Typeface characteristics, pp.76–81

The following examples are all 60 words long and set to approximately the same size visually (not necessarily the same point size).

1 You are unsettled by the wild jumble of their troops, my Prince. All those
2 banners and icons and crosses and multicoloured emblems, and the
3 trumpets, and the long and resonant names and titles of their dukes and
4 counts, and then the musicians and poets poised to sing the glory of each
5 and every one of them for generations to come.

Stone Print, 10.5 pt
Stone Print is very narrow which makes it useful when you want a large font in a narrow measure. At smaller sizes it can look too dense.

1 You are unsettled by the wild jumble of their troops, my Prince. All
2 those banners and icons and crosses and multicoloured emblems, and
3 the trumpets, and the long and resonant names and titles of their
4 dukes and counts, and then the musicians and poets poised to sing the
5 glory of each and every one of them for generations to come.

Joanna, 10.5 pt
Joanna is comparatively light in colour so can be set quite tightly.

1 You are unsettled by the wild jumble of their troops, my Prince. All
2 those banners and icons and crosses and multicoloured emblems,
3 and the trumpets, and the long and resonant names and titles of
4 their dukes and counts, and then the musicians and poets poised to
5 sing the glory of each and every one of them for generations to come.

Garamond, 11 pt
Garamond is the smallest-looking of these fonts. It is set half a point larger than the Stone Print and Joanna.

1 You are unsettled by the wild jumble of their troops, my Prince.
2 All those banners and icons and crosses and multicoloured
3 emblems, and the trumpets, and the long and resonant names and
4 titles of their dukes and counts, and then the musicians and poets
5 poised to sing the glory of each and every one of them for genera-
6 tions to come.

Bauer Bodoni, 10.2 pt
Bauer Bodoni is the least readable of these. This is because of the contrast between thick and thin strokes. It is better used as a display font in larger sizes.

MAKING EXTENT

Fitting x words and y pictures into z pages

When the design of a publication is being commissioned, it is not unusual for the format and extent to be fixed by the publisher. This decision will be based on a number of factors – practical, financial and aesthetic. It falls to the designer to fit the material into the given space without compromising the text or illustrations in any way that may reduce readability or lessen the reader's understanding and pleasure.

Computerized typesetting has made this task much easier, especially if the whole text is provided to design the trials. However, if the book contains illustrations or if only a sample of text and a word count is available to the designer, a series of (albeit rough) calculations are necessary.

1 Establish how much space is available for main text

Pages will be taken up with prelims and endmatter which are subtracted from the total first. If a book has part titles – say, on a recto with a blank verso following – these are also taken into account. A book of 224 pages, for example, may contain:

PRELIMS		IN THE MAIN TEXT	
p.1	half title	3 part-titles of 2 pages each	
p.2	blank	ENDMATTER	
p.3	title page	pp.211–218	endnotes
p.4	imprint	pp.219–220	bibliography
p.5	contents	pp.221–223	index
p.6	blank	p.224	blank

leaving 198 pages. As endmatter material is not always available at the design stage, an educated guess may have to be made at how many pages to leave for each section. The editor should be able to give some guidance on the length of endnotes, bibliography and index. Looking at other books of a similar format will help.

2 Calculate the number of pages likely to be occupied by illustrations

If a book contains illustrations placed throughout the text, the editor may well have strong feelings as to the size at which they should be reproduced. A set of instructions – for example, *8 full-page illustrations, 15 half-page illustrations, 27 quarter-page illustrations* (taking up space equivalent to just over 22 pages) – is invaluable at this stage, but if none is available an average illustrations-per-page ratio can be used as a rough guide. So one could say that 50 illustrations at an average size of between half and a third of a page will occupy space of between 17 and 25 pages. This allows for a certain amount of flexibility when placing the pictures.

One factor that will influence this calculation is whether the text is to run around the illustrations. If space is tight this can make the setting more economical, though at the expense of the text which becomes less readable when set at a narrow measure. If text is not run around, an illustration that is quarter-page in size will actually occupy half of the text panel.

It is quite common for editors to ask for illustrations to be 'half-page' or 'quarter-page' regardless of whether the format makes this possible. If in doubt talk to the editor.

3 Consider the effect of part-titles and chapter headings

In some books, such as collections of short stories, each new part or chapter should start on a recto. However, the law of averages would suggest that the previous part or chapter will only finish on the verso in approximately 50 per cent of cases, resulting in a blank page if it ends on the previous recto. This should be factored in when calculating extent. Using large chapter headings with the text starting low down the text panel will also use more space:

12 chapter openings occupying ⅓ of a page equals 4 pages
12 chapters ending on average half way down a page equals 6 pages left blank
which equals space equivalent to 10 pages occupied by chapter openings and endings

This can be added into the final calculation of extent.

4 *The final calculation*

So far the following calculation has been made:

Total pages	224
minus prelims (6 pages)	218
minus endmatter (14 pages)	204
minus part-titles (6 pages)	198
minus illustrations (22 pages)	176
minus chapter openings/endings (10 pages)	166

When flowing in a whole text, remember to include page turns. If there are footnotes, insert them in the text next to their indicators to include them in extent calculations. This will also make them easier to find when laying out the book.
See *Preparing text for setting*, p.378

which leaves space equivalent to 166 pages in which to fit text. If the whole text is available it can be flowed into a new document and the process of designing the text panel can begin. If only a word count is provided divide the number of words by the number of text pages to give an approximate number of words per page:

50,000 words divided by 166 pages = 302 words per page

This figure refers to the number of words on a full page of text without illustrations or chapter drops. At this stage it is possible to see if the calculations leave a reasonable space for the text. If not it may be necessary to go back to the illustrations and increase or reduce the illustrations-per-page ratio, or talk to the publisher about the possibility of changing extent.

The necessity of fitting text into a limited space can be frustrating, but it is always worth taking time to resolve problems at the start of the process; making changes once the book is set will be labour intensive and expensive. Most important of all, decisions should be made with the ultimate aim of benefiting the reader.

Flowing in text

Computers have made the designing of a text panel a more organic process. Rather than consulting copyfitting tables, the designer can flow in the text and make adjustments until satisfied with the result. For the beginner, it is important to understand the basic principles of how these adjustments work, and what is actually happening to the text when such changes are made.

Type size and measure

Changing the type size or the measure will affect the extent of the book because there will be fewer or more words on a line.

Small changes in extent can be achieved in this way, but the amount by which the extent increases or decreases depends on the content. For example, if most of the text is solid prose:

> they signed off a year, or even two years, later. And there were the contracted men, who had signed themselves up for serfdom on the plantations for five years before they would be set on their own feet again. If they could even stand by that time.

reducing the number of words on a line will create more lines:

> they signed off a year, or even two years, later. And there were the contracted men, who had signed themselves up for serfdom on the plantations for five years before they would be set on their own feet again. If they could even stand by that time.

but a text with lots of short lines, such as dialogue:

> 'Sorry, I didn't mean to kick you.'
> 'It doesn't matter,' Sole assured him.
> But, as he apologised, Hadouch bent down and looked under the table. He whistled in admiration.

will not be much affected:

> 'Sorry, I didn't mean to kick you.'
> 'It doesn't matter,' Sole assured him.
> But, as he apologised, Hadouch bent down and looked under the table. He whistled in admiration.

and will require more radical changes.

Whether you decide to change the type size *or* change the measure depends on other adjustments you wish to make. Changing the type size will require that the leading is also adjusted.

Miller text
10 on 15 pt
Measure: 98 mm

Miller text
10 on 15 pt
Measure: 95 mm

Minion
10.5 on 14 pt
Measure: 96 mm

Minion
10.5 on 14 pt
Measure: 92 mm

Leading and depth

Changing the leading or the depth of the text panel will affect the extent of the book because there will be more or fewer lines on a page. This will have a greater impact on extent than adjusting the type size or measure because every full page of text will gain or lose lines.

The key to this is the number of chapters starting on new pages. Imagine a book that has 200 pages of text composed of one long continuous chapter. Reducing the number of lines on a page from 36 to 35 will turn over 200 lines of text, which at 35 lines-per-page makes six more pages.

Now imagine a book that has 200 pages of text composed of 20 chapters, each approximately 10 pages long. Reducing the number of lines on a page will turn over lines, but if a chapter has enough space at the end, it will simply absorb these lines:

The end of this chapter can accommodate many lines without pushing the subsequent chapters on a page.

Only chapters which finish closer to the foot of the page will be affected enough to make a new page:

The end of this chapter is near to the foot of the text panel, so an increase in the leading or depth of page is likely to have an effect.

As this demonstrates, books with many short chapters are harder to manipulate. If they have lots of dialogue as well there may be little you can do to change extent – you may just have to accept the text as it falls.

Putting theory into practice

The following is an example of flowing text into the text panel and making adjustments to make extent. The book is 256 pages, 6 of which are prelims. This leaves 250 pages to fill with the main text, which is continuous.

1 Use the master pages of the typesetting program set trial margins. These are simply a starting point from which to make changes. The chosen typeface is Quadraat.

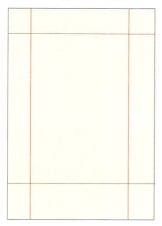

2 The text is flowed into the document. The number of pages created is shown on the document layout. Print out a spread and see how it looks. Text: 11 on 13 pt, 56 characters-per-line, 32 lines-per-page.

3 Text too large with not enough leading. Reduce type size to 10 pt and increase leading to 14 pt. Text: 10 on 14 pt, 62 characters-per-line, 28 lines-per-page.

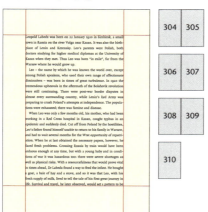

4 Increase the depth of the text panel. Text: 10 on 14 pt, 62 characters-per-line, 31 lines-per-page.

5 Widen the measure. Text: 10 on 14 pt,
66 characters-per-line, 31 lines per page.
This is still over extent.

6 Widen the measure a little more. Text:
10 on 14 pt, 70 characters-per-line, 31 lines-per-
page. This gives an extent of 248 pages.

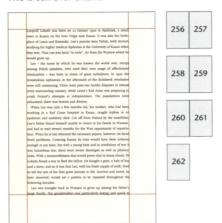

At 248 pages the extent is now close to the required 250 pages. It is acceptable to leave a couple of pages short of extent; these will be made up as the text is massaged and revised or left blank. The final text is set in 10 pt on 14 pt leading. There is an average of 70 characters-per-line and 31 lines-per-page.

> Leopold Labedz was born on 22 January 1920 in Simbirsk, a small town in Russia on the river Volga near Kazan. It was also the birthplace of Lenin and Kerensky. Leo's parents were Polish, both doctors studying for higher medical diplomas at the University of Kazan when they met. Thus

The most important part of the process is to print out a full-size spread at each stage and check the readability of the text and the look of the page. Some compromise may be necessary when working to a publisher's specification, but a judgement must be made on what is an acceptable page of type. If the specification cannot be fulfilled satisfactorily talk to the editor or production manager about how they wish to proceed.

See *Progressive
formats*, pp.334–7

If the book is to be re-issued later in a smaller format, print out a reduction to make sure that this, too, is readable.

When fitting text into a limited space, do not be tempted to . . .

Make the word-spacing too wide or too narrow:

conviction, not allowing for the slightest interruption. 'You are unsettled by the wild jumble of their troops, my Prince. All those banners and icons and crosses and multicoloured

Minion
10.5 on 15 pt

conviction, not allowing for the slightest interruption. 'You are unsettled by the wild jumble of their troops, my Prince. All those banners and icons and crosses and multicoloured emblems, and the trum-

Minion
10.5 on 15 pt

adjust the inter-character-spacing to squeeze or stretch text:

conviction, not allowing for the slightest interruption. 'You are unsettled by the wild jumble of their troops, my Prince. All those banners and icons and crosses and multicoloured

Minion
10.5 on 15 pt
8 ICS

conviction, not allowing for the slightest interruption. 'You are unsettled by the wild jumble of their troops, my Prince. All those banners and icons and crosses and multicoloured emblems, and the trumpets,

Minion
10.5 on 15 pt
minus 5 ICS

or use horizontal scaling to make characters wider or narrower:

conviction, not allowing for the slightest interruption. 'You are unsettled by the wild jumble of their troops, my Prince. All those banners and icons and crosses and multicoloured

Minion
10.5 on 15 pt
Horizontal scale: 110%

conviction, not allowing for the slightest interruption. 'You are unsettled by the wild jumble of their troops, my Prince. All those banners and icons and crosses and multicoloured emblems, and the trumpets, and the long

Minion
10.5 on 15 pt
Horizontal scale: 90%

PART NINE

TYPESETTING

SETTING A FONT FAMILY

Check that you have all the necessary faces within a font, and are using the proper italics and small caps, rather than generating them with the formatting palette of your layout program.

A line of text may contain more than one face – roman for the main text, italic for a name, superior figures to indicate an endnote, etc. As these faces are designed in families, they should match for size and colour, but sometimes a little fine adjustment is necessary to ensure that they sit well together in the line.

Setting italics within roman text

Italics are used for the titles of books, plays and films, or to give emphasis to a certain word, or to indicate a word or phrase in a foreign language. As the italic is sloped, it may give the appearance of increasing the space before and reducing the space after the italicized words:

Fournier roman
and italic

November of that year the *Evening Standard* published an

This can be corrected with kerning – adjusting the space before and after the italic:

Fournier roman
and italic

November of that year the *Evening Standard* published an

Clashes can occur where italic words are next to roman punctuation:

Garamond roman
and italic

as reported by the *Daily Mail*? It is unlikely considering

Stone Sans roman
and italic

year (since contributing to the *Washington Post*). Once he

This can also be corrected with manual kerning:

Garamond roman
and italic

as reported by the *Daily Mail*? It is unlikely considering

Stone Sans roman
and italic

year (since contributing to the *Washington Post*). Once he

Caps and small caps

Capitalized words and acronyms may stand out from a page of text if they are set in caps:

> whilst on a visit to the country arranged by UNICEF in April 1992

Minion

Adding some letter-spacing or setting them in small caps may make them less noticeable:

> whilst on a visit to the country arranged by UNICEF in April 1992

Minion

> whilst on a visit to the country arranged by UNICEF in April 1992

Minion and Minion Expert

Superior characters

Some word-processing programs will automatically set superior figures for 1st, 2nd, 3rd as 1st 2nd 3rd.

This can have the effect of overly drawing attention to them when they are set within a passage of text. This default should be turned off.

Superior figures are used most commonly as indicators for notes, where they are likely to be placed directly after punctuation. Clashes with question marks, closing parentheses and closing quote marks need to be watched and spaced where necessary:

See *Indicators*, p.215

> Congress of the Communist Party of the Soviet Union (CPSU)[35] Lenin announced a crucial change to the 'New Economic Policy'[36] which ended

> Congress of the Communist Party of the Soviet Union (CPSU)[35] Lenin announced a crucial change to the 'New Economic Policy'[36] which ended

Collis, 9.5 on 13.5 pt
These indicators clash with the preceding punctuation. A little space between the characters solves this problem.

Make sure that the space following the superior figure is not also set as superior as this will reduce it in size.

SETTING PUNCTUATION

Punctuation is a subject that can arouse strong reactions in readers if they feel it is being used incorrectly. Thankfully for the designer, the job of getting the dots and dashes in the right order is the responsibility of the editor, though knowing the basic rules may help you too, especially if you find yourself keying in late changes to the text.

Quotation marks ''

Quotation marks – an opening quote before the word and a closing quote after it – can be used to denote speech, an extract of text, or in some cases titles. They can take the form of single quotes:

Double quotes are used more in America and have the advantage of not being confused with apostrophes. Single quotes, being smaller, look less 'spotty', especially on pages with lots of dialogue.

‘like this’

or double quotes:

“like this”

The decision to use either double or single quotation marks depends on house style and so is usually a matter for the editor. Whichever form you use, the other will be used for quotes within quotes, for example:

Bembo, 10.5 on 13 pt

If a double and single quotation mark are set together, there should be enough space between them to show that they are two independent elements.

> he wrote in what would be his last notebook: "Aren't all true healers – from the prehistoric shaman on – all 'thundermen'?"

> he wrote in what would be his last notebook: 'Aren't all true healers – from the prehistoric shaman on – all "thundermen"?'

When a quotation mark appears the wrong way round it is usually because a word-space is in the wrong place

A quotation mark should not touch any other character or punctuation mark, but when following a full point or comma, can be kerned back just a little to almost sit over the top of it:

from ‘here,’ to ‘here,’

When setting a text with a lot of dialogue it is worth making sure the font's pre-set kerning pairs are set properly for quotation marks, ensuring even spacing. Kerning them individually will take a long time:

See *Fit*, pp.81–3

> 'Do you even know what Thérèse's boyfriend does for a living?' Half Pint asked from behind his rose-tinted glasses.
> No, I didn't even know what he did for a living.
> 'Books!'

Minion, 11 on 16 pt Opening quotes, often followed by a capital letter, are more likely to need adjusting.

> 'Do you even know what Thérèse's boyfriend does for a living?' Half Pint asked from behind his rose-tinted glasses.
> No, I didn't even know what he did for a living.
> 'Books!'

In this example a little space has been added between the opening quote and the capital letter at the start of the first and fourth line, and between the question mark and the closing quote on line 2.

Hanging out opening quotes

If a text starts with dialogue or speech, the opening quote can be *hung out* so that the first letter aligns with the rest of the text. This is particularly useful if the first line is set as display, or if a drop cap is used:

> '**C**AN I HAVE my bed back?'
> Someone asked me this question in the pit of my sleep.
> Someone I knew.

Minion, 11 on 16 pt Drop cap of 2 lines, first three words in Minion small caps with 20 ICS

Foot and inch marks

A frequently-made mistake – often due to the vagaries of word-processing programs – is to use foot and inch marks instead of quotes. These should be avoided.

'foot' marks, "inch" marks   ' ' " "

'serif' "quotation" marks   ' ' " "

'sans serif' "quotation" marks   ' ' " "

Apostrophes '

An apostrophe takes the same form as a single closing quotation mark. It is used to indicate possession or missing letters or syllables. It also appears in some proper names.

Where an apostrophe falls in the middle of a word it should be set without touching the characters either side and spaced evenly:

I've   shouldn't   So'ton   Earl's Court

I've   shouldn't   So'ton   Earl's Court

Where an apostrophe falls at the beginning of a word, some typesetting programs may automatically turn it round into an opening quotation mark. It may be necessary to put in two and delete the first:

'80s   ''80s   '80s

Colons, semi-colons and commas : ; ,

Colons, semi-colons and commas are used to divide up sentences. In English-language texts there is no word space before the punctuation, and just one word space afterwards. French setting has a word space before semi-colons and colons.

The spacing of these punctuation marks may be uneven following words which have been put into italics:

> *From left to right*: Jacques Raverat, Gwen Raverat *with back to camera*, Sonia Lewitska *seated*, unidentified and Jean Marchand

Small adjustments to the kerning can put this right:

> *From left to right*: Jacques Raverat, Gwen Raverat *with back to camera*, Sonia Lewitska *seated*, unidentified and Jean Marchand

The colon is also used to introduce an extract or illustration:

> In the winter of 1689 he announced news of the following:
>> a strange light and fire, which has been observed, and a great number of huge, fiery rocks, red as artificial light and glistening like stars,

Joanna, 11 on 15 pt
Extract: 10 on 13 pt

A line ending with the colon should not fall on the last line of a page.

Lists are often divided up using commas:

> biology, chemistry, astro-physics, sociology, literature, geography

Stone Sans, 9.5 pt

Where lists are more complicated, semi-colons are used instead:

> Early Printed Books; Humanities; Medicine; Science; Architecture; Standard Sets; 15th- to 20th-century Literature; Modern First Editions in Literature; Art and Photography; Bindings

Stone Sans
9.5 on 15 pt

But if a list is divided spatially, there is no need for added punctuation:

Early Printed Books	Standard Sets
Humanities	15th- to 20th-century Literature
Medicine	Modern First Editions in Literature
Science	Art and Photography
Architecture	Bindings

Stone Sans
9.5 on 14 pt

Semi-colons may be used to divide up sub-entries of an index if there is no room to start each sub-entry on a new line:

See *Indexes*, p.197

> Llosa, Mario Vargas 432, 491
> London 39, 82–4, 86, 102, 109, 137–8, 140, 195, 236, 260, 355, 369, 397, 407, 439, 518; British Museum 92, 313; Dorchester Hotel 119; Ealing 86, 95, 103; Eaton Place 110, 399, 406, 439, 442, 455, 537; Grosvenor Crescent Mews 109, 111, 130, 145, 157, 228, 513; Kynance Mews 221, 235, 244, 251, 442, 514; Mount Street 157, 163, 165–6, 174–5; Victoria & Albert Museum 96
> London, Jack 62

Stone Print
8 on 10 pt

A combination of semi-colons and commas is used to separate the elements in lists of sources. The semi-colons separate different sources and the commas separate elements within each source:

Albertina roman
and italic
9.5 on 13 pt

11 David Watkin, *Sir John Soane: Enlightenment Thought and the Royal Academy lectures*, Cambridge, 1996, p. 619; quotes RA Lectures, Second Series, Lecture IX, 2 March 1815.

Full points .

Full points (known outside the trade as full stops, or, in America, periods) indicate the end of sentences, and are also used to indicate abbreviations.

Despite what many people are taught at typing school, a full point should not be followed by two word spaces – which create uneven white spaces throughout the text – one is sufficient. Double spaces should be replaced with single spaces before the text is set.

When are full points unnecessary?

Full points are not used at the end of displayed headings.

When setting small amounts of text, such as captions, the rule is that if the text forms a complete sentence, containing a subject and a verb, it should end with a full point:

Albertina small
caps and italic, 9 pt

FIG. 24 *The architect relished the prospect of a fat fee as costs rocketed.*

If the text does not form a complete sentence, it does not need a full point:

Albertina small
caps and italic, 9 pt

FIG. 25 *Sale catalogue of Nash's Library*

However, editors and house rules may choose to ignore this rule for the sake of consistency and end all captions, or none of them, with a full point.

Texts which take the form of short, listed entries, such as endnotes or indexes do not need full points at the end of each entry:

342 *The Dance* from *Daphnis et Chloé*, 1928–31, 74 × 100
343 Title page to *The Cambridge Book of Poetry for Children*
345 *The Back of the Farm* from *Farmer's Glory*, 1933–34, 58 × 88

Royal Academy, 36, 51, 114, 116, 350
Royal Academy Schools, 75, 117, 156
Royal College of Art, 224, 355, 382
Royal Medical Corps, 357
Royal Society of Painter-Etchers and Engravers, 321
Royal Society, 4, 25, 104

Left: Scala roman and italic, 8 on 11 pt

Right: Scala 7 on 9 pt

Abbreviations which consist of upper case initials do not need full points if they are commonly used and likely to be recognized by the reader:

Some house styles omit full points on all abbreviations.

USA   BBC   PLC   NATO   MP

Garamond, 12 pt

Full points and abbreviations

An abbreviated word is usually treated as a complete word and followed by a word space, but there are exceptions to this. Where words such as 'page' or 'figure' are abbreviated to 'p.' or 'fig.' and followed by a number, the space can be removed:

This rule is not followed by all publishing houses, so consult with the editor if there is inconsistency within the supplied text.

p.17   pp.94–7   Fig.37   Cat.21   Pl.66   vol.3   no.28

Publishing houses have different house rules as to whether people's initials should be set closed up or spaced:

painted by J.M.W. Turner, 1820   painted by J. M. W. Turner, 1820

Caslon, 11.5 pt

Raised points

In display lines, a raised point can be used to separate elements. This works particularly well in capitalized lines. The raised point is set halfway up the height of the capital and centred between words:

SIMON WHISTLER · ON A GLASS LIGHTLY

Trajan, 12 pt, 15 ICS

Hyphens -

A hyphen is used to join words together to form a compound – *twentieth-century* art, *middle-class* households – and to divide a word between two lines like this: hyphen-ation. Hyphens are set unspaced, falling at the end, never at the beginning, of a line.

No more than two successive lines should end with a hyphen. A page or column of text should not end with a hyphen.

Some typefaces have hyphens which are slanted:

twentieth-century   twentieth-century

En dashes –

An en dash is longer than a hyphen and can be set unspaced or spaced. When set unspaced it has the meaning 'to' or 'between' and is most often found between numbers:

1972–88   pp.63–9   May–July 2002

Unspaced en dashes will often need kerning, particularly if the numbers are set in an expert font:

23–98 71–64 49–25 32–14 20–62
23–98 71–64 49–25 32–14 20–62

Spaced en dashes are used parenthetically in pairs:

Small beer – will it be believed! – was the only drink with which unhappy gentleman soothed the fever of their previous night's potation.

Em dashes —

An em dash is twice the length of an en dash and is rarely used in British setting. In America it is set unspaced to perform the same function as the British spaced en dash:

> Small beer—will it be believed!—was the only drink with which unhappy gentleman soothed the fever of their previous night's potation.

In British setting, it is used to indicate words or names which the author does not wish to print in full:

> that still seems like a shadow crossing my soul. The next morning, when I came to say goodbye, I had to look for C— for a long while. At last I found her in the kitchen garden, which was overgrown

Em dashes can also be used in bibliographies to replace names which are repeated:

> Eeghen, I. H. van, Uit het dagboek van broeder Wouter Jacobsz., Groningen, 1959.
> — "Coenraad van Beuningen", in Tijdschrift Genootschap Amstelodamum, 1970, p. 107.
> Elias, J. E., De vroedschap van Amsterdam, 1578–1795, two vols., Haarlem 1903–05.
> Emeis, M. G., Amsterdam buiten de grachten, Amsterdam, 1983.
> Fuchs, J. M., Amsterdam, een lastige stad, Baarn, 1970.
> — Nou hoor je het eens van een ander, buitenlanders over Amsterdam, Den Haag, 1975.

Some writers use em dashes, rather than quotation marks, to indicate dialogue, with a dash at the start of each line of speech:

> — Your brother will always have a great advantage over you.
> — What advantage? I asked.
> — He's the brother of an ex-Resistance fighter, while you, you're the brother of an ex-smuggler.

Ellipses . . .

An ellipsis can indicate a missing section of text; it also suggests dialogue that tails off or pauses. It takes the form of three points.

These points should be spaced – about the same as a word-space – and should also have a word-space before and after. Using kerning tables to space them, or using a fixed-size word-space will make them consistent throughout the text:

Minion, 10 on 14 pt

> it had all been very nice . . . the coffee . . . the chat . . . the cognac, of course, and the trust he had in me . . . plus the honour shown to my sister . . . all extremely . . .
> 'One last thing, Benjamin.'

There are two ways of setting ellipses. In some publishing houses, the ellipsis is always set as three points with a word space either side, as above.

Other houses will set it as three points if it falls mid-sentence, but ellipses falling between two sentences are preceded by a full point to end the first sentence. This is set close up to the last word of the sentence as usual. The sentence after the ellipsis then starts with a capital letter, for example:

Albertina
10 on 14.5 pt

> style to work in and it has no room for tolerance at all. His detailing was very simple but costly. . . . Since then I've come to the conclusion that it's better to go back a long way

The entire ellipsis should always be on the same line, not split between lines.

If a passage of text contains many ellipses, try to set them so they don't align vertically, which creates a white hole in the text like this:

Minion, 10 on 14 pt

> crystallising cloud . . . those faces looming up from a shallow pit . . . that spontaneous genera-tion of an image . . . that unstoppable incarnation . . . and then that wonderful commemoration of

Leaders ...

Leaders are three points produced by a single keystroke. The space between the points is fixed and is smaller than is desirable with an ellipsis.

Leaders were traditionally used for making dotted lines, sometimes seen in contents pages, to join a chapter title to a page number:

15 Out of His Depth 174   Bembo, 11 on 14 pt
16 The Archaeologist 188
17 A Season in Hell 201

This has fallen out of fashion and is rarely used now.

Parentheses ( ) and square brackets [ ]

Parentheses are used to contain references to other parts of the text, or a person's birth and death dates:

in some cases titles (*see* p.63). They can take the form of   Albertina, 12 pt

LUDWIG VAN BEETHOVEN (1770–1827)   Bembo, 12 pt

When setting parentheses look out for clashes between them and the text contained inside. This is more likely to happen if the enclosed text is italic and should be corrected with kerning:

used to indicate abbreviations (*for usage see previous chapter*).   Albertina roman
used to indicate abbreviations (*for usage see previous chapter*).   and italic, 12 pt

Though most italic fonts include italic parentheses, they are best set in roman even if the text is completely italic:

addressing the issue of modern (steel or concrete) construction.   Minion italic, 12 pt
addressing the issue of modern (steel or concrete) construction.

Where two parentheses are set next to each other a thin space should be inserted between them:

Stone Print, 10 pt

> van der Rohe, whose architecture has obvious classical roots (see cat.15)).
>
> van der Rohe, whose architecture has obvious classical roots (see cat.15)).

For the use of brackets in the setting of plays, see pp.321–2.

Square brackets are used mainly to indicate that text has been inserted by some-one other than the author or speaker. They are set following the same principles as parentheses, always in roman, with attention paid to kerning:

Stone Sans, 10 pt

> 'They're crazy about fine things [in Hollywood]. Dickens and

Question marks ? and exclamation marks !

Question marks and exclamation marks are set close up to the last word of a sentence to indicate a question or exclamation. A full point should not be used as well. Both these marks are used most often in dialogue and their height makes clashes with quotation marks possible, so kerning may be necessary:

> 'What?' "Stop!" 'What?' "Stop!"

Using more than one of these marks for extra emphasis suggests informality and is most likely to be found in reproductions of diary entries and personal correspondence:

Scala Sans, 10 pt

> I thought, Oh my God!!! what's he doing?!?!!

Some editors choose to tone this down for publication.

Italicizing punctuation

The rule for italicizing punctuation is as follows: if the punctuation is part of the phrase which is italicized, then it too is italicized.

For example, the title of the book

Will You Please be Quiet, Please?

contains a comma and a question mark. If this title was to be quoted in text, both these marks would be italicized:

> was not until *Will You Please be Quiet, Please?* was published in 1976 that

Stone Print roman
and italic, 11 pt

Punctuation that does not form part of the italicized phrase is set in roman even if it is set closed up with an italic word:

> three collections of stories, *What We Talk about When We Talk about Love, Cathedral* and *Elephant. Fires*, a collection of essays, poems and

Stone Print roman
and italic, 11 on 14 pt

In the above example the commas and full point are in roman.

When romans and italics appear next to each other it is always worth looking at the relationship between them:

> *Cathedral?   Elephant)   'Fires*

Here, the question mark clashes with the 'l', the closing parenthesis is too close to the 't' and there is too much space between the opening quotation mark and the 'F'. These will need adjusting:

> *Cathedral?   Elephant)   'Fires*

SETTING DISPLAYED TEXTS

A text will sometimes contain short sections of text which are to be *displayed*. These include extracts, quotations and poetry and should be set in a way that differentiates them from the rest of the main text. This is predominately a feature of non-fiction, although novelists may want to display a piece of text that forms part of their narrative, such as a letter.

Extracts and quotations

An extract is a passage of text from a different source which the author wishes to use to illustrate a point; a quotation is something that someone has said. Both are treated in the same way. Short extracts are set within the text, contained in quotation marks, but longer passages are set as separate blocks of text.

The most common treatment is to indent the extract on both the left and right, and leave line or half-line spaces before and after. The extract, when set like this does not need quotation marks:

Scala
10 on 14.5 pt
Extract
indented by
6mm. Line
space of 7.25 pt
above and
below extract

second edition, however, issued soon after the first, he added the phrase 'by the Creator' to his final sentence, thereby re-admitting the notion of divine agency, possibly to mollify his readers.

> There is grandeur in this view of life, with its several powers, having been originally breathed by the Creator into a few forms or into one; and that, whilst this planet has gone cycling on according to the fixed law of gravity, from so simple a beginning endless forms most beautiful and most wonderful have been, and are being, evolved.

Despite this and other alterations, Darwin's theories undermined orthodox religious teaching, chiefly because, as Noel Annan has pointed out, *The Origin*

See *Massaging text*, pp.106–9

If an extract is divided between two pages, there should be at least two lines of it on both. A full line space will be needed before and after to keep the main text on the baseline grid. If an extract is three lines or less it should not be split.

Avoid setting the extract with just one line of text above or below it on the page:

> whilst this planet has gone cycling on according to the fixed law of gravity, from so simple a beginning endless forms most beautiful and most wonderful have been, and are being, evolved.

Despite this and other alterations, Darwin's theories undermined orthodox

If the extract is introduced by a sentence ending in a colon, this should not fall on the last line of a page:

> flavour of the ghost' of Charles Darwin hung about the whole place, 'house garden and all', as Gwen recalled:

Setting down extracts

Extracts can be set at a smaller type size than the main body of the text. This is called *setting down* and reduces the space occupied by words which are not the author's own. The disadvantage is that some readers may skip past them:

the Creator' to his final sentence, thereby re-admitting the notion of divine agency, possibly to mollify his readers.

> There is grandeur in this view of life, with its several powers, having been originally breathed by the Creator into a few forms or into one; and that, whilst this planet has gone cycling on according to the fixed law of gravity, from so simple a beginning endless forms most beautiful and most wonderful have been, and are being, evolved.

Despite this and other alterations, Darwin's theories undermined orthodox religious teaching, chiefly because, as Noel Annan has pointed out, *The Origin*

In the example above, the type size has been reduced from 10 pt to 9 pt and the leading has also been reduced. The line spaces before and after the extract are adjusted so that the main text lines up with the baseline grid.

Setting poetry within the text

Where poetry is quoted in a text, it is set with a half-line space before and after. If there is more than one stanza, there should be a whole line space before and after. The poetry block may be centred visually within the text panel or the longest line may be centred and the poem aligned with that:

Collis, 10 on 16 pt
The longest line is
centred in the text
panel. Line spaces
of 8 pt before and
after poem.

For further
guidance on
setting poetry
see pp.323–9

> On this the White Rabbit blew three blasts on the trumpet, and
> then unrolled the parchment scroll, and read as follows:–
>
> The Queen of Hearts, she made some tarts,
>   All on a summer day:
> The Knave of Hearts, he stole those tarts,
>   And took them quite away!
>
> 'Consider your verdict,' the King said to the jury.
> 'Not yet, not yet!' the Rabbit hastily interrupted. 'There's a great
> deal to come before that!'

If two stanzas from the same poem, or two poems written in the same form appear separately on a page, they should align on the left. Indentation of individual lines should follow the original published form of the poem.

Setting poetry continuously within text

Where just a few lines of poetry are being quoted, the editor may decide to set them continuously within the text. In this case they are set within quotation marks and lines are separated by a forward slash. Take care that the slash does not clash with the characters either side of it:

Iowan Old Style
10 on 14.5 pt

> She had compressed a great deal into these small prints, including a
> row of poplars, 'The poplars in the fields of France / Like glorious
> ladies come to dance', and a moonlit road winding into the distance.
> The poetry in her images is certainly a match for Frances's words;

Italicizing poetry

The author or editor may wish to italicize poetry displayed within the text. If this request is made, ensure that you choose a typeface which has a legible italic:

Albertina
10 on 13.5 pt
Poem: Albertina italic

people's faces. The time has come to realize an ambitious Icelandic paradox, like the one I referred to earlier:

> *The fish can sing just like a bird,*
> *And grazes on the moorland scree,*
> *While cattle in a lowing herd*
> *Roam the rolling sea.*

I say, and have always said, and will always say: the fish that does not sing throughout the whole world is a dead fish. It is

Displaying lists within the text

Lists are set ranged left and indented. The size of the indent depends on the length of the items in the list. As with extracts, a half-line space is inserted before and after the list. There is no need for punctuation at the end of each item, unless it changes meaning, for example a question mark:

Stone Print
10 on 13 pt
List indented by 8 mm

led to his fundamental law of electrodynamics. Ampère's discoveries were supplemented by those of

> François Arago (1786–1853) on 'magnetism of rotation' (1824)
> F. Lenz (1804–1865) on the direction of induced currents (1833)
> Franz E. Neumann (1798–1895) on *self-induction* (1845)
> Léon Foucault (1819–1868) on *Foucault currents* (1855)

These researches were brought towards culmination by many other physicists, notably the Scot Lord Kelvin (William Thomson, 1834–1907)

Bullet points

Bullet points, though popular in word-processing documents can make a page look unattractive. This is because they are usually drawn at too large a size:

Stone Print
10 on 13 pt
Bullets: 10 pt

- François Arago (1786–1853) on 'magnetism of rotation' (1824)
- F. Lenz (1804–1865) on the direction of induced currents (1833)
- Franz E. Neumann (1798–1895) on *self-induction* (1845)
- Léon Foucault (1819–1868) on *Foucault currents* (1855)

If the author or editor requests that they be used, set them in a small size, or use a tint or an outline shape to lessen their visual impact:

Stone Print
10 on 13 pt
Bullets: 6.5 pt

- François Arago (1786–1853) on 'magnetism of rotation' (1824)
- F. Lenz (1804–1865) on the direction of induced currents (1833)
- Franz E. Neumann (1798–1895) on *self-induction* (1845)
- Léon Foucault (1819–1868) on *Foucault currents* (1855)

Stone Print
10 on 13 pt
Bullets: 8 pt
40 % tint

- François Arago (1786–1853) on 'magnetism of rotation' (1824)
- F. Lenz (1804–1865) on the direction of induced currents (1833)
- Franz E. Neumann (1798–1895) on *self-induction* (1845)
- Léon Foucault (1819–1868) on *Foucault currents* (1855)

Stone Print
10 on 13 pt
Bullets: 8 pt
outline

- François Arago (1786–1853) on 'magnetism of rotation' (1824)
- F. Lenz (1804–1865) on the direction of induced currents (1833)
- Franz E. Neumann (1798–1895) on *self-induction* (1845)
- Léon Foucault (1819–1868) on *Foucault currents* (1855)

If an item is more than one line long, the second and third lines should align with the text in the first line, rather than with the bullet point:

- Planimeters, designed to measure the area enclosed by a plane curve; the first was made in 1854 by Professor Amsler of Schaffhausen, for measuring areas on maps and plans
- Integrometers and integraphs, which give the numerical values of functions defined by their derivative
- Harmonic analysers and tide predictors, of which the earliest forms were invented by Lord Kelvin in 1878

There are various ways, other than bullet points, of indicating where each item on a list starts.

The first line may hang out to the left:

Planimeters, designed to measure the area enclosed by a plane curve;
    the first was made in 1854 by Professor Amsler of Schaffhausen,
    for measuring areas on maps and plans
Integrometers and integraphs, which give the numerical values of
    functions defined by their derivative
Harmonic analysers and tide predictors, of which the earliest forms
    were invented by Lord Kelvin in 1878

Stone Print
10 on 13 pt
First line hung
out by 4 mm

or extra space may be added between the items. You may need to close up the leading of the entries to make this work:

Planimeters, designed to measure the area enclosed by a plane curve; the first was made in 1854 by Professor Amsler of Schaffhausen, for measuring areas on maps and plans

Integrometers and integraphs, which give the numerical values of functions defined by their derivative

Harmonic analysers and tide predictors, of which the earliest forms were invented by Lord Kelvin in 1878

Stone Print
10 on 13 pt
1 mm space
between items

If content allows, headwords at the beginning of each item may be set in a different font, such as small caps or semi-bold:

Planimeters, designed to measure the area enclosed by a plane curve; the first was made in 1854 by Professor Amsler of Schaffhausen, for measuring areas on maps and plans

Integrometers and **integraphs**, which give the numerical values of functions defined by their derivative

Harmonic analysers and **tide predictors**, of which the earliest forms were invented by Lord Kelvin in 1878

Stone Print
10 on 13 pt
Headwords in
semi-bold

A combination of these methods may be used, but should be consistent throughout the book.

See *Numbered lists*,
p.272

Displaying letters and diary entries within the text

Both novels and biographies will at times contain letters and diary entries. In academic works these are simply set as extracts with date, place, and – in the case of letters – sender noted in the text.

Letters

If a letter is to be shown in full, it may be indented as with an extract, or set in italic, differentiating it from the rest of the text:

Trinité
11.5 on 14 pt
Letter extract:
Trinité italic
11.5 on 14 pt
Indents: 6 mm

transept (Poets' Corner) and the Chapter House. There it remained all night, dimly lit by two oil lamps, covered with a cloth of black velvet and watched over by a guard.

> *My dearest George,*
>
> *Father was taken very ill last night with great suffering. They sent Dr Allfrey and he staid [sic] the night and was a great support to Mother. She was all alone with Bessy. They sent for Dr Moxon and he came just to see him take his last breath. Mother said he was happy to die and sent us all an affectionate message. He told her he was not the least afraid to die. Mother is very calm but she has cried a little.*
>
> *You will come at once.*
>
> *Your H.E.L.*

By mid-morning the next day the coffin had been moved to the porch of the Chapter House, inside which had gathered aristocrats, statesmen, scientists and representa-

Insertions by the author/editor are made in roman, enclosed in square brackets.

If the letter contains a place and date, this is set above the greeting:

Centaur
12 on 15 pt

> Timsah
> 6 March 1863
>
> Dear Doctor,
> At twilight every evening I go for a stroll along the lakeshore. At the sound of a rifle shot, an army of flamingos rises like a

Diary entries

When a diary is being published, the entries are treated as main text with section breaks between, and each entry dated.

When extracts of a diary appear, they may be indented, as with other extracts, or set in italics with a half-line space above or below. Italicizing diary entries is preferable, especially in autobiographies, where it distinguishes between different styles of text written by the same author:

> unresolved from their marriage. Emotionally restrained, he was flirtatious with ideas and relished strong intellectual relationships.
>
> *15 July*
> *Oeufs molles en gelée, cold salmon trout with mayonnaise, tomato and cucumber salad, strawberries arrosées in brandy & with cream; cheese; bottle of chilled Sancerre. Bruce C. very good value and should be a pleasure to teach.*
>
> 'Sotheby's is having fits, of course,' Elizabeth wrote to Gertrude. She had left Wilson's employ soon after her engagement was

Bembo, 10.5 on 13 pt

Diary entry: Bembo italic, 10.5 on 13 pt
Indents: 6 mm

Re-creating handwritten material

Handwritten letters and diaries are often written in a very expressive way, with phrases underlined or capitalized for emphasis. This can be re-created to a certain extent, keeping in mind what is necessary to aid comprehension and what may simply distract the reader. Some editorial explanation of abbreviations and names may be necessary. This is done inside square brackets:

> *I think more and more that what we have to do is just let IT or THEY speak through us – not get in the way . . . Work is just making your mind empty and listening. It's not I that speaks nor Shakespeare: it's the land and the people. It's God . . . And Jacques [Raverat]? . . . He is French. He joins on to all the people who sculpted Auxerre and Vézelay – twelfth-century people.*

Scala italic
10 on 14 pt

Setting interviews

Interviews are set with the name of each speaker followed by a colon preceding their words. Quotation marks are unnecessary. After the first mention of each name, they may be indicated by initials only if preferred.

Questions and answers may be set in different fonts to help the reader, but if more than one person is being interviewed do not set each speaker in a different font as this will look messy.

Quadraat
10 on 14.5 pt
Questions:
Quadraat italic
Names: Quadraat
small caps

Q: *You've managed to get out of Komsomolskoe. What next?*

LEMA: It's no problem to get past army posts in the night. I won't tell you exactly how we do it, though.

Q: *You mean you paid the feds on the army posts and during 'cleansing' operations?*

RUSLAN: We never pay to get past their posts. But we do buy weapons and ammunition, of course, from Russian officers. The feds have a lot of the latest weaponry and they sell it.

Q: *When did you yourself last buy weapons from the soldiers?*

R: About a month ago.

Re-creating typographic styles in the text

When representing printed matter within the main text, there is always the temptation to reproduce the style in which the item would have been originally set. This approach might be described as theatrical and tends to be more popular in advertising and marketing material. Frequently used (or overused) styles include:

notes written by typewriter:

Typeka
10 on 14 pt, 20 ICS

```
PHONE HOPELESS COME ALGIERS 9 OCT STOP
BRING DESERT SHOES ONE DRESS AND NOT
LESS THAN 250 POUNDS WILL REPAY WILL GO
CENTRAL SAHARA BRUCE
```

invitations in a fancy script:

Doña Adela de Otero
requests the presence of the fencing master
Don Jaime Astarloa

Shelley Andante
Script, 16 on 22 pt

text on a computer screen:

"That's It! Let's Ask Murakami!" Say the People and They Try Flinging 282 Big Questions at Haruki Murakami, But Can Murakami Really Find Decent Answers to Them All?

Chicago
9.5 on 14 pt

and ye olde documents:

Martínez Carmona, Ramón. Calle del Prado, 16, Madrid
Miravalls Hernández, Domiciano. Calle Corredera Baja,
Cazorla Longo, Bruno. Plaza de Santa Ana, 10, Madrid

Wittenberger Frakt
12 on 16 pt

Though there is fun to be had with display faces, think very carefully before proceeding down this route and talk to the editor about it. Using display fonts in the main text of a book will dramatically change the authorial tone of voice in a way that may not be appropriate. Readers may regard it as a gimmick and become irritated, especially if the text is hard to read.

Playing games with typographic style is best attempted only in collaboration with a willing author, and/or with a text that is suitably playful. Try to avoid resorting to clichés, and most importantly, make sure the text can be read. Also, think about the technological processes you are trying to recreate and use an appropriate style of layout – setting text justified or centred on a manual typewriter is easier said than done!

PART TEN

NUMBERS

SETTING NUMERALS

Lining and non-lining figures

Numbers are usually available in two styles for each typeface. *Lining figures*, sometimes called *modern* figures, line up with the font's capital alphabet:

Galliard, 14 pt

$$\text{A B C D E F G 1 2 3 4 5 6 7 8 9 0 H I J K L M}$$

making them appropriate for use in capitalized display lines:

$$\text{FRIDAY 18 JUNE 2004}$$

Non-lining figures, also called *old-style* figures, blend with lower case characters:

Requiem, 14 pt

$$\text{a b c d e f g 1 2 3 4 5 6 7 8 9 0 h i j k l m}$$

making them too small for capitals:

$$\text{FRIDAY 18 JUNE 2004}$$

but appropriate for use within a continuous setting or with small caps:

Stone Print, with non-lining figures

50 · DANIEL LYSONS 1762–1834
The volumes were prepared at 'unlimited expense' for William Wyndham Grenville of Dropmore (1759 – 1834) from the existing Lysons volumes published in 1813.

lining figures on the other hand, look too big and stand out from the text:

Stone Print, with lining figures

50 · DANIEL LYSONS 1762–1834
The volumes were prepared at 'unlimited expense' for William Wyndham Grenville of Dropmore (1759 – 1834) from the existing Lysons volumes published in 1813.

In some circumstances lining figures may be preferable in continuous text. For example, when setting a company annual report, where figures appear in the text and in tables, lining figures may be used throughout for the sake of consistency.

The set of lining figures

The difference between lining and non-lining figures is not just in the height. Lining figures are usually designed with the same *set*, that is, they occupy a space of the same width. Non-lining figures, however, have a set determined by the width of the characters themselves:

lining figures		non-lining figures	
1111111111	6666666666	1111111111	6666666666
2222222222	7777777777	2222222222	7777777777
3333333333	8888888888	3333333333	8888888888
4444444444	9999999999	4444444444	9999999999
5555555555	0000000000	5555555555	0000000000

Caslon, 10.5 pt
This is how these figures appear when keyed in. No extra space has been added between the lining figures on the left.

The advantage of lining figures is that they can be put into columns that will automatically line up vertically. This makes them the ideal choice when designing tables, especially if rules or boxes are required:

3,682	458	19	4,294	129
4,297	663	198	587	99
557	51	1,586	933	746
108	496	224	7,071	692
4,962	1,210	2,008	8,591	1,537

3,682	458	19	4,294	129
4,297	663	198	587	99
557	51	1586	933	746
108	496	224	7,071	692
4,962	1,210	2,008	8,591	1,537

Garamond, 7.5 pt
The lining figures on the left align in rows and columns. The distance between the figures and the rules is constant. The non-lining figures on the right appear to move around within the boxes.

Bear in mind the set of figures as the demands of the text changes. The vertical alignment of lining figures, which is so useful in tables, can give them an uneven look in display (*left*), and should be adjusted with individual letter-spacing (*right*):

11005746111900 0358   11005746111900 0358

Garamond, 14 pt
Narrow figures, such as '1', have more space either side of them than the wider figures. This should be adjusted in display lines.

The close set of non-lining figures, which blends them into lower case text, can make long strings of digits – such as telephone numbers – harder to read (*left*), so they should be letter-spaced where necessary (*right*):

0 ICS   03915 5159721 / 6241926   03915 5159721 / 6241926   12 ICS

Garamond, 12 pt

Numbered lists

A book may contain many numbered lists: contents pages, lists of illustrations, endnotes, etc. Finding a consistent treatment for these elements will produce a more cohesive whole. A possible treatment is to range right numbers and range left the text:

> 98   *View of Longwood, 1820* by Louis Marchand.
> 99   *The Emperor on St Helena Dictating his Memoirs to General Gourgaud.*
> 100 *The Eylau Cemetery* by Baron Gros.
> 101 *The Last Phase* by James Sant.

This has the advantage of maintaining an equal space between the number and the following text throughout, which in turn has the advantage of visually separating the elements so that there is no need to place a full point after the number.

Hanging numbers out to the side will aid the reader when looking for a particular entry as they are easily visible and identifiable:

> 98   *View of Longwood, 1820* by Louis Marchand (p.39). *Courtesy of Réunion des Musées Nationaux.*
> 99   *The Emperor on St Helena Dictating his Memoirs to General Gourgaud* (p.82). A lithograph by Lanzedelly after a painting by Carl August von Steuben. *From the Collection Archiv für Kunst und Geschichte, Berlin (AKG, London).*
>
> 100 *The Eylau Cemetery* by Baron Gros (p.102). *Courtesy of Photo © Daniel Arnaudet.*
> 101 *The Last Phase* by James Sant (p.176). *Courtesy of Kelvingrove Art Gallery and Museum, Glasgow.*
> 102 *Napoleon's Apotheosis* by Horace Vernet (p.233). *Reproduced by Permission of the Trustees of the Wallace Collection.*

In small tightly set lists, a little extra space between entries can also enhance readability further:

> 98   *View of Longwood*, 1820 by Louis Marchand (p.39). Courtesy of Réunion des Musées Nationaux.
> 99   *The Emperor on St Helena Dictating his Memoirs to General Gourgaud* (p.82). A lithograph by Lanzedelly after a painting by Carl August von Steuben. From the Collection Archiv für Kunst und Geschichte, Berlin (AKG, London).
> 100 *The Eylau Cemetery* by Baron Gros (p.102). Courtesy of Photo © Daniel Arnaudet.
> 101 *The Last Phase by James Sant* (p.176). Courtesy of Kelvingrove Art Gallery and Museum, Glasgow.
> 102 *Napoleon's Apotheosis by Horace Vernet* (p.233). Reproduced by Permission of the Trustees of the Wallace Collection.

Numbered illustrations

Captions to illustrations are often numbered, sometimes preceded by 'Fig.' (for figure) or 'Pl.' (for plate). Following the number with an en space will make a second full point unnecessary:

Fig.26 View over the Lake from the Doric Temple

If captions frequently appear grouped together, using a different type style for the number – for example, small caps – will help the reader distinguish between them. This should be consistent throughout the captions though not repeated in the text:

FIG.26 View over the Lake from the Doric Temple

FIG.27 The Ionic building on Grotto Island as illustrated in the Lysons volume

FIG.28 The Tuscan Pavilions

Numbered catalogue entries

Catalogues should be designed with their end use in mind. A catalogue for an art exhibition should be numbered in a way that can be read easily by someone walking through the gallery. Setting the numbers at an adequate size with plenty of space surrounding them will aid the reader. This can be achieved by hanging them out or putting them on a separate line to the title:

2 *Longitudinal section of house*

Insc: *Section of Wotton House in 1820*
Pencil and pen with grey and washes
497 x 675 mm

The forlorn shell of the great house is dramatically illustrated in this section taken through the garden front. It shows the

2

Longitudinal section of house

Insc: *Section of Wotton House in 1820*
Pencil and pen with grey and washes 497 x 675 mm

The forlorn shell of the great house is dramatically illustrated in this section

Columns and tables

For a further discussion of setting tables, see *Tables*, pp.340–3

When setting numbers in columns or tables, some thought should be given to the relationship between them. If the numbers in a column are added together so that the foot of the column gives their total, they should be aligned vertically, ranged on the right. Using lining figures will ensure that the units, tens and hundreds, etc. line up properly. If the numbers are not to be added, they should be set centred or ranged left within the column:

2,682	458	4,294	2,682	458	4,294
4,297	663	587	4,297	663	587
557	1,586	933	557	1,586	933
496	5,071	692	496	5,071	692
485	428	1,058	485	428	1,058
691	221	184	691	221	184
9,208	**8,427**	**7,748**			

The totals are usually separated from the figures in the column above by a rule. Putting the totals in semi-bold will make it easier for the reader to find them in complicated table work.

In financial reports negative amounts are indicated by round brackets and nil amounts by a dash ranged right:

2,682	(458)	4,294
–	–	(587)
557	1,586	933
496	5,071	–
3,735	**6,199**	**4,640**

Tables should contain the minimum amount of rules and boxes needed to make the information clear:

	A	B	C	D	E
MARCH	245.55	952.85	543.38	875.63	749.54
APRIL	35.21	49.98	88.59	21.24	73.05
MAY	64.58	93.22	167.57	87.34	47.34
JUNE	6.40	7.58	9.25	7.12	9.75
	351.74	1103.63	808.79	991.33	879.68
	9%	27%	19%	24%	21%

Minion, 8.5 pt
These columns of figures add up with a total at the bottom, so they are set ranged right.

Decimals and fractions

Decimals and fractions are most likely to be used in books containing measurements. Decimalization means that fractions are less common in the UK, but will still crop up in books aimed at the American market.

Decimals

In the UK a decimal point is used (France and Germany use a decimal comma). For numbers smaller than one, the decimal point should always be preceded by a zero:

$$0.57 \quad not \quad .57$$

Numbers which have four digits or more are grouped into threes using commas (France and Germany use spaces):

$$3,128 \quad 25,662,740 \quad 91,549$$

Exceptions to this are years, page numbers, reference numbers, mathematical workings, and numbers denoting columns and lines of poetry.

Fractions

Some expert fonts contain a set of ready-made fractions, though these tend to be limited to halves, thirds, quarters and eighths:

$\frac{1}{8}$ $\frac{1}{4}$ $\frac{1}{3}$ $\frac{3}{8}$ $\frac{1}{2}$ $\frac{5}{8}$ $\frac{2}{3}$ $\frac{3}{4}$ $\frac{7}{8}$

These may look too big, especially next to old style figures – reduce if necessary:

$2\frac{1}{8}$ $3\frac{1}{4}$ $4\frac{3}{8}$ $5\frac{1}{2}$ $6\frac{5}{8}$ $7\frac{3}{4}$ $8\frac{7}{8}$ $2\frac{1}{8}$ $3\frac{1}{4}$ $4\frac{3}{8}$ $5\frac{1}{2}$ $6\frac{5}{8}$ $7\frac{3}{4}$ $8\frac{7}{8}$

$2\frac{1}{8}$ $3\frac{1}{4}$ $4\frac{3}{8}$ $5\frac{1}{2}$ $6\frac{5}{8}$ $7\frac{3}{4}$ $2\frac{1}{8}$ $3\frac{1}{4}$ $4\frac{3}{8}$ $5\frac{1}{2}$ $6\frac{5}{8}$ $7\frac{3}{4}$

The denominator is the number below the diagonal, the numerator is that above it.

Fractions can be made using lining figures, reduced in size, with the denominator sitting on the baseline and the numerator moved up by using baseline shift. The diagonal stroke is not the standard forward slash / but has more of a slant ⁄ :

$\frac{1}{16}$ $\frac{3}{8}$ $\frac{2}{3}$ $\frac{15}{16}$ $\frac{29}{32}$

The fractions will need careful kerning. In particular, the figure '1' has a very wide set in lining fonts so will need closing up to any figure next to it. The elements of the fraction should be close but not touching.

If the fractions are to be seen next to full-size numbers, they may look light because of the reduction in type size. This can be countered by using a semi-bold:

$3\frac{1}{16}$ $12\frac{3}{8}$ $6\frac{2}{3}$ $19\frac{15}{16}$ $8\frac{29}{32}$

$3\frac{1}{16}$ $12\frac{3}{8}$ $6\frac{2}{3}$ $19\frac{15}{16}$ $8\frac{29}{32}$

Weights and measures

Units of measurement are usually abbreviated:

millimetres: mm	inches: in	grams: g	minutes: min
centimetres: cm	feet: ft	pounds: lb	seconds: sec
metres: m	yards: yd/yds	ounces: oz	
kilometres: km	kilograms: kg	hours: hr/hrs	

They are set with a word space between number and unit.

Times

There are a number of ways of giving the time. The author of a novel may wish to spell it out in full: seven o'clock, half past three.

If using a 24-hour clock, the decimal point should be used to separate the hours from the minutes: 20.03.

A 12-hour clock is often used with 'a.m.' and 'p.m.', but saying '12 noon' and '12 midnight' will avoid confusion.

Dates

In the UK, dates are given in the order: day / month / year. Spelling out the month in full will avoid confusion: 11 April 2005.

There is no need to use 'st', 'nd', 'th' in dates – '1st', '2nd', '5th' – unless in dialogue:

'It happened on the 21st.'

The abbreviations BC and AD should be used in this sequence:

400 BC   AD 400

Elided numbers

Ranges of numbers are expressed by using an unspaced en dash to mean 'to':

267–315

It is common practice to reduce the number of digits to as few as possible:

21–6, 147–9

This should be done with reference to how the words are said, so 115–117 would be reduced to 115–17, because we say 'one hundred and fifteen to seventeen', not '. . . fifteen to seven'.

When printing a range of years, many editors have the rule that the last two digits are always shown:

1835–38, 1921–24

Terms of office and years which do not coincide with the calendar year, such as tax years, are indicated using a slash: 1984/5.

When a range of dates is given which contains word-spaces, the en dash should also be spaced:

15 April 1921 – 24 July 1936

Setting the en dash unspaced would have the effect of joining the numbers together in a way that would confuse the reader:

15 April 1921–24 July 1936

Roman numerals

Roman numerals set in capitals are used for titles (of people and chapters):

George III   Chapter V

Roman numerals set in small caps are used for volumes of journals, and acts in operas or plays:

Act II   vol. XXVII

Lower case is used for the pagination of prelims and scene numbers:

p. xiv   scene ii

Titles should not be followed by: 'th', 'Henry VIIIth'. Roman numerals should not be followed by a full point unless they fall at the end of a sentence.

Confusion may arise if small cap roman numerals are used alongside non-lining figures: II may look like two or eleven. Using capitals (consistently throughout) will make it clearer to the reader: II is two.

Spelling out numbers

In non-mathematical works the editor will make a decision on *spelling out* numbers, that is, using a word 'eight' rather than a number '8'. This is usually limited to numbers between one and ten or between one and a hundred, depending the wishes of the editor.

There will be some exceptions to the rule. For example, it would look strange to switch from spelt-out numbers to digits mid sentence:

The five children were aged 16, 13, 11, nine and seven.

It is better to spell out the whole sentence:

The five children were aged sixteen, thirteen, eleven, nine and seven.

It is also preferable not to start a sentence with a digit:

last year. 15 people were injured in the fire, which started when

Spelt-out numbers from twenty-one to ninety-nine are hyphenated.

1	I
2	II
3	III
4	IV
5	V
6	VI
7	VII
8	VIII
9	IX
10	X
11	XI
12	XII
13	XIII
14	XIV
15	XV
16	XVI
17	XVII
18	XVIII
19	XIX
20	XX
30	XXX
40	XL
50	L
60	LX
70	LXX
80	LXXX
90	XC
100	C
200	CC
300	CCC
400	CD
500	D
600	DC
700	DCC
800	DCCC
900	CM
1000	M

PLACING ILLUSTRATIONS WITHIN TEXT

See *Plate sections*, p.288

There are two ways of placing illustrations into a book of text. One is to group the illustrations together on a set of pages known as a *plate section,* usually printed on a different paper stock. The second is to place illustrations throughout the book so they appear when they are referred to in the text. These are known as *scattered* illustrations. Scattering illustrations is the more expensive option if the images are to be printed in colour, because then the whole book, and not just one or two signatures, has to be printed on a four-colour press. Advances in print technology and paper quality have, however, made scattering black and white images possible on all but the lowest quality papers.

The size of scattered illustrations

The editor will often specify which illustrations should be large and which should be small. Before laying the book out, it is worthwhile calculating how much space they will fill. For example:

> 6 large pics at 1 page each = space equivalent to 6 pages
> 15 medium pics at ⅔ page each = space equivalent to 10 pages
> 12 small pics at ⅓ page each = space equivalent to 4 pages

See *Making extent*, pp.234–6

makes an equivalent to 20 pages of text. This number can then be put into your extent calculations. If necessary the average size can be reduced:

> 6 large pics at 1 page each = space equivalent to 6 pages
> 15 medium pics at ½ page each = space equivalent to 7½ pages
> 12 small pics at ¼ page each = space equivalent to 3 pages

making a total of 16½ pages. Knowing the approximate size of your illustrations before you start will enable you to layout the book with some confidence that the extent will be about right. What you are trying to avoid is having to make the illustrations towards the end of the book too large or too small to fit the available space. Or, even worse, having to go back to the beginning of the layout process and start again.

Positioning illustrations

When an illustration refers to a specific passage of text, it should, of course, be placed as close to it as possible, ideally on the same spread, although this cannot always be achieved. If the text contains a reference to the illustration – 'see Fig.24' – the illustration should always be placed *after* the reference.

If an illustration is referred to more than once, the editor should indicate at which point the illustration should appear.

There should be at least a line space between the illustration and text and this space should be consistent throughout. If any text falls above or below the illustration, this text should be at least four lines long.

If the illustration is at the foot of the page it should align with the baseline of the text. If it is at the head of the page it should align with the top of the text panel:

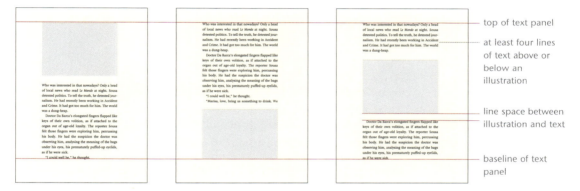

— top of text panel

— at least four lines of text above or below an illustration

— line space between illustration and text

— baseline of text panel

Where many illustrations are referred to in a short passage of text, grouping them together may make it easier to place them closer to the reference in the text:

Proportions

Illustrated books may contain many images with a variety of proportions. If the decision is made to fit all illustrations to the width of the measure, this will have the effect of determining picture size not by the significance or content of the illustration, but by its format. The portrait-format illustrations will all be much larger than the landscape-format ones:

Illustrations at full-measure

Rather than fixing the width of illustrations, they can be given equal weight by making the area they cover approximately the same:

Making the portrait-format illustration (left) 75 per cent of full measure means that it covers the same area as the landscape illustration (right).

A standardized set of image widths will give the book consistency throughout. For example, all illustrations could be set to either 60 per cent, 80 per cent or 100 per cent of the text measure, depending on their proportions and content.

Unusual shapes

Illustrations which are long and narrow can be particularly difficult to place. A page with a wide fore-edge margin will accommodate them more easily:

Cut-outs

Illustrations which have been *cut out* and are therefore irregularly shaped should be treated with care. Forcing them into a grid may result in unbalanced negative space. It is preferable to reduce them in size, leaving more surrounding space to counter this. They should be placed visually within the space, rather than working out margins mathematically:

Cut-outs which are regular in shape, such as circles and ovals, also benefit from having a little more space around them.

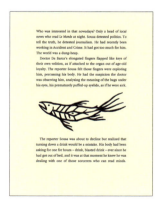 

Cut-out illustration at full-measure

Cut-out illustration at 80 per cent of full-measure

Grids for illustrations

You will get increased flexibility when laying out illustrations if you use a more complex grid – one that allows text and illustrations to be independent of each other. This frees you from making the illustrations too small to match the measure, or making the measure too wide to suit the illustrations.

The simplest way to do this is to introduce a second column, narrower than the text panel, which can contain illustrations, captions, or be left as a wide margin:

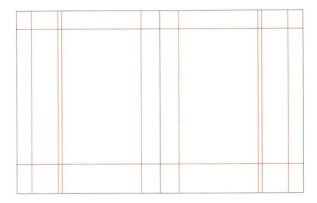

This provides a variety of possible picture widths without breaking out of the basic grid. It has the added benefit of creating more space on the page and making the text appear less dense:

Asymmetric layouts

A grid does not necessarily have to be symmetrical. Pages can be set with the large margin always on the left or always on the right:

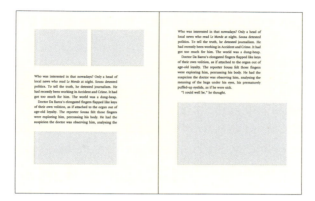

If opting for an asymmetric layout, ensure that your choice of stock does not allow too much show-through in the wide margins.

Double-column layouts

Using two columns of text can be restrictive when it comes to placing illustrations. Anything other than single-column width or double-column width illustrations will look uncomfortable:

Double-column layouts are better suited to large-format illustrated books – especially landscape-format – and catalogues.

Plate sections

Printing illustrations can be expensive. They require better quality paper than plain text, and colour illustrations need to go through a four-colour press. One way of reducing the cost is to print illustrations in a plate section. This allows you to use a different paper for this section, and to run it through a different press than the text.

A plate section is made up of a single signature (usually 8, 16 or 32 pages), which is folded and bound into the book between two signatures of text. This limits where it can be positioned within the text and some books have several plate sections throughout. If a plate section is printed on a different stock and is obviously a separate section within the book, it does not have folios: the text is numbered excluding the plate section.

Laying out a plate section using the same margins as the text will give the book a more consistent look, but it is not essential. If the text has generous margins you may decide to reduce them so that illustrations can be reproduced at a larger size. This is perfectly acceptable as long as it is consistent throughout the plate sections. Be careful not to make the margins too small, as some of the margin may be reduced further when the book is bound.

Your grid may be adapted when laying out a plate section. In this example reducing the margins increases the area available for pictures by 30 per cent.

LARGE-FORMAT ILLUSTRATED BOOKS

Choosing a format

The formats of large illustrated books are driven by their illustrations, resulting in a wide variety of shapes and sizes. When developing a format, consider the following factors:

Illustrations: the format of the illustrations will be the main influence, especially if some of the images are to be bled out. If the illustrations vary in shape, the format and layout of the book will need to be flexible enough to allow both portrait and landscape images to be reproduced at an adequate size. Using extreme proportions for the format – tall and thin, or a wide landscape format – may make the placing of some of the images difficult.

Text: if the book contains substantial text, the shape of the text panel must also be taken into account. If the text is to be in a double column, the page needs to be wide enough to accommodate this. You will also need the space in which to place captions.

Paper/press size: talk to the printer to find out how economically your proposed page size cuts out of a sheet. Changing it very slightly may reduce the paper cost.

Previous titles: publishers may wish a book to resemble the style of a previous title (not necessarily one of their own) which has been successful.

Marketing/sales: booksellers have to consider practical matters such as the size of their shelves, and selling a large, oddly-shaped book into bookshops may prove difficult. Landscape-format books seem to arouse particularly antagonistic feelings in those who find them difficult to handle and store.

Retail price: illustrated books are very expensive to produce. It is important that they can be sold at a price which will cover this cost.

As with all publishing decisions, it is a matter of finding a balance between aesthetic, practical, technical and business considerations.

Before laying out an illustrated book, you will be asked to supply trial spreads to the publisher. The trial pages may be used by the editor to help secure co-editions with overseas publishers and also for sales purposes, so it is important that they are well presented.

Spending time in bookshops and becoming familiar with what is currently on the market is always useful. It will help in discussions with marketing departments who may want some input into the design.

The format of illustrations

Your approach to designing a book format will depend on whether all the illustrations have the same proportions. If this is the case, as is likely in photographic books, then the page can be built around these. This does not necessarily mean copying the proportions exactly, although this will be necessary if you want to bleed out images without cropping them:

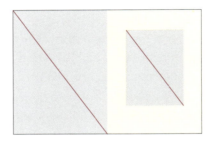

Illustrations with the same proportions as the page

If images are not to be bled out and captions or text are to be placed on pages with illustrations, this will affect the shape of the page:

The format of the spread on the left is deeper than the illustrations in order to accommodate captions. Making a book too tall may make it hard to sell as it will not fit on bookshops' shelves. The spread on the right is shorter and wider: a more popular solution with many publishers.

If a book has illustrations in a variety of proportions, choosing a format for the book is a matter of balance between the differing needs of these illustrations. A look at the art books currently on the market will give a good idea of how most publishers address this. Formats tend to be portrait, heading towards the square with proportions of around 5:4.

Landscape formats are best used for books which only have landscape illustrations, or which contain enough text to balance the pages. A portrait-format illustration alone on a landscape page will always look awkward.

Large-format grids

A larger page allows for greater variety when designing a grid. Multiple columns may be used and the margins increased. Both these elements result in a page which has more space. For example:

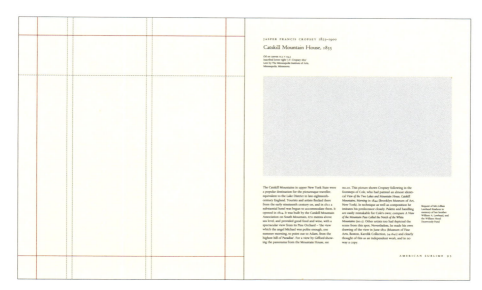

The text panel can be divided into columns if a book is wide in format. The narrower measure does mean that text may benefit from being set ranged left rather than justified.

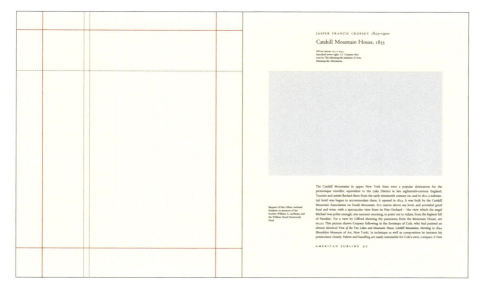

A single column of text with wide margins can look very elegant. Illustrations can be set to measure or hung out into the wide margin.

Grids for catalogues

Some illustrated books, such as art exhibition catalogues, are divided into two distinct sections: the first part containing essays and small comparative illustrations, and the second part containing large illustrations with extended captions. A grid is thus needed that is flexible enough to work with both these forms of material:

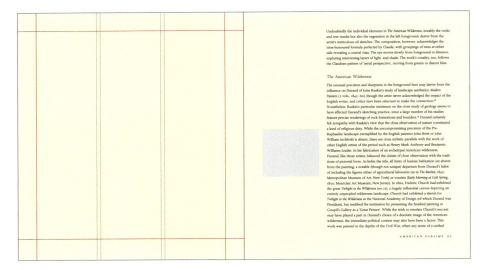

This grid has three columns, two of which are used to form a single column in the first section, with the third used as a margin for illustrations, captions and sidenotes.

In the second section all three columns are used to contain text and to reproduce illustrations at different widths.

Planning four-colour work

If an illustrated book contains few colour pictures, with all the rest in black and white, it may be possible to plan in such a way that the number of sheets which are printed in four colours is reduced. If you are considering this, talk to the printer first to find out whether the cost saving will be worthwhile.

The printer should be able to provide you with a plan from which you can choose which sheets to print in four-colour. In the plan below, for example, if you were to choose signature 2, side A and signature 4, side B, you would be able to print colour on pages 17, 20, 21, 24, 25, 28, 29, 32, 50, 51, 54, 55, 58, 59, 62 and 63.

signature 1		signature 2		signature 3		signature 4		signature 5		signature 6	
	1 A		17 A		33 A		49 A		65 A		81 A
2 B	3 B	18 B	19 B	34 B	35 B	50 B	51 B	66 B	67 B	82 B	83 B
4 A	5 A	20 A	21 A	36 A	37 A	52 A	53 A	68 A	69 A	84 A	85 A
6 B	7 B	22 B	23 B	38 B	39 B	54 B	55 B	70 B	71 B	86 B	87 B
8 A	9 A	24 A	25 A	40 A	41 A	56 A	57 A	72 A	73 A	88 A	89 A
10 B	11 B	26 B	27 B	42 B	43 B	58 B	59 B	74 B	75 B	90 B	91 B
12 A	13 A	28 A	29 A	44 A	45 A	60 A	61 A	76 A	77 A	92 A	93 A
14 B	15 B	30 B	31 B	46 B	47 B	62 B	63 B	78 B	79 B	94 B	95 B
16 A		32 A		48 A		64 A		80 A		96 A	

These numbers will not match your folios if you are numbering your prelims with roman numerals. If you have, for example, 8 pages of prelims, your page 1 will fall on page 9 of the plan.

Choosing signature 1, side B would give you the opportunity to use colour on the title page.

This planning necessitates that the whole book is printed on a stock suitable for colour printing.

Typography in large-format illustrated books

Text in large-format illustrated books often takes the form of extended captions. Here the designer is less restricted by the constraints of setting type for long continuous text as the reader is reading for shorter periods of time – in between looking at the pictures.

Finding a text font which compliments the illustrations is always an interesting challenge. Bear in mind the weight of the type: is it too dark or too light for the pictures? One approach is to use fonts which are of the same period or nationality as the illustrations. Sans serif fonts are commonly used because of their neutral feel – like the white walls of a gallery.

In catalogues containing both essays and entries, different type styles may be used for each form of text: the essays treated as continuous text and the catalogue entries set in a smaller type size and narrower columns:

The two examples below show how the text panel and type style can be changed when the function of the text changes. The first is simply a reduction in size, leading and measure. The second has a matched serif face, set justified, for continuous text, with a sans serif set ranged left, for catalogue entries.

The Catskill Mountains in upper New York State were a popular destination for the picturesque traveller, equivalent to the Lake District in late eighteenth-century England. Tourists and artists flocked there from the early nineteenth century on, and in 1822 a substantial hotel was begun to accommodate them. It opened in 1824.

This shows Cropsey following in the footsteps of Cole, who had painted an almost identical *View of the Two Lakes and Mountain House, Catskill Mountains, Morning* in 1844 (Brooklyn Museum of Art, New York). In technique as

Essay: Stone Sans, 9.5 on 14.5 pt
Catalogue: Stone Sans, 8.5 on 13.5 pt

The Catskill Mountains in upper New York State were a popular destination for the picturesque traveller, equivalent to the Lake District in late eighteenth-century England. Tourists and artists flocked there from the early nineteenth century on, and in 1822 a substantial hotel was begun to accommodate them. It opened in 1824. It was built by the

This shows Cropsey following in the footsteps of Cole, who had painted an almost identical *View of the Two Lakes and Mountain House, Catskill Mountains, Morning* in 1844 (Brooklyn Museum of Art, New York). In technique as well as composition he imitates

Essay: Joanna, 10.5 on 14 pt
Catalogue: Gill Sans, 9 on 12.5 pt

Captions

Captions are set in a smaller size than the main text and may be italicized or set in a complimentary typeface.

They can be placed beneath or to the side of the illustration, depending on the format of the picture box. The space between caption and image and the relationship of caption to text should also be consistent throughout.

When placing captions beneath illustrations they may be set ranged left, justified or centred, as long as the setting is consistent throughout, and set on a measure equal to the width of the illustrations:

The Ionic building on Grotto Island as illustrated in the Lysons volume

The Ionic building on Grotto Island as illustrated in the Lysons volume

Left: Stone Print
9.5 on 12 pt
ranged left
Right: Stone Print
9.5 on 12 pt, centred
If an illustration falls
at the foot of a page,
the last line of the
caption should
fall on the text
panel's baseline.

When placing captions to the side of illustrations, they should either all be on the fore-edge side or all on the gutter side. In an asymmetrical layout, they should all on the left or all on the right. Aligning them with either the top or bottom of the illustration will give the neatest look.

Captions can be set ranged against the illustrations, but ranged right captions may be difficult to read if they are extensive. In this case set them all ranged left:

FIG. 41, *right*: The South Drawing Room in August 1825, watercolour by J M Gandy. The two black tripod stands either side of the fireplace were sold by the Trustees after Soane's death.

FIG. 42, *below*: Pencil sketch of Mrs Soane by John Flaxman

FIG. 43, *opposite page*: The South Drawing Room

FIG. 41, *right*: The South Drawing Room in August 1825, watercolour by J M Gandy. The two black tripod stands either side of the fireplace were sold by the Trustees after Soane's death.

FIG. 42, *below*: Pencil sketch of Mrs Soane by John Flaxman

FIG. 43, *opposite page*: The South Drawing Room

Stone Sans
7.5 on 10.5 pt
The ranged
right captions sit
nicely next to the
illustration, but the
text is easier to
read in the ranged
left version.

For the numbering
of captions
see *Numbered
illustrations*, p.273

Bleeding out illustrations

When an illustration covers the page right up to the trimmed edge it is described as *bled-out*. The illustration is printed slightly larger than the page size, so that when the pages are trimmed no white areas remain at the edges. The area of the illustration that is trimmed off is called the *bleed*, and is usually about 3 or 4 mm wide.

The top left corner of a bled-out page (verso). The page trim is indicated by the red line. Any image falling outside that area would be cut off. Bleeds are only used at the trimmed edges of the book. The image should not be extended at the gutter margin.

page trimmed to this crop

Full-page bled-out illustrations

The advantage of using full-page bled-out illustrations is that they are shown as large as possible and the page looks cleaner with fewer edges, but there are other considerations to bear in mind when deciding whether or not to bleed images out.

Computers do make it possible – though time consuming – to add on image for the bleeds, using a technique called *cloning*. This may not be appropriate for some images, such as works of art. Talk to the editor and production manager before using it. See *Working with images*, pp.304–9

Unless the format of the book has been designed to match the format of the illustrations, some of any bled-out image will need to be cropped. Check with the editor that this is allowed and make sure that the content of the illustrations can be fitted to the format of the page without losing vital parts of the image. Whatever the format, a little of the image will be lost in the bleeds. The smaller the size of the page, the larger the percentage of the image will be lost.

Bleeding out is a good treatment for enlarging details of illustrations which are reproduced elsewhere – provided the quality of the original is good enough – and may be used for section openings or title pages.

Cross-fold bleeds

An illustration that is placed across the gutter of a spread is called a *cross-fold bleed*. It is a useful solution for placing images that are particularly wide:

In some cases, such as academic works, it is vital that none of the image is lost in the gutter. The image should be split in two with a gutter margin of 3–5 mm.

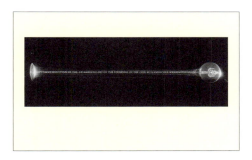

The success of this treatment depends on the method and quality of the binding – a sewn, case-bound book is the best – as well as judicious picture placement. Make sure the gutter does not fall through a vital part of the image:

See *Binding*, p.350

gutter

It is better to move the illustration to one side to avoid this:

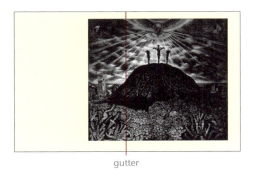

gutter

There are occasions when breaking out of grid may be advisable. When placing a difficult cross-fold bleed, the content of the illustration must be considered the priority.

Fold-outs

A *fold-out*, or *throw-out*, is a page that is larger than the pages in the rest of the book and folded to fit into it. Using fold-outs is a way of reproducing large-format illustrations without bleeding across the gutter margin.

An example of a fold-out shown from above. The back of the page that folds out is usually left blank.

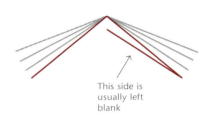

This side is usually left blank

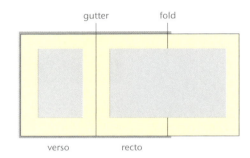

gutter   fold

verso   recto

Size of fold-outs

The dimensions of a fold-out are critical and the printer should be consulted before you lay it out. The folded edge of the page needs to fall within the trimmed page size by a few millimetres, so that when the book is bound and trimmed, the fold is not trimmed off. The part of the page that folds back into the book should fall short of the gutter so that it can be unfolded easily. For example, a book with a width of 245 mm, would have a fold-out with the following measurements:

An example of possible measurements for a fold-out section. There are many factors that can affect these, including the binding method and the page size. Taking advice from the printer should help to avoid any problems.

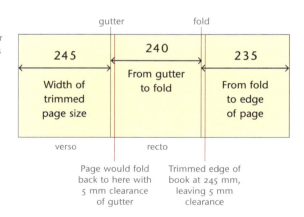

gutter   fold

245   240   235

Width of   From gutter   From fold
trimmed   to fold   to edge
page size   of page

verso   recto

Page would fold   Trimmed edge of
back to here with   book at 245 mm,
5 mm clearance   leaving 5 mm
of gutter   clearance

Position of fold-outs

Most printers will have strong views about where they are willing to place fold-outs within a book, and should be consulted at the outset. The most common positions are between signatures, or in the middle of a signature.

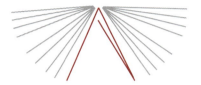

Fold-out sections between signatures (left) and in the middle of a signature (right).

The recto page following the the fold-out will lose a few millimetres from the gutter margin where the fold-out is glued in.

Fold-outs are printed separately from the normal text pages and inserted at the binding stage. They are output as separate documents which include the back and front of the fold-out sections. The following diagrams show how a fold-out section falling between two signatures would be output.

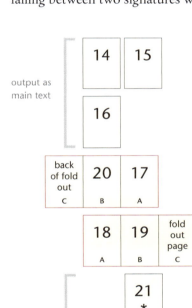

output as main text

back of fold out

C | B | A

fold out page

A | B | C

output as main text

* new section

The main text is output as usual and the imposition is carried out by the printer. Fold-out sections can be imposed by the designer. The two sheets, shown here bordered in red, form the front and back of a fold-out section. A, B and C indicate how they back up:

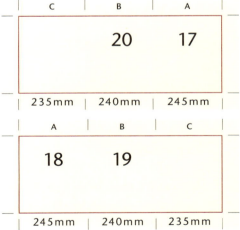

Far left: A fold-out section (pages numbered 17–20) falling between two sections.

This shows how the output document for the fold-out section may look. In this example the page width is 245 mm. If in doubt, it is always worth folding a sheet of paper and writing the numbers on it to see how the pages back up. Make sure the measurements match up for back and front.

Co-editions

Producing large, full-colour illustrated books is a costly process, so publishers will often sell co-edition rights to foreign-language publishers. This allows the cost of origination (design, etc.) and repro (scanning and proofing images) to be shared between the publishing houses. The book is then produced in a number of different languages.

A co-edition is printed using five plates rather than the usual four. The illustrations are colour-separated and printed in the usual way – cyan, magenta, yellow and black – and the text is printed using a separate black plate. The black text plate is changed for each language.

Any text which will appear in a different language can only be printed with the black text plate, so when designing a co-edition for foreign-language publishers, the following rules apply:

Do not . . .	*But you may . . .*
Print text in colour	Print text in a tint of black
Reverse text out of blocks of colour	Reverse text out of a tint of black
Reverse text out of illustrations	Overprint illustrations in black

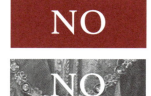

For co-editions between publishers in the same language, the only usual changes are the title page and imprint page. Covers or jackets may be different and are produced separately.

Blads

While putting together trial designs for an illustrated book, you may be asked to produce a *blad*. This is a printed document, usually of 8 or 16 pages with a cover, in the same format as the book, showing samples of the pages. Blads are also used by publishers to secure co-edition deals.

Blads may also be supplied to sales representatives to show to bookshops.

The flat plan for the inside of an 8-page blad may look like this:

The idea of a blad is to show how the finished book will look, so a selection of different sorts of pages should be used. Remember that this is a sales tool so choose the most impressive images.

The blad will be required early in the production process, as publishers need to make their financial contracts before the book goes to print and the print run is decided.

The publication details – p.8 on the flat plan – help to sell the book, so will be different to those which appear on an imprint page:

> Format: 354 × 263 mm, hardback cloth-bound
> 208 pages with 160 full page 4-colour illustrations
>
> UK publication: April 2005; retail price £45
> US publication: May 2005; retail price $85
>
> ISBN: 1 86046 345 2

	title page
	1
frontispiece illustration	contents page
2	3
illustration	section opening
4	5
text	illustration
6	7
publication details	
8	

Information on the author and artist/photographer will also need to be included.

The alternative to a blad is a dummy binding, produced by the printers, with sample pages glued into it.

WORKING WITH IMAGES

Printing technology has reduced the cost of reproducing illustrations in books, and the designer is often called upon to handle images from layout to output. The treatment of images will vary according to the type of book that is being illustrated. Images you may be asked to work with may include:

> works of art for exhibition catalogues and art books
> collections of informal family photographs for biographies
> technical elements for academic and scientific publications
> commissioned illustrations and drawings
> decorative elements for the designer to use as wished

Cropping illustrations

Most images will require adjustment when they are laid out onto designed pages. *Cropping*, the cutting of parts of the image so that it fits into a picture box, is the first stage of that process. Old photographs may have irregular borders; obvious extraneous portions may need cropping out to enlarge the photograph's main characters within the area available in the layout:

Typical old family photographs to be used in a biography.

Buildings that have no interest are cropped out, enabling enlargement so that individuals can be more easily recognized.

If the crops are left to the designer, above all, take account of the content of the image. What you leave in or take out is usually a matter of common sense and observation of what makes for an attractive composition. The author or editor may indicate what elements are to be the main focus of the picture.

The uncropped photograph shows the painter in her studio. The second concentrates on the artist and her desk. The third, zooming in, might be requested by the editor for use on the jacket.

Original unposed photographs may cut off people at the edges. It is always better to sacrifice that part of the image unless it is the only known photograph of an important person in the book.

When cropping and enlarging or reducing a picture, bear in mind the negative spaces created by the elements of the composition. Try to balance the composition without losing any essential information:

The dark area of the hedge and the light area of the sky detract from the statue and mansion. Enlarging the image and cropping both the hedge and sky results in a more interesting composition.

Cropping works of art

How a work of art is cropped depends on the context in which it is being reproduced. Where the work of art itself is the subject, it should not be cropped any more than is necessary to straighten and tidy up the edges.

If a picture has been photographed with its frame, the frame is not usually shown. However, in some works of art the frame is considered intrinsically important and a request may be made to feature it. If a shadow has been cast by the frame onto the picture when the photograph was taken, it may need closer cropping, reducing the area of the work or retouching the shadow.

When the item has an irregular shape it may be *cut out*, removing the background. This adds to the clarity and impact of the image.

Where the work is used to illustrate a point in the text, say a portrait of an historical figure who appears only in a part of the picture, it may be cropped to focus on that area. However, in all these cases it may be that the holder of the picture's copyright will not allow cropping. Check with the editor for any restrictions.

Using image details

An enlarged detail is often used to illustrate an area of particular interest within a picture: this should be made clear in the caption using the bracketed word (*detail*).

If the complete image has been used elsewhere in the book, details are an intriguing way of introducing new views of the work and give the designer freedom to find further qualities within the image. Experiment with different enlargements.

There may be a limit to how much an area can be enlarged. This depends on how large the original photograph is and what scanning equipment is available. If you are hoping to use a very small area of a transparency, first check with the repro house that the result will be satisfactory and in sharp focus. When using files that were originated digitally, the extent of any possible enlargement will depend on the size and resolution at which they were taken.

These details are from the Stowe Bowl, designed and engraved by Simon Whistler. The image of the bowl (*top left*) has been enlarged to the following percentages:

1: 184%
2: 216%
3: 272%
4: 360%
5: 480%

Photograph by John Pasmore

Horizontals and verticals

Few pictures will be perfectly straight. When aligning pictures a flat horizon, such as the sea, should be horizontal and the vertical lines of buildings should be properly vertical. If the verticals of a building do not run parallel, due to a distortion in the perspective of the photograph, choose one which is near the centre of the image. In the example below, making the large door on the left of the picture vertical (*left*) gives a less satisfactory result than getting the corner of the room vertical (*right*). At least this makes the floor look level.

An image can be straightened out using computer software, but if it is very distorted it may have to be re-photographed.

Rotating an image can result in the loss of portions of the image. If any of these are critical areas, it should be re-photographed:

The photograph on the left is out of vertical by 3°. When it is rotated to correct this, there is a loss of usable image.

Differences in scale

When more than one illustration with a similar subject or content appears on a page, it may be desirable to make the subjects match a common scale. Portraits in particular benefit from this treatment.

Here the difference in the size of the subject's heads create an imbalance.

Keeping the heads level and in the same position within the picture box gives the portraits greater equivalence.

This treatment would be appropriate in a biography or history book where the portraits are used to illustrate how specific people appeared. However, if the book is about portraiture or a painter and the paintings themselves are the subject, it would be an inappropriate treatment.

When reproducing works of art it is not usually possible to show them all at the same scale as the sizes of the originals will vary greatly. However, it is illuminating for the reader if size can be suggested in your layout by making large paintings bigger and small sketches smaller.

DIGITAL IMAGES

Image refers to
any original source,
be they drawn
images, photo-
graphic prints
or transparencies.
Images created
in illustration
programs such
as Illustrator® will
already be in a
digital form.

The use of an image requires its digitization so that printing plates can be made.
The process of scanning transforms the original image into digital information.

The pixel and resolution

The *pixel* – *pix*(picture)+ *el*(ement) – is the form in which the hues and tones of an
image are gathered in the scanning process. A pixel is a minute square element of
a single hue – in the case of a coloured image – or a single tone in the case of a
black and white image. Thus hundreds of thousands of pixels, each containing a
single colour, are necessary to reproduce the range of colours present in a colour
image. Similarly, the reproduction of the shades of grey and black present in a
black and white image requires the use of hundreds of thousands of pixels, each
consisting of a single shade of grey or black.

The quality of the digital image depends on the number of pixels that are collected
at the scanning stage. That is determined by two settings:

> The *resolution*, expressed as *dpi* – pixels per inch – can be set on scanner and
> is usually in a range from 72 to 4,000 dpi.

> The *scale* at which the image is scanned. The scanner setting allows the image
> to be scanned at a range of scales, usually from 10% to 2,000%.

Dpi was an pre-
digital term for
'dots per inch';
it has continued
in use to refer to
pixels per inch.
Resolution may also
be defined as pixels
per centimetre.
120 *ppc* is the
equivalent to
304.8 dpi.

The number of pixels that the scan achieves is the area of the scaled scan multiplied
by the resolution. As an example, take a photograph which is 2 inches by 2.5 inches.
You wish to use the image in a book at twice that size. 300 dpi is a good minimum
resolution for plate-making purposes. So scan the image in at 200% at 300 dpi.

This image scan will contain: If scanned in at 72 dpi and to the same scale:

The 300 dpi image thus contains nearly 18 times more information.

Scanning at the required size and resolution

When scanning a picture for printing, it is important to know what size your final image will be. The digital file should be at least the same size at which it will be printed and have a minimum resolution of 300 dpi.

If you do not know at the time of scanning how an image is to be used, you should scan it at a larger size than you could possibly need, and at a higher resolution. When the final size is decided, the scan can be scaled down without a reduction in picture quality. This is vital. It is straightforward to reduce the size of an image, but images cannot be enlarged in size without suffering in quality. Once an image is scanned there is no way in which the amount of digital information can be increased other than by re-scanning.

1. The original image

2. Scanned in at low resolution the pixel form is seen, each with a single tone or hue.

3. As scanning resolution increases, the step effect is less marked but evident.

Stepping may also be referred to as *pixellating*.

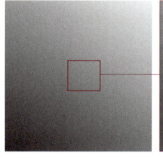 

The digital information of a scan contains a finite number of pixels. If you enlarge a scan, the same finite number of pixels are spread over a larger area, stepping occurs and there is a reduction of picture quality.

4. Only a scan at 300 dpi and 100% scale produces a usable digitized image.

5. But if an area of a 300 dpi scan is enlarged beyond 110%, there is insufficient information to spread over this small area.

The two common file formats for scans are the JPEG and the TIFF. The JPEG is a compressed form which produces a small file size but may not contain enough pixel information. The TIFF format will accurately transmit all pixel information.

TIFF stands *for Tagged Image File Format.*

JPEG stands for *Joint Photographic Experts Group.*

Colour modes – RGB and CMYK

Colour printing uses four colours: cyan, magenta, yellow and black – referred to as CMYK – to reproduce coloured images. The scanning equipment of a repro house will scan an image using CMYK but many images that you receive may be in the red, green and blue mode – referred to as RGB. This is especially so in the case of images from digital cameras. Many special filters and effects to adjust images can only be carried out in the RGB mode. Although programs such as Photoshop® convert from the RGB mode to CMYK automatically, it is wise to discuss this conversion with the repro house before carrying it out yourself.

Not all colours can be reproduced by the CMYK process. Some bright, vivid colours can only be reproduced by printing additional plates with special ink colours.

Duotones

A duotone is not a colour mode but a method by which black and white images can be enhanced. The image is printed in a colour, usually a grey or brown and then in black, enriching the depths of the tones. The choice of the second colour is best made by looking at a range of printer's examples.

Duotones are commonly used for books of photographs.

How scans are used

When an image is to be printed, it will be converted into a *half-tone* in order to render the graduations of tone of a black and white picture, or tone and hue in the case of a coloured image. To create this half-tone the image is screened, translating the tonal graduations of the original into a series of dots of varying sizes. In the case of four-colour images, the four colours, cyan, magenta, yellow and black from which all images are made, are screened separately. The technical processes of screening and plate-making are beyond this book's scope: your concern is the relationship between the digital values of high resolution images and the way they perform in the plate-making process.

Development in the reproduction of images continues. Techniques such as *stochastic screening* – where all the dots are the same size and a greater or lesser number of dots create the tonal areas – offer further increases in quality.

There is a progression in the fineness of the screens used for this, depending on the demands of the final printed product. A picture in a newspaper demands a lower level of reproduction compared with a book of works of art in four colours.

The fineness of a screen is defined by the number of *lines of dots* in an inch – *lpi*. A coarse screen would be at 80 lpi: a fine screen at 200 lpi or higher is required to achieve high quality reproduction of an image. Ask the printer what screen is to be used. As a rule of thumb, if you multiply the lpi needed for the screening of the images by one and a half times, the resulting figure should not be greater than the resolution of the scanned image. If an image is to be screened at 175 lpi for plate-making, the minimum resolution must be 175 x 1.5 = 263 pixels per inch. An image scanned at 300 pixels per inch will function with screens of up to 200 lpi. If the figure exceeds the resolution a drop in the quality of the reproduction occurs. These considerations only apply to high resolution scans; in many cases you may not be dealing with them.

175 lpi or 200 lpi are the usual fine screens for art books.

Picture management

Laying out illustrated books requires accurate and efficient management of photographs, transparencies, artwork and digital images. Whatever their original form, they will be placed in the layout as digital images. Scans are derived in several ways:

1 Low resolution scans done by the designer
2 Low resolution scans provided by the repro house
3 High resolution scans provided by the repro house or publisher
4 Digitized images from photographers or other sources

The work of progressing the layout of an illustrated book and then including the final images in your layout document will differ in each of these circumstances.

A low resolution scan is done at between 72 to 100 dpi. High resolution scans are done at a minimum of 300 dpi or 120 pixels per cm.

Low resolution scans done by the designer

In the early stage of a design you may be provided with a mixture of photographs and transparencies. If some pictures have yet to be sourced by the publisher you may receive only photocopies. Scan in all of these at a low resolution – 100 dpi, in colour or black and white depending on their final use. If the editor has numbered or titled the pictures use this name exactly to label each file. If not, name the image as clearly as possible so as to identify it easily. Looking for an image can be time-consuming and confusing if you have only named them 1, 2, 3 etc. If there are several chapters or sections in the book, sub-divide your picture files into folders corresponding to those parts. Again this makes searching for an

As all printed four-colour work is done with CMYK files it is a good habit to scan images using CMYK mode.

image quicker. If your scanner and computer capacity allow you to scan at high resolution and to the approximate final size, there can be an element of security in scanning at a high resolution as a back-up. Should any loss or damage occur to the original pictures then there is something to be rescued.

Low resolution scans provided by the repro house

OPI stands for Open Pre-press Interface. It is critical to the working of the OPI system that you do not change the name of any picture file.

OPI Image Replacement is a process sometimes used by repro houses. When the repro house is given the chosen picture crops and sizes by the designer, scans are done by them at high resolution and you are sent a set of low resolution scans with the same file names as the high resolution scans. You place these low resolution scans and output the final layout document. When you send back the completed layouts, the repro house links the document to the OPI system and the high resolution pictures automatically replace the low resolution ones before plates are made. Check the printer's proof carefully for correct placements as errors can occur.

Sometimes, if there is a tight deadline, the repro house will provide low resolution scans derived from high resolution scans before the sizes of the picture are known. This is inefficient as the pictures may later have to be re-scanned to the final size.

High resolution scans provided by the repro house

If you are supplied with high resolution scans, place, crop and size the images. Check any enlargement that is needed to fit the picture boxes in your layout. There is a small margin of allowable size enlargement, up to 110%, that you can apply in fitting a scan without loss of print quality. If an enlargement above that percentage is needed to fit, then the picture should be rescanned.

The industry standard for referring to enlargement or reduction is based on the use of the term 100% to mean the original size of the scan. Thus an enlargement of 10% is referred to as one to 110%. A reduction of 10% is referred to as one to 90%.

At the same time the repro house will produce a set of colour proofs of the images. These should be viewed and passed as correct by the editor, production manager and yourself. Any comments on colour and possible adjustments are passed onto the repro house. This is important if the images require accurate colour representation, as in the reproduction of works of art.

Final output to the printer may be in the form of a PDF – a *portable document format*. This format encapsulates all the pictures and fonts. To produce a PDF of sufficient quality for plate-making, high resolution CMYK images must be used.

Digitized images from photographers

Digital photography has developed to a level that can produce high quality images. Cameras that have complex 'back-end' programs are capable of additional subtle adjustments to pictures. The digital files that are produced are in RGB format. The conversion of RGB files into CMYK suitable for four-colour printing is a matter for the repro house. They have *press profiles* – settings for individual plate-makers and presses – to carry out this conversion. Note that RGB files should not be used for the creation of PDFs for print.

You may receive a camera-originated digital file which you cannot place in your layout. One reason for this may be that it is a *16-bit* image. This is the highest quality type of image – whether derived from a scan or produced with a digital camera. The advantage of a 16-bit image is that it can be comprehensively adjusted without deterioration of the digital information, though this is done in specialized programs. The 16-bit image should be converted to the 8-bit image for placement in the layout program.

Colour adjustments of scans

Adjustments of colour, saturation, brightness and contrast to 8-bit images may radically reduce the amount of digital information that the file carries resulting in poor picture definition. If colours need correcting after you have seen the initial proofs it is wise to instruct the repro house to carry this out and ensure you see a set of corrected proofs for approval before printing.

Naming and filing images

In working on an illustrated book with many pictures, it has already been noted that you must establish a system for labelling what may be hundreds of pictures. When you send originals to the repro house to be scanned, ensure that you label each picture with the page number and its position on the page, matching the layout. If you are working with a photographer who is providing digital files, have an early discussion to ensure that the files are named or described accurately to relate to the book's content. And bear in mind that you may have no specialist knowledge of a book's contents, and may be unable to identify any of the pictures by their appearance. Ask the editor for annotated photocopies to help you.

Some digital camera sources may produce images of great size at a low resolution of 72 dpi. Increase the dpi to 300 and reduce the dimensions of the image but be sure that the total 'pixel dimension' is not greater than the original file.

Do not be tempted to make these adjustments yourself as you, not the repro house or printer, will bear the responsibility for the final result if it does not satisfy the client. Limit any changes to scans to sizing and rotating.

The output of scanned images

There are four ways in which your final document may be output to the printers:

1 as a document in your layout program, together with the original transparencies and photographs
2 as a layout document with low resolution images to be replaced by OPI
3 as a layout document with high resolution images already in place
4 as a portable document file – a PDF file

What follows is only for guidance – every repro house and printer will differ in the exact processes they use. Ask at the outset how they prefer to work.

In a layout document

A greyscale is a half-tone black and white print-out of pictures and text.

If you have used low resolution scans in the layout of the book's illustrations do not send these scans with the document. The repro house will use your 100% sized greyscale to scan the pictures at the correct sizes. The scans will be placed into your layout document and the plates made from the resulting combined document. Always check the correct placing and identification of pictures when you receive the printer's proofs.

In a layout document with low resolution images to be replaced by OPI

The OPI images at low resolution provided by the repro house are fitted into the layout. The layout document is output with these images.

In a layout document with high resolution scans in place

The repro house will supply the high resolution scans and they are then fitted to the picture boxes in the layout. When these sizes and positions have been approved by the editor, it is necessary to size the scans to as near the actual size – 100% – as possible. If a scan can only be fitted by enlarging it, there is a definite limit to this enlargement before the scan deteriorates. To be safe, no more than a 110% enlargement should be considered before the repro house is asked to re-scan the original to the larger size. Pictures with a simple colour content may tolerate a greater enlargement, but scans of pictures requiring accurate colour reproduction must be as near 100% size as possible. This process is carried out as shown opposite.

1. Picture as supplied at 300 dpi 72 x 50 mm

2. Picture fitted into layout picture box at 50%
X%: 50% Y%: 50% 36 x 25mm

You may take the view that the repro house can carry this process out. It does give you a final opportunity to double check the pictures and ensure that none have been distorted in fitting.

3. Picture is re-sized in Photoshop®; the dpi is unchanged, only the dimensions are changed.
Now re-fitted at 100%
X%: 100% Y%: 100% 36 x 25mm

Pixel Dimensions: 519K

Width:	600	pixels
Height:	864	pixels

Document Size

Width:	5	cm
Height:	7.2	cm
Resolution:	304.8	pixels/inch
or:	120	pixels/cm

Ensure that the linkages between proportions are constrained.

Pixel Dimensions: 129K (was 519K)

Width:	300	pixels
Height:	432	pixels

Document Size

Width:	2.5	cm
Height:	3.6	cm
Resolution:	304.8	pixels/inch
or:	120	pixels/cm

Do not hesitate to talk to the repro house if any problems occur. The more problems that can be resolved before proofs and plate-making take place the better.

As a PDF file

The PDF format is becoming a popular choice for output, but it can only be used if the designer has been provided with high resolution scans. The format also obviates the need for font purchases by the repro house. When the scans have been fitted and sized as above, the document can be translated into a PDF file. There are many settings and profiles for creating print-quality PDFs. Before creating a PDF contact the printer to ensure that your PDF settings are suitable or ask for the printer's preferred profile and work with that.

See p.76

PART THIRTEEN
FURTHER TEXT TREATMENTS

SETTING PLAYS

In continuous texts the identity of speakers of dialogue is revealed within the sentences – with phrases such as 'he said' – or implied by the narrative flow. In either case the beginning of a speech is marked with a paragraph indent:

> 'Elisabeth!' called Gérard in an urgent whisper. 'Open the door. It's us.'
>
> 'I shan't open the door!' remarked a small stubborn voice from the other side of it. 'I'm sick to death of boys. Turning up at this hour of the night – you must be mad. I'm fed up with you.'

In plays, characters' identities are shown by setting their names at the beginning of their lines, ranged left and full out. This avoids any confusion as to the speaker's identity. As plays are, in effect, all dialogue, no quotation marks are used.

A change of character is emphasized by hanging out the characters' names, and indenting successive lines. The use of small caps for the names, followed by a colon, further helps the reader to see this change:

Joanna regular and small caps for the characters 11 on 14 pt

> SOLNESS: – build it together with a princess, whom I love –
> HILDE: Yes, tell him that! Tell him that!
> SOLNESS: Yes. And then I'll say to him: Now I'll go down and throw my arms round her and kiss her –
> HILDE: – many times! Say that!
> SOLNESS: – many, many times, I'll say.
> HILDE: And then – ?
> SOLNESS: Then I'll wave my hat – and come down to earth – and do what I told him.

Ensure that the leading is adequate. A space inserted between speeches would separate these more, but this would increase extent and is uneconomical. Sometimes it is used in publishing expensive large-format books celebrating a famous playwright's works.

Plays include stage directions as well as characters and dialogue. The combined text becomes a script from which actors' attitudes, responses and movements can be identified and directed.

Acting instructions are italicized and set within either square brackets [*gloomily*] or with parentheses (*gloomily*) to separate them from the dialogue. The use of square brackets is preferred, as it distinguishes instructions from any parentheses that might appear within the dialogue itself:

HILDE: [*with outstretched arms*]: Now I see you again as I did when there was a song in the air!

SOLNESS: [*looking at her with bowed head*]: How did you come to be what you are, Hilde?

HILDE: How did you make me what I am?

SOLNESS: [*shortly and firmly*]: The princess shall have her castle.

HILDE: [*clapping her hands with joy*]: Oh, Master Builder – ! My beautiful, beautiful castle! Our castle in the air!

SOLNESS: With a foundation under it.

[*In the street a number of people have gathered, who can be seen distinctly through the trees. The music of wind instruments is heard from a distance behind the new house. MRS SOLNESS with a fur collar around her neck, DR HERDAL with her white shawl on his arm, and some ladies come out on the veranda. RAGNAR BROVIK comes up at the same time from the garden.*]

MRS SOLNESS [TO RAGNER]: Is there to be a band. too?

Stage directions:
Joanna italic
11 on 14 pt
Characters' names appearing within the directions:
Joanna small caps

The name of any character within a stage instruction is set in small caps.

Play texts are sometimes held in the hand at rehearsals and actors may highlight their own lines and use the shape of the text as a mnemonic – an aid to memory. So choose a face, such as Joanna, that has clearly differentiated roman and italic forms. Bracketing the stage directions ensures their visual separation from the parts the actor must commit to memory. Footnotes should be avoided.

If characters' names are long, abbreviated forms may be used to reduce the space occupied by them – for example:

Rosencrantz is set as – ROS and *Guildenstern* becomes – GUIL

Plays are divided into acts and scenes. An act is the equivalent of a chapter and acts should start on a new page. The first act should be on a recto: subsequent acts fall as they will, on either a recto or verso page. Scenes should be indicated with a sub-heading.

Running heads are an aid in longer plays:

The prelims of a play are essentially the same as in a book – with half-title, title contents and any introduction treated in the same way. A list of characters – called the *dramatis personae* in earlier plays – will be included. Sometimes a note on the date, venue and actors in the first performance of the play appears before the main text. The list of characters is styled to correspond with the typographic treatment of the characters in the play, accustoming the reader to this treatment. The list may be placed on the recto page preceding the recto of the first act or on the verso page opposite the first act opening recto.

Joanna regular
small caps
and italic
11 on 14 pt

CHARACTERS

HALVARD SOLNESS, *the master builder*
ALINE SOLNESS, *his wife*
DR HERDAL, *the family doctor*
KNUT BROVIK, *formerly an architect; now an assistant in Solness's firm*
RAGNAR BROVIK, *his son, a draughtsman*
KAJA FOSLI, *his niece, a book-keeper*
HILDE WANGEL
Some ladies and a crowd in the street
The events take place in Solness's house

Occasionally you may have the opportunity for a more generous setting with individual lines for the characters, directions and dialogue:

Garamond regular
small caps and italic
11 on 14 pt
To indicate an action
an opening square
bracket is used with
the italic; no closing
bracket is added.

HILDE:
[with outstretched arms
Now I see you again as I did when there was a song in the air!

SOLNESS:
[looking at her with bowed head
How did you come to be what you are, Hilde?

SETTING POETRY

Setting a book of poetry is a complex job. You should pay attention to:

> The poet's marking up of line indents, capitals and punctuation
> The positioning of the poems in the text panel
> The positioning of the poem's title and the numbering of verses and lines
> The running on of a poem over pages and turning of long lines
> Type choice and word-spacing

Line indents and capitals

The poet's use of indents, capitals and punctuation must be matched exactly as they are an intrinsic part of poetic rhythm and expression. There are many variations:

> You were she who abode
> By those red-veined rocks far West,
> You were the swan-necked one who rode
> Along the beetling Beeny Crest,
> And, reining nigh me,
> Would muse and eye me,
> While Life unrolled us its very best.

Bembo
10.5 on 12 pt
Thomas Hardy

> But that's all shove be'ind me – long ago an' far away
> An' there ain't no 'buses runnin' from the Bank to Mandalay;
> An' I'm learnin' 'ere in London what the ten-year soldier tells:
> 'If you've 'eard the East a-callin', you won't never 'eed naught else.'
> No! you won't 'eed nothin' else
> But them spicy garlic smells,
> An' the sunshine an' the palm-trees an' the tinkly temple-bells;
> On the road to Mandalay . . .

Bembo
10.5 on 12 pt
Rudyard Kipling

> That the sight,
> though strange to me,
> must be a common one,
> is clear: there are such flowers
> with such leaves
> native to some climate
> which they can call
> their own.

Bembo
10.5 on 11 pt
William
Carlos Williams

Before considering how to deal with the setting of a book of poems it is wise to go through the the whole manuscript, making a line count of each poem and noting the lengths of the longer lines. This will give you an early impression of how you might place the poems in a text panel.

The editor may have directed you to set the poems to the left of the page or visually centred within the text panel, poem by poem. In either of these two arrangements, you must still observe the individual poem's indents. The editor will also instruct you as to whether the poems are to be set on each page or run on, where the verses of a poem may run over pages. The word *stanza* may be used by editors and can be taken as another word for verse.

Positioning of poems in the text panel

Setting to the left margin is the simpler setting arrangement. You will already have listed the line lengths. From this draw up a text panel wide enough to accommodate the majority of lines without turning over too many long lines:

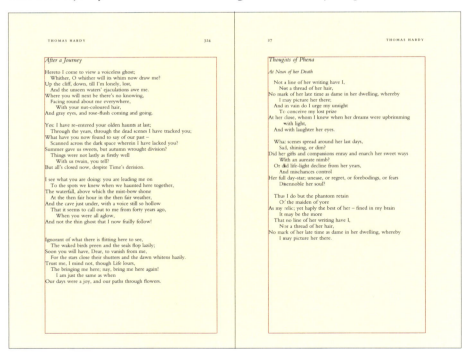

Many of the decisions you have to make in positioning the text panel will be based on aesthetic judgements – especially the balance between the printed and unprinted areas. And unlike the solid panels of continuous text, these values will also vary from spread to spread.

After you have flowed in all the poems review the position of the left-hand side of the text panels. If on average the lines of the poems are short then you may have to move the panel to the right to reduce the white spaces on the right side. Do this in your master pages and review the effect throughout the spreads of the layout.

In the example below with poems of short lines, the text panels are moved further to the right than the example opposite so as to achieve a better balance:

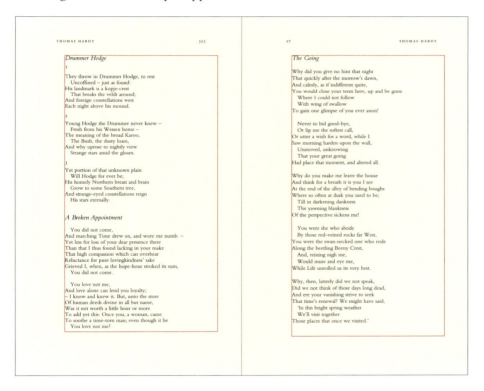

Rather than moving the text panel on individual pages, you may apply a left indent to each page's poems. This will maintain the text panel as it is in the master pages and allows any later changes to the master pages to take effect overall.

Visually centred setting requires that you place the poems one after another with a sufficient indent from the left edge of the panel to create the centred appearance on the page whatever the line lengths of the individual poems. This process is more time consuming than the ranged left setting. The exact value of the indented position of each poem is a matter for your judgement. Poems with shorter, even line lengths are easier to place than those with long and short lines:

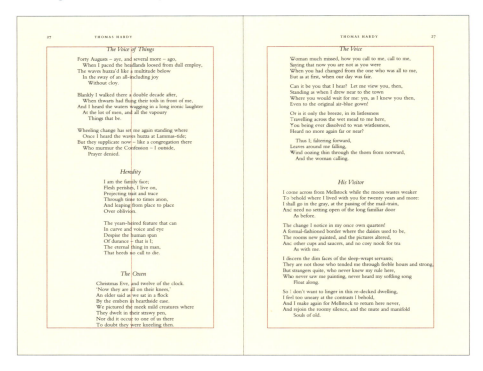

Positioning of poem titles, sub-titles and verse numbering

When the poems are set ranged left, the poems' titles will also be set ranged left. In a poem with short lines, a long title may look overpowering – turn over the title to make two lines.

When the poems are visually centred in the text panel the title is centre set. If you centre it in the text panel it may not appear to be centred on the poem because of the varying line lengths. A useful rule is to centre it to the longest line on the page. If there is more than one title on a page, they should be centred on the same axis.

If the verses of the poem are numbered, then set the numbers to match the setting position of the title – if ranged left, to the left, or centred if it is centred.

Frequently, a poem will have a sub-title – a quotation or a point of reference for its creation. Again, follow the positioning style of the title and if it is a long line – as it often is – turn it over to make two lines:

Drummer Hodge

1

They throw in Drummer Hodge, to rest
   Uncoffined – just as found:
His landmark is a kopje-crest
   That breaks the veldt around;
And foreign constellations west
   Each night above his mound.

2

Young Hodge the Drummer never knew –
   Fresh from his Wessex home –
The meaning of the broad Karoo,
   The Bush, the dusty loam,
And why uprose to nightly view
   Strange stars amid the gloam.

Harp Song of the Dane Women

("The Knights of the Joyous Venture"
   – Puck of Pook's Hill)

What is a woman that you forsake her,
And the hearth-fire and the home-acre,
To go with the old grey Widow-maker?

She has no house to lay a guest in –
But one chill bed for all to rest in,
That the pale suns and the stray bergs nest in.

She has no house to lay a guest in –
But one chill bed for all to rest in,
That the pale suns and the stray bergs nest in.

In academic publishing there may be a need to refer precisely to each line of poetry. These line numbers are then used as references for notes and discussion. There is no need to number each line; every 4th, 6th or 10th is sufficient. The figure is best placed 2 to 3 ems to the right, set in a size less than that of the text. Line '1' is not numbered.

I look into my glass,   237
And view my wasting skin,
And say, "Would God it came to pass
My heart had shrunk as thin!"

For then, I, undistrest   241
By hearts grown cold to me,
Could lonely wait my endless rest
With equanimity.

Whatever interval of numbering, it must be consistent throughout.

Running on poems

You will often need to run a poem onto a second or third page. Avoid dividing a verse: it is better to have a varying number of lines on a page. If the poem to be divided is on a recto, try to find a verse which does not end in a full point so that the reader does not think the poem has ended. On the occasions when a verse does end with a full point, an asterisk or dash may be used to signal a continuation.

Turning long lines

Whatever width of text panel you choose there will always be exceptionally long lines that will need turning over:

> Yes: I have re-entered your olden haunts at last;
>   Through the years, through the dead scenes I have tracked you;
> What have you now found to say of our past –
>   Scanned across the dark space wherein I have lacked you?
> Summer gave us sweets, but autumn wrought division?
>   Things were not lastly as firstly well
>   With us twain, you tell?
> But all's closed now, despite Time's derision.
>
> Yes: I have re-entered your olden haunts at last;
>   Through the years, through the dead scenes I have
>   tracked you;
> What have you now found to say of our past –
>   Scanned across the dark space wherein I have lacked
>   you?
> Summer gave us sweets, but autumn wrought division?
>   Things were not lastly as firstly well
>   With us twain, you tell?
> But all's closed now, despite Time's derision.

The turned-over words – 'tracked you;' and 'you?' – are indented to the right, further than the three indents already specified for the poem. This clearly indicates to the reader that these words are a continuation of the line above.

Word-spacing and typeface choices

Poems are not set justified and the word-spacing throughout should be perfectly even. Maintain equal spacing between all the words by setting the minimum, optimum and maximum to the same value.

See *Word-spacing in text composition* p.100

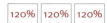

This ensures that long lines coming close to the right of the text panel are not fitted with a narrower word space which would contrast with lines above and below.

Typeface choices for poetry are an aesthetic judgement for you to make. Contemporary poetry can be set in contemporary fonts and sometimes in sans serif faces. Poems of earlier centuries are better suited to classical faces such as Garamond, Bembo or Fournier. Generous leading always enhances the appearance of poetry.

Dual-language poetry setting

Dual poetry texts, in which the language of the original and the English translation are printed within the same book, can be dealt with in three ways:

> the original below the translation, at the bottom of a page
> the original at the end of the book, as an appendix
> the original on the verso, opposite the translation

The last solution is attractive and educational, although some translators may feel uncomfortable with the direct comparison:

<table>
<tr><td>

VII

Otras canciones a lo divino
de Cristo y el alma.

Un pastorcico solo está penado,
Ajeno de placer y de contento,
Y en su pastora puesto el pensamiento,
Y el pecho del amor muy lastimado.

No llora por haberle amor llagado,
Que no le pena verse así afligido,
Aunque en el corazón está herido;
Mas llora por pensar que está olvidado.

Que sólo de pensar que está olvidado
De su bella pastora, con gran pena
Se deja maltratar en tierra ajena,
El pecho del amor muy lastimado.

</td><td>

VII

Other songs concerning Christ
and the soul

A shepherd lad was mourning his distress,
Far from all comfort, friendless and forlorn.
He fixed his thought upon his shepherdess
Because his breast by love was sorely torn.

He did not weep that love had pierced him so,
Nor with self-pity that the shaft was shot,
Though deep into his heart had sunk the blow,
It grieved him more that he had been forgot.

Only to think that he had been forgotten
By his sweet shepherdess, with travail sore,
He let his foes (in foreign lands begotten)
Gash the poor breast that love had gashed before.

</td></tr>
</table>

Trinité
The original in italic and the translation in roman.

The texts are usually provided in two separate documents, one for each language. If the layout is as above, it is best to keep them separate and draw up unlinked text boxes in the master pages, manually linking successive pages as the poems of each language are flowed in. If the texts are provided with alternate poems in both languages, then the text boxes can be automatically linked.

In prose translation English uses fewer words than most other languages. But with poetry, the English translation tends to use more words. Set the left-hand margin for the English text panel closer to the gutter to adjust the visual balance.

SETTING DUAL-LANGUAGE PROSE

In continuous prose, English uses fewer words than other languages. French will usually occupy five to seven per cent more and German seven to ten per cent more than English. Rarely will you be asked for a page-by-page dual setting but in that case the only way in which the fewer lines of English can be balanced with the other language is to increase the leading of the English text panel. In the case below the French is leaded 17 pt and the English 18.2 pt:

→ LA SALLE DE BAL →

La salle de bal, qui donne d'un côté sur le jardin, de l'autre sur la cour, est située dans la partie sud de l'hôtel, rajoutée en 1873 par un des fils du premier propriétaire. Elle servait à l'origine de galerie d'art. De nos jours, cette grande pièce accueille des réceptions et des cérémonies, telles que des remises de décorations, mais on y donne parfois des concerts sur le grand piano à queue qui trône près des fenêtres sur cour.

En face de la porte qui ouvre sur le Salon Jaune est accrochée la « Tapisserie de l'évanouissement d'Esther », une des trois magnifiques tapisseries des Gobelins exposées dans la salle de bal. Tissée en 1738 en laine et en soie, d'après le peintre d'histoire Jean-François de Troy, nommé depuis peu directeur de l'Académie de France à Rome, elle appartient à une série biblique composée de sept pièces représentant des scènes tirées du Livre d'Esther. Le thème avait été choisi par de Troy et approuvé par le duc d'Antin, Intendant des Bâtiments du Roi et donc des Manufactures. Les cartons, qui ont demandé à de Troy quatre années de travail, sont aujourd'hui conservés au Louvre.

La tapisserie de la Résidence met en scène le passage de l'Ancien Testament où la très belle Juive Esther, épouse du roi Assuérus (ou Xerxès) de Perse, tente de sauver ses coreligionnaires de l'extermination décidée par Aman, favori du roi. La reine se présente devant le roi et « tombe comme évanouie, la couleur de son teint se changeant en une pâleur ... ». Les autres tapisseries de la série représente « La Toilette d'Esther, Le Couronnement d'Esther, Le Dédain de Mardochée, Le Repas d'Esther, Le Triomphe de Mardochée et La Condamnation d'Aman ».

Le succès des cartons, exposé au Salon parisien en 1737, est immédiat, ce qui vaut à de Troy la commande d'une « Histoire de Jason ». La tenture d'Esther est mise sur le métier à la Manufacture des Gobelins en 1738. Entre cette date et 1797, cent tapisseries sont exécutées, la majorité d'entre elles tissées en haute lisse, en laine et soie. Celle de la Résidence, comme toutes celles qui sont tissées jusqu'en 1768, a une bordure représentant un cadre en bois sculpté et doré, orné de coquilles et de guirlandes de fleurs, avec fleurs de lys et cartouches aux armes de France. Ce modèle de bordure est l'oeuvre de Pierre-Josse Perrot.

La première tenture en sept pièces est livrée en 1744 au Garde-Meuble de la Couronne pour être accrochée ensuite au Château de Versailles, dans les appartements de la nouvelle Dauphine, fille de Philippe V d'Espagne. Elle reste à Versailles jusqu'à la Révolution, mais heureusement n'est pas vendue pendant la grande vente du mobilier du château qui entraîne la dispersion de tant de magnifiques oeuvres d'art. Quatre tapisseries de la série sont conservées au Château de Compiègne depuis le Second Empire. Une tenture complète, tissée nettement plus tard, se trouve aujourd'hui au Château de Windsor.

Dans l'autre partie de la salle de bal sont accrochées deux grandes tapisseries en laine et soie, également tissées à la Manufacture des Gobelins, entre 1675 et 1681, d'après des dessins de Charles Le Brun. Elles appartiennent à la série des « Mois », dite aussi des « Maisons royales », une des plus célèbres tentures du règne de Louis XIV.

→ THE BALL ROOM →

The long Ballroom runs the whole depth of the house, from the garden to the courtyard, and occupies the one-storey extension added to the south side in 1873 for José de Murrietta, which originally housed an art gallery as well as a ballroom. It is now used for receptions and concerts – a large grand piano dominates the courtyard end of the room.

It is entered from the Yellow Drawing-Room and is divided into two halves by an archway. Opposite the entrance hangs one of three important Gobelins tapestries displayed in this room. This one, woven in 1738, was designed by Jean-François de Troy, a leading history painter who had just been appointed director of the French Academy in Rome. It depicts an Old Testament episode, taken from the Book of Esther, in which the beautiful young Esther, wife of King Ahasuerus of Persia, falls down at the king's feet as she pleads with him to save her fellow Jews from Haman the Agagite's plan to exterminate them.

The tapestry is one of a series designed by de Troy with scenes from The Book of Esther. It seems that the subject-matter was his own choice and that his sketches were approved by the Duc d'Antin, the Royal Buildings Intendant, who was in charge of all the royal workshops. He then spent four years painting the cartoons, which showed, as well as the scene in the Residence, Esther getting dressed in her royal apparel before pleading with the king; the king setting the crown on Esther's head; her adopted father Mordecai being treated with scorn; Esther feasting; Mordecai's triumph; and Haman being condemned. These cartoons are now in the Louvre. The paintings were much admired and their success led to de Troy being commissioned to work on a series of episodes from the story of Jason and the Golden Fleece. The Gobelins workshop started weaving the first Esther tapestry in 1738 and continued producing the series over a long period, right down to 1797. Altogether a hundred tapestries were produced, in silk and wool, the earlier ones, like the one in the Residence, set within a frame designed by Pierre-Josse Perrot to imitate a carved wooden picture frame, decorated with shells and garlands of flowers and France's coat of arms. The later models, made after 1768, had a different frame, this time designed by Maurice Jacques.

The Residence's tapestry was part of that first series, which was delivered in 1744 to the Royal Furniture Repository and was subsequently hung at Versailles, in the first-floor rooms occupied by the new Dauphine, the daughter of Philip V of Spain. The tapestries stayed at Versailles until the French Revolution, but were not auctioned off four years later, as so many of the palace's furnishings were. Four others in the series are now in the Château de Compiègne. A complete set, woven considerably later, hangs at Windsor Castle.

Two more large Gobelins tapestries are displayed in the other half of the ballroom. They were designed by Mr

Text setting in multilingual co-editions

Origination includes all those processes up to the point of printing. The work of authors, editors, illustrators, designers, photographers, typesetters and proof readers.

It is common practice for publishers from several countries to co-operate in the production of illustrated books in order to share the high cost of their *origination* and printing. Layout of a co-edition book is done by the designer of the publishing house which is organizing the edition. The four-colour pictures are printed with the normal set of four colour plates – cyan, magenta, yellow and black. An additional fifth black plate is used to print the text. This fifth plate is changed for each language. A large number of copies are printed with successive changes of the fifth plate as each language edition is produced. Considerable economies of scale are achieved doing this. There are two ways in which you may be involved in a multilingual co-edition. If you are the originating designer, working in English, you must design a text panel and type size that leaves sufficient space to accommodate the other 'longer' languages. This is not a difficult task as texts in most illustrated books are limited to short introductory essays and captions. You send the completed layout to the other publishers' designers so their text can be fitted into it. Alternatively you may be sent a layout to fit the English text into. In either case the position of the pictures must not be changed.

See *Co-editions* p.300

If you have set the English text in your layout and are then supplied with the foreign languages to fit, you must depend completely on the supplied text. Unless you are fluent in a language, do not be tempted to make corrections.

Marked-up corrections are the only guide you should use.

There are foreign usages which do not follow English usage, for example:

In French a space is placed before the punctuation marks , ; :

> *L'italique , en général , est plus mince que le romain.*

and quotation marks are rendered with *guillemets* – chevrons – with a space:

> « Je ne les estime la valeur d'un poil. »

In German, unfamiliar ligatures also are used:

> The double 'ss' has a ligature – *eszett* – form ß as in schloß for schloss.

Accents and special sorts

Accents

The English language does not use accents but within English texts words with accented letters will occur. Their presence affects the word's pronunciation in the original language. These accents must be reproduced. This is especially true for individual's names – without the accents you are not respecting the person.

> Senor Jose Marias *is not the same person as* Señor José Marías

Many accents do not transfer from word-processing programs to typesetting programs and this can make it difficult to ensure they are in place and accurate. Once the text is flowed into the layout, careful page-by-page checking is needed to find the words and add the correct accents.

See *Preparing text for setting* p.378

English language keyboards do not offer accented characters in a single keystroke. They have to be made by using two keystrokes. The first, known as a *dead key-stroke* is usually made by pressing two keys successively. This instructs the creation of the accent but it will not appear on screen until the character you wish to accent is pressed. For example, in most keyboards if you wish to make an 'e grave', you will hold the alt or option key down and then key in `. Release these keys and press the 'e' and è will be created. Keyboards are supplied with a list of keystrokes for each accent and the automatic creation of these combined characters. Occasionally a typeface will not have a full set of accents; you should check this when you buy it.

Some programs allow you to choose from a menu of special characters.

The normal range of European accents available on the keyboard with a dead keystroke sequence is shown below:

à	À	a acute	ï	Ï	i diaeresis
á	Á	a grave	ñ	Ñ	n tilde
â	Â	a circumflex	õ	Õ	o tilde
ä	Ä	a diaeresis	ø	Ø	o slashed
ã	Ã	a tilde	ó	Ó	o acute
å	Å	a angstrom	ò	Ò	o grave
ç	Ç	c cedilla	ô	Ô	o circumflex
é	É	e acute	ö	Ö	o diaeresis
è	È	e grave	õ	Õ	o tilde
ê	Ê	e circumflex	ü	Ü	u umlaut
ë	Ë	e diaeresis	ú	Ú	u acute
í	Î	i acute	ù	Ù	u grave
ì	Ì	i grave	û	Û	u circumflex
î	Î	i circumflex	ÿ	Ÿ	y diaeresis

Accents may also be referred to as *diacritics*.

Other accents may be found in the keyboard layout but will not combine automatically with the character. They have to be placed using kerning:

ˇ – a *breve* – can be made by tracking back the character until it is over the accent:
ˇa tracked back -120 ICS to form ă or ˇg ğ
^ – a *caron* – is also made in this way: ^a â or ^s ŝ

The editor should forewarn you if unusual special accents are needed.

If you are setting a text which contains many accented characters that cannot be made on the keyboard or by combining accents and characters it may be necessary to search out and buy a specialist font family. Alternatively these extra characters can be drawn for a particular font in a font drawing program, but this is time-consuming and expensive.

Special sorts

This phrase refers to symbols and signs, other than routine English punctuation marks, that are available on the keyboard for specific purposes. Less frequently used punctuation marks, such as additional paragraph marks, are directly available on the keyboard:

† ¶ ‡ §† which vary in design from font to font.
These † ¶ ‡ §† are in Caslon and these † ¶ ‡ § † in Quadraat

or mathematical signs such as: ° ¬ μ π √ ∞ ≠ ≤ ≥ ÷

or frequently used trade symbols ® ™ ©

Each typeface family will have special sorts that may differ from those above and some may not have an entire range.

Special fonts with wider ranges of symbols are also available but seldom find an application in bookwork:

⊗ ⊘ ▢ 🚌 🚲 ! ✈ ◪ ✔ ? ♥ 🚑 📠 ⊸ () ⌠ 🏛 ✗ 🏔 ⊖ 📮 ⓘ ⊸ 🚂 💬 ‖ ✚ ✹ ⊸   Webdings

Non-Latin alphabets

Typesetting in languages such as Hebrew, Japanese and Greek which use non-Latin alphabets is a specialist field and is not dealt with here. Odd phrases in non-Latin languages may occasionally be required within a text. In European literature Greek names or phrases will occur:

Non-Latin fonts are available but may require additional software to allow the keyboard to function correctly with them.

Apollodorus (Ἀπολλόδωρος) said 'You couldn't have asked anyone better.'

If you have an appropriate Greek font use that. Or you may be supplied with the words as bitmapped artwork to be dropped into a space in the text setting, as in the example above.

PROGRESSIVE FORMATS

In trade publishing, many books are not just published once. They are re-issued later in different formats – smaller and cheaper – to maximize sales. The same setting, reduced in size, is used in the later formats. As the editing and origination has already been done, these subsequent versions are cheaper to produce. When designing a book, it is crucial to know at the outset what plans there are for future format changes as this will affect your decisions about the text panel.

The successive formats of a book will be something like this:

1   Royal hardback, 234 × 153 mm – this is how the first edition appears
2   Royal paperback, 234 × 153 mm – issued with or after the hardback
3   B-format paperback, 198 × 129 mm – the most common paperback size
4   A-format paperback, 178 × 111 mm – the cheapest mass-market edition

These are just examples, each publishing house will have its own system.

Seen to scale, these three different page sizes look like this:

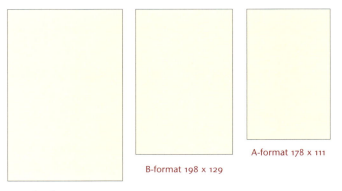

A-format 178 x 111

B-format 198 x 129

Royal 234 x 153

The proportions of the Royal and the B-format are very similar. The width of the B-format is 85 per cent that of the Royal and the height is 84 per cent.

The A-format is proportionally narrower. The width of the A-format is 73 per cent that of the Royal, and the height is 76 per cent.

Reducing the text panel

Taking a text panel from a Royal, for example, and placing it on a page which is 85 per cent of the width and height, does not necessarily result in the text being 85 per cent of the size. If the Royal has been set with generous margins these may be reduced allowing for a proportionately bigger text panel in the reduced formats:

Royal with text panel
at 100%

The text panel on this Royal spread could be reduced to 90 per cent, and fitted onto a B-format page with smaller margins. The A-format reduction here is 82 per cent:

A-format with text panel at 82%

B-format with text panel at 90%

When producing grids for the smaller format pages it is important not to reduce the gutter margin by too much or the text panel will become hard to read. This may mean compromising the relative proportions of the margins, but it is better to do this than to reduce the type to an illegible size. When designing the text panel for the first edition, it is useful to produce trials of the subsequent reductions so any potential problems can be sorted out at an early stage.

The effect of reducing type

The following samples show the same setting reduced to 95 per cent, 90 per cent, 85 per cent, 80 per cent and 75 per cent:

100%   room so as not to be seen for what he is, get the books out of the laundry basket at least, how are you going to explain to Julie what John of the Cross is doing amid the dirty socks? Get them out

95%   room so as not to be seen for what he is, get the books out of the laundry basket at least, how are you going to explain to Julie what John of the Cross is doing amid the dirty socks? Get them out

90%   room so as not to be seen for what he is, get the books out of the laundry basket at least, how are you going to explain to Julie what John of the Cross is doing amid the dirty socks? Get them out

85%   room so as not to be seen for what he is, get the books out of the laundry basket at least, how are you going to explain to Julie what John of the Cross is doing amid the dirty socks? Get them out

80%   room so as not to be seen for what he is, get the books out of the laundry basket at least, how are you going to explain to Julie what John of the Cross is doing amid the dirty socks? Get them out

75%   room so as not to be seen for what he is, get the books out of the laundry basket at least, how are you going to explain to Julie what John of the Cross is doing amid the dirty socks? Get them out

Choice of typeface is important in this circumstance: if the font is too dark the smaller panels will look dense, too light and they will look weak and spindly.

Typefaces which work well at small sizes have a large x-height and medium colour. They should be set with plenty of leading.

REFERENCE WORKS

Reference books function in a different way to narrative books. Rather than reading the text straight through from beginning to end, the reader wants to quickly locate and read individual entries as needed. The approach to designing a reference book, or a reference section within a book, is therefore slightly different.

Navigation

Typographic devices which aid *navigation* are of particular importance in reference books. Headings, sub-headings, running heads (or feet) and folios, as well as a contents page and index will help direct the reader through the text.

Indexes and contents pages

The index may be the most used part of a reference book. Entries should be clearly laid out and at a legible type size. It is helpful to use a semi-bold font to indicate the main entry for a subject. For readers who are less sure as to what they are looking for, a detailed contents page will be their first stop. The editor should decide which levels of heading to include here.

See *Indexes*, pp.194–7 and *The contents page*, pp.181–5

Headings and sub-headings

Readers scanning the pages need to see headings quickly. Avoid using display typefaces of poor legibility. If there is more than one level of heading, set the most frequently used level in the most legible form of type – usually roman, upper and lower case.

See *Sub-headings*, pp.126–41

If a second colour is available, using it for headings will help them stand out from the text. It will aid the reader even further if you can hang headings into the margin.

Folios and running heads

Placing the folio and the running head close together helps the reader to see them both as they flick through the pages. Place them at the fore-edge of the page.

See *Folios and running heads*, pp.200–7

Multi-column layouts

The word *gutter* can mean the space between columns, not to be confused with the *gutter margin*.

Minion, 10 pt
Gutter: 2 mm

Extensive reference works will often be set in a small type size using a multiple-column layout. This does not adversely affect the function of the text as it is not to be read continuously for long periods.

Multi-column layouts – usually two, three or four columns – work best on wide pages. The *gutter* between columns should be narrower than the margins – the text panel should still look like one block – but should be wide enough to prevent the eye from jumping from one column to the next:

3000–2900 BCE. The figures of the Egyptian number-system appear (see Chapter 14).

2700 BCE [W]. The cuneiform characters (in the form of angles and wedges) of the Sumerian writing system appear on their clay tablets (see Chapter 8). The Semites of Mesopotamia borrow the cuneiform the Sumerian number-system appear (see Chapter 8).

2700–2300 BCE. For doing arithmetic, the people of Sumer now abandon their old calculi and invent their abacus, a kind of table of successive columns, ruled beforehand, which delimit the successive orders of magnitude of their sexagesimal number-system. By clever manipulation of small balls or rods on the abacus, they are able to perform all sorts of calculations.

2600–2500 BCE. Egyptian hieratic writing appears, a cursive abbreviation of hieroglyphic writing and used alongside the latter for the sake of rapid writing on manuscripts (see

3000–2900 BCE. The figures of the Egyptian number-system appear (see Chapter 14).

2700 BCE [W]. The cuneiform characters (in the form of angles and wedges) of the Sumerian writing system appear on their clay tablets (see Chapter 8). The Semites of Mesopotamia borrow the cuneiform the Sumerian number-system appear (see Chapter 8).

2700–2300 BCE. For doing arithmetic, the people of Sumer now abandon their old calculi and invent their abacus, a kind of table of successive columns, ruled beforehand, which delimit the successive orders of magnitude of their sexagesimal number-system. By clever manipulation of small balls or rods on the abacus, they are able to perform all sorts of calculations.

2600–2500 BCE. Egyptian hieratic writing appears, a cursive abbreviation of hieroglyphic writing and used alongside the latter for the sake of rapid writing on manuscripts (see

Minion, 10 pt
Gutter: 3.5 mm

Type style

Headwords at the beginning of entries are best highlighted in semi-bold (as above). This is effective in alphabetical and chronological lists. A space dividing entries will make it clear to the reader how much they have to read and help draw the eye to the beginning of the entry. If abbreviations are used, they should be explained in a prominent position at the start of the text.

MULTI-VOLUME WORKS

Works that are too large to be published in a single volume are divided into two or more volumes. These are by nature complicated works and the division of the content and the order of the prelims and endmatter will be tailored by the editor to suit the needs of each work. The following serves only as a guide.

The convention is that works which are to be published and sold separately are treated as single-volume books, paginated from one, and each with its own contents page and index. A list of the other volumes should appear in the prelims.

Works sold as sets

Pagination

If a multi-volume work is to be sold only as a set, the volumes may be paginated separately or consecutively. If the former, cross-references will need to include a volume number as well as the page number. In the latter case volume numbers are not necessary but will be an aid to the reader.

In volumes with consecutive pagination, only the arabic numbering is carried through all the volumes, always starting with an odd number on a recto page. The prelims, using roman numerals, start from i in each volume.

Prelims and endmatter

The half-title and title page are repeated in each volume and should include the volume number.

It is useful to the reader if volume 1 contains a full list of contents for all volumes. Contents pages in subsequent volumes need only contain a list of what is in that volume. Each volume should have its own list of illustrations.

Those parts of the book which aid the reader, such as the glossary and list of abbreviations are best repeated in each volume.

The index appears in the final volume. The first page reference for each volume should include the volume number:

> 1.19, 27–8, 95; 2.481, 520

TABLES

There are three ways of placing tables in a book. The first is to put them together at the back in the form of an appendix. The second is to place them as you would illustrations, as close as possible to the reference in the text with a figure number and a caption. The third is to treat them as part of the text, following on from the paragraph above. The editor and author will decide which of these methods to use and should instruct the designer accordingly.

When setting tables you should ask the editor for a hard copy of the table's content showing how the columns and rows are to align. Formatting can be lost in the translation from word-processing document to layout program.

Column width

The width of the columns is determined by the longest entries. Ideally there should be consistency in column width where content is similar. Where column width varies it should be by a significant amount:

In this table each column is a different width depending on the content of the column. The column on the far right is very wide just to accommodate one entry.

date BC	zone	climate phase	climate	vegetation
c.14000	Ia	Oldest Dryas	cold	tundra
	Ib	Bolling interstadial	warmer	
	Ic	Older Dryas	readvances of ice	
c.12000	II	Allerod interstadial	warmer	birch and pine woodland
c.10000	III	Younger Dryas		tundra

In this table the two columns on the left are the same width and the three columns on the right are the same width. The long entry on the right has been turned onto a second line.

date BC	zone	climate phase	climate	vegetation
c.14000	Ia	Oldest Dryas	cold	tundra
	Ib	Bolling interstadial	warmer	
	Ic	Older Dryas	readvances of ice	
c.12000	II	Allerod interstadial	warmer	birch and pine woodland
c.10000	III	Younger Dryas		tundra

It will be necessary at times to turn over long entries onto a second and third line. This can be indicated by indenting the extra lines or by using space between entries to make clear where each begins:

(Mesolithic) increase of alder	(Mesolithic) increase of alder
(first farmers c.1500) Early	(first farmers c.1500) Early
Neolithic forest clearance –	Neolithic forest clearance – elm
elm decline	decline
Increase of ash and birch (late	Increase of ash and birch (late
Neolithic – early Bronze Age)	Neolithic – early Bronze Age)
Increase of ash, birch,	Increase of ash, birch,
hornbeam and beech; decline	hornbeam and beech; decline
of lime (middle and late	of lime (middle and late
Bronze Age)	Bronze Age)
(Iron Age) birch and beech	(Iron Age) birch and beech
more prominent	more prominent

Formata light
8.5 on 11 pt

Type size

The problem most frequently encountered when setting tables is that of lack of space. It is important to remember that text set within a table should obey the same principles of legibility and function as other text. Tables often have a practical use and need to be referred to quickly. Using type that is too small, setting content at odd angles or distorting the typeface itself will make the table unusable.

A better solution is to set your tables in a different typeface to the text, giving you the opportunity to find an economic typeface, legible at smaller sizes. A complimentary sans serif will clearly distinguish between body text and table. Sans serifs with large x-heights are suitable for setting within tables. Choose one that is not too light so that it will permit reduction. A little inter-character spacing may be necessary to aid legibility at small sizes:

Stone sans	Formata	Scala sans	Quadraat sans	7 pt, 0 ICS
Stone sans	Formata	Scala sans	Quadraat sans	7 pt, 5 ICS

Rules

Most tables are laid out with rules to divide up the columns and rows. External rules (those which define the edge of the table) should be heavier than internal rules (those inside the table).

Using rules to divide every single element is unnecessary and looks too busy:

DATE	SYSTEM	CLASS	TYPE
−200	Learned Chinese	C	1
−180	Hebraic alphabetic	A	3
−150	Nabataean	B	1
+100	Khatraean	B	1
+100	Palmyrenean	B	1
+270	Coptic alphabetic (Egypt)	A	3
+292	Maya (long form of dates)	B	5

Use the minimum number of rules necessary to make the structure clear:

DATE	SYSTEM	CLASS	TYPE
−200	Learned Chinese	C	1
−180	Hebraic alphabetic	A	3
−150	Nabataean	B	1
+100	Khatraean	B	1
+100	Palmyrenean	B	1
+270	Coptic alphabetic (Egypt)	A	3
+292	Maya (long form of dates)	B	5

Vertical rules are not usually used except in very complex tables.

Extensive tables

Where a table runs onto a second page, the column widths should be the same on both pages. The rule at the foot of the first page should be omitted to show the table has not finished. On the second page the headings are repeated.

Where a table appears by itself on a page, it may be rotated 90° if this shape is more suitable for the page.

Chronologies

Biographies and histories will sometimes feature a chronology, listing significant points in a person's life, or the key events in a particular period of history, alongside lists of other world events that were happening contemporaneously.

The first column contains the dates and the second column contains the events that are relevant to your particular book. Subsequent columns may include local or international events or cultural landmarks.

The events for each year are listed chronologically, separated by full points. Remember to use italics for titles where appropriate. Using a line space or half a line space between years will help the reader:

	Gillray's life	Home affairs	International news
1784	Published *Love in a Coffin*, 30 December.	Dissolution of Parliament. Fox re-elected for constituency of Westminster in the March General Election. Pitt is made prime minister.	
1785		George, Prince of Wales, marries Mrs Fitzherbert.	In Paris, Jacques-Louis David exhibits *Oath of the Horatii*.
1786	Resumes satirical work. Published primarily by William Holland and Samuel W. Fores.	Edmund Burke (1729–97) introduces an impeachment process against Warren Hastings (1732–1818) of the East India Company after concern about the moral standards of the British in India are raised.	
1787	Publishes *Ancient Music*, 10 May, and *Monstrous Craws*, 29 May.		Anglo-French commercial treaty.
1788		George III's madness is announced provoking a political storm. Fox conspires with the Prince of Wales to establish a Regency. Hastings sent to trial before the House of Lords.	

If the chronology runs onto further pages, the headings for each column should be repeated at the top of each page.

SETTING TEXT FOR SPECIAL NEEDS

Setting text for dyslexic readers

The requirements of text setting are different for people who find reading difficult. The emphasis is on legibility – making words easier to decipher – rather than readability – encouraging speed and rhythm.

Further information on this subject is available from the British Dyslexia Association.

Dyslexic readers have to concentrate harder to comprehend and remember what they have read. Any design element that disturbs concentration will make the reading process more difficult. The following guidelines can aid legibility for dyslexic readers.

Choice of fonts

A rounded font will be easier to read for longer periods.

Characters should not be very close together. Add a little ICS if the fit is tight.

Avoid fonts which have a marked contrast between the thick and thin strokes, and those which contain unusually formed characters.

Type style

Type should be set in a size which gives an x-height of at least 2 mm.

When highlighting words, a bold font – with sufficient letter-spacing – is preferable to an italic font which can appear to run characters together. Do not set whole words in capitals.

Sufficient leading is vital to legibility. Use a leading of about double the type size.

Paper

If too much glare comes off the printed surface it will be difficult to read. Use lightly-coloured or off-white papers rather than white, with a matt finish. The paper should be heavy enough not to allow show-through.

Layout

Keep lines to about 60 to 70 characters and set them ranged left. The slightly uneven word-spacing of justified text can lead to the appearance of rivers of white space flowing down the page which will distract the reader. Margins should be wide.

Avoid large blocks of dense text. Set short paragraphs separated by line spaces. Try to avoid starting a new sentence at the end of a line. Do not divide words between lines.

Boxes can be used to highlight certain words. Do not reverse-out text or surround it with complicated graphics.

Stone Sans medium with semi-bold highlights 12 on 24 pt

In 1772, Robert and James Adam planned a street northwest of Chandos House which was named after the Lord Chief Justice, the Earl of Mansfield.

The Adam style has many details that recall **Ancient Rome**. Ancient buildings had columns thought to have derived from bundles of reeds.

The capitals on top of the columns are decorated with anthemion, a Roman and Greek version of honeysuckle flowers. Rams were offered as sacrifices to Roman gods. **Husk swags**, garlands made of dead seeds and **florettes**, single flowers, were popular Roman decorations.

Setting text for partially sighted readers

Further information on this subject is available from the Royal National Institute for the Blind.

Setting text for partially sighted readers is not a simple matter of making it bigger. Reading can be a slower process for those whose vision is impaired, so rather than setting type in a way that encourages speed and rhythm, emphasis is on clarity, of both letterforms and text structure.

Choice of fonts

Choose fonts which are of a heavier weight: some readers even prefer the semi-bold forms. Sans serifs will look clearer.

Avoid fonts which have a lot of contrast between the thick and thin strokes, and those which contain unusually-formed characters.

Use bold for emphasis, rather than italics or capitals.

Type size and leading

Type should be set in a size which gives an x-height of between 2 mm and 4 mm. 'Large type' books are usually set at a type size between 16 pt and 22 pt.

Leading should be 1.5 to 2 times the type size.

Contrast

Black type on a white background provides the best contrast for partially sighted readers, but avoid glossy papers that will produce a glare. Type may be reversed out if the background is flat and dark, but do not lay text over illustrations.

Paper should be heavy enough to avoid show-through.

Line length

Lines should be approximately 60 to 70 characters long. Paragraphs should be kept reasonably short and be separated by line spaces.

Alignment

Text should be set ranged left with even word-spacing. Do not divide words between lines.

Do not run type around illustrations or set it vertically.

If setting in columns, make sure there is sufficient space between the columns. If space is limited use a vertical rule.

Aids to navigation

Place headings and folios in the same position on each page. Give an indication, such as a rule, to show where each section ends. A list of contents at the start will be useful.

Univers 55
15 on 26 pt

The Adam Style

The Adam style has many details that recall Ancient Rome. Ancient buildings had columns thought to have derived from bundles of reeds.

The capitals on top of the columns are decorated with anthemion, a Roman and Greek version of honeysuckle flowers. Rams were offered as sacrifices to Roman gods. Husk swags, garlands and florettes, single flowers, were popular Roman decorations.

PART FOURTEEN
BINDING, COVERS AND JACKETS

BINDING

The intricacies of the mechanics of binding are complex and it is not the purpose of this section to deal with all of these. Binding styles are described here in order to understand the way in which they affect jacket and cover layout.

Hard-bound books

In the traditional hand-made method the gathered signatures are individually sewn, then sewn together, and lightly glued. The joined signatures – the *book block* – are then beaten to produce a rounded spine shape. The threads are incorporated into a coarse muslin sheet overhanging the spine of the signatures; strips of stronger linen are then glued onto the muslin.

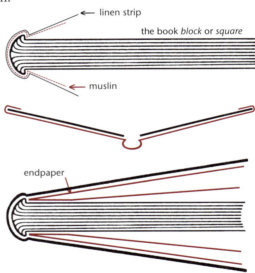

The two boards that will make up the outer case of the book are glued to the cloth covering and a spine is created.

The muslin and linen strips of the joined signatures are glued onto the boards. Any foil blocking on the spine or front board is done before the book block is fixed in.

The endpaper can be of a coloured paper or a colour-printed paper to add appeal to the book's appearance.

To cover the linen strips and further fix the signatures to the boards, a folded sheet of paper, the *endpaper*, is glued to the board and a portion of the first sheet of the text. The endpaper may also be referred to as the *flypaper*.

Case-bound books

In cased books the endpaper is potentially the weakest link in the binding. Choose a strong paper.

Hand-binding is an expensive process. In the mass production of hard-bound books the linen/muslin attachments are replaced by a fibrous strip and the sewn signatures glued to the boards by the endpaper; a mechanically weaker solution. A book bound in this way is referred to as *case-bound*. The finished book may be *flat-backed* or *round-backed* – the latter will maintain shape longer in use.

Spine and front board blocking

The decorative impressing of a foil design and text on the spine, less frequently on the front board, is an essential part of hardback books. It enables identification if the jacket is discarded – through wear or by preference. The texts and logos used in the design of the spine of the jacket usually form the basis of the design which is supplied to the binder as artwork. The quality of the blocking effect depends on the smoothness of the cloth. Fine typefaces should be avoided.

Foil blocking is a process in which a metallic foil is impressed into the binding cloth. A gold or silver foil is usually used though other colours are available.

Paperback books

There are two principal methods of binding a paperback book, *perfect binding* and *sewn and drawn-on binding,* often referred to as *limp-sewn*:

Perfect binding: the gathered signatures are not sewn, but glued directly into the folded cover. The signatures have grooves cut into them to allow the glue to penetrate the individual sheets. The mechanical stability of this least costly binding mechanism is limited and is usually reserved for light works that are not likely to be re-read often.

The cuts made into the paper and the subsequent gluing reduce the gutter margins. The text panel designed for a book to be bound in this way, should have a wider gutter margin to enable the reader to read along the text lines without bending the book back and breaking the glued signatures and spine.

text panel

Sewn and drawn-on binding is a mechanically sounder binding for paperbacks. Signatures are individually sewn and then sewn together, usually in a single process. The creased and folded cover is glued and pulled onto the book block creating a stronger bond than perfect binding. To increase the bond, the book is subjected to pressure along the spine; this produces a compression along the spine which extends for 5 mm and renders a completely flat opening of the book impossible. Allowance must be made in the gutter margin for this. Where a *simultaneous* hardback and paperback edition is planned, bear this effect in mind in planning margins.

A compromise is made for simultaneous editions in which the margin of the paperback is a little less than ideal but reduces what would be an excessive margin in the hardback.

COVERS AND JACKETS

The jacket may be referred to as the *dust jacket* or *wrapper*

A jacket is the printed paper that wraps round a hard-bound book, whereas a cover is the outer card cover of a paperback book.

Cover components

There are two distinct styles of paperback cover.
A *flush paperback* where the cover is trimmed to the page size:

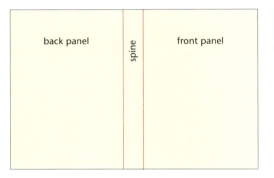

flush paperback

A *flapped paperback* where the cover has flaps, the folded cover extending 1–2 mm over the fore-edge of the trimmed pages; only the head and foot of the cover is trimmed flush to the page depth:

flapped paperback

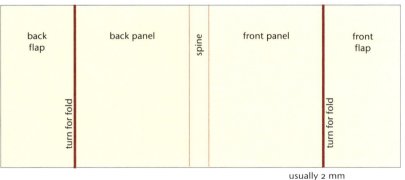

usually 2 mm

Cover dimensions and layout

The depth of the cover panels of both styles is that of the trimmed page depth. For a flush paperback the front panel width is that of the trimmed page. The binder will supply a figure for the spine bulk when the extent is known.

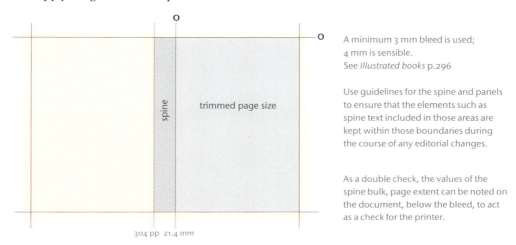

spine

trimmed page size

304 pp 21.4 mm

A minimum 3 mm bleed is used; 4 mm is sensible.
See *Illustrated books* p.296

Use guidelines for the spine and panels to ensure that the elements such as spine text included in those areas are kept within those boundaries during the course of any editorial changes.

As a double check, the values of the spine bulk, page extent can be noted on the document, below the bleed, to act as a check for the printer.

There may be many changes to the cover design and the spine bulk before layout is finalized. To make it easier to increase or decrease the spine bulk, set the axes of the document vertically to the left margin of the front panel and horizontally to the head. If changes are made to the spine bulk, only the components on the left of the front panel have to be moved; the remainder is constant.

The folded cover of a flapped paperback extends over the trimmed fore-edge. The width available for the flaps and the fold *turn* value are obtained from the printer.

The size of printer's presses may impose a limit on the width of the flaps. Check this with the printer.

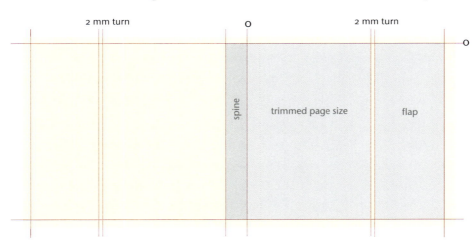

2 mm turn

2 mm turn

spine

trimmed page size

flap

Jacket components

The components of a jacket are called the *front flap, front panel, spine, back panel* and *back flap*. The element between the panels and the flaps that wraps around the hardback binding board is known as the *turn* or *run-round*.

The signatures when sewn and glued together before binding are referred to as the *book block* or *square*.

When the jacket is wrapped round the binding board, the turn runs from the front edge of the board to the book block of the pages.

back flap	back panel	spine	front panel	front flap
	back turn		front turn	

Jacket dimensions and layout

The binder will supply the dimensions of the bound book based on the trimmed page size. The front and back boards usually overlap the trimmed page by 3 mm at the head and foot and 4 mm at the fore-edge. If the trimmed page size is 234 × 156 mm, the back and front panels are drawn up to 240 mm (234 + 6 mm) by 160 mm (156 + 4 mm). The width or *bulk* of the spine is calculated by the thickness of the paper stock plus the thickness of the two boards making up the case.

As soon as the paper stock is chosen, ask the printer for a *dummy* – a book made up of sheets of the paper bound exactly as the final printed book will be. This will allow you to check the binding dimensions.

The flaps should be wide enough to accommodate the text legibly. Consult with the printer at an early point and ask for the limit of the flap width and advice on the width of the turns. These depend on the presses and paper sizes. The printer will supply a figure for the spine bulk. There will be different values for round-backed and flat-backed binding styles. Tables of values of paper bulk exist but it is always safer to confirm bulk and binding style with the printer and ask for a dummy.

The complete jacket layout will appear like this:

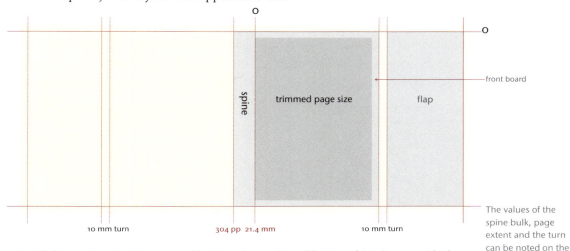

spine

trimmed page size

flap

front board

10 mm turn

304 pp 21.4 mm

10 mm turn

As with the cover layout, minimum 3 mm bleed is used; 4 mm is sensible. It is useful to draw up guides for the spine and panels to ensure that the elements such as flap text included in those areas are kept within these boundaries during the course of any editorial changes. The axes of the layout are placed vertically to the left margin of the front panel and horizontally to the head.

The values of the spine bulk, page extent and the turn can be noted on the document, below the bleed, to act as a check for the proof-reader, printer and yourself.

You may find it easier to lay the jacket out in three separate components:

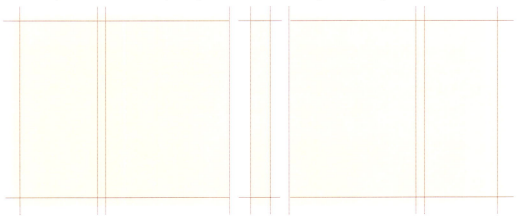

If you do this, you are leaving it to the repro section of the printers to combine them. Passing on that task will still leave you with the responsibility of checking the complete jacket at proof stage – and it is not easy to measure the printer's proof accurately. It is very difficult, if not impossible, to make this method work when a jacket image occupies the front and back panels and the spine.

Jacket front panel and flap layout

In laying out the front panel and flap the effect of wrapping a printed paper around the book has to be taken into account. To compensate for the inevitable outward spring of wrapper to the fore-edge, text should be set 3 mm to the right if it is to be visually centred in the front panel. On the back panel, that movement is to the left.

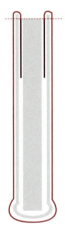

Any solid colour or illustration on the front or back panels should occupy the turn area as well as the panels.

When the book is closed no part of the flap, shown in black, should show.

turn

French-fold jackets

A French-fold jacket is made by extending the printed area at the head and foot by 80 to 100 mm. After trimming, the jacket is folded to the vertical dimensions of the book giving a double layer of paper at the head and foot. This makes the jacket less prone to damage at the head and foot when handled.

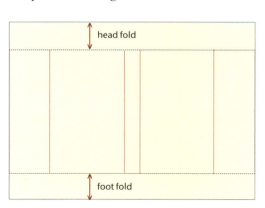

head fold

foot fold

The final folding and fitting of the jacket is done by hand. It is usually reserved for expensive large format illustrated books.

The folded jacket in cross section

Printed cases

As an alternative to a jacket for a hard-bound book, a printed sheet can be used to cover the boards and spine of the case. This is referred to as a *printed case*. This technique is frequently used in the production of books for children where a jacket is often lost or destroyed.

Any image or design to be used on the sheet should exceed the dimensions of the case by at least 15 mm. The binder trims the sheet to the edge of the image before fixing it to the boards.

Then the paper is glued onto the whole case; the overlapping portion is wrapped round the board. When the endpaper is glued onto the inner boards, only 3 to 4 mm of the image is left and shows on the inside of the boards.

Jacket and cover finishes

The printed jacket or cover must be sealed and then laminated to protect it in the bookshop. Matt laminate finishes have a sophisticated look and feel but can be marked by hard objects. Gloss varnishes add to more vivid designs and are more resistant to damage. A combination of the two, with some particular element of the artwork picked out in a gloss varnish, may produce an attractive result. Embossed lettering is sometimes used to add marketing impact.

Note: if you do not specify what particular laminate finish you want, the printers will use a gloss varnish.

Combining cover and jacket image with text

The choice of an image for a jacket or cover is usually made by the publisher. It may be a decision arrived at without assessing the proportions of the image or the effects of placing the title and author text over it.

Fitting the image

You should confirm various points with the publisher at the outset:

Is the image to fit only the front panel or extend to include the spine and the back panel? The proportions of the image may not fulfil this requirement.

Is the image to be bled out? This may involve cropping essential parts of the image.

This shows the complete image placed in the layout. Only the front panel and front panel turn have to be filled with the image.

The paintings used in these examples are by Richard Shirley Smith.

The portion of the image central to the use of the picture is moved onto the front panel and cropped. The area in the top left corner suggests itself for the title and author. The type sizes of the text depend on the length of the wording.

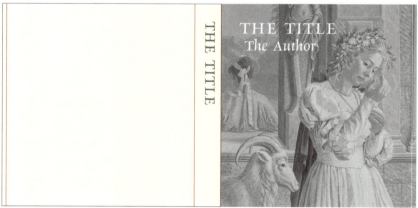

THE TITLE

THE TITLE
The Author

Here the requirement is to use the picture to fill the entire jacket. This changes the focus, concentrating on the upper part of the woman's body. The image of the girl fortuitously fits the back panel. The area which suggests itself for the title and author is now changed to the bottom right corner. The type size will depend on the length of the title.

Has thought been given to the use of a framed image? This is a way of treating an image whose composition and proportions cannot fit the format if bled out.

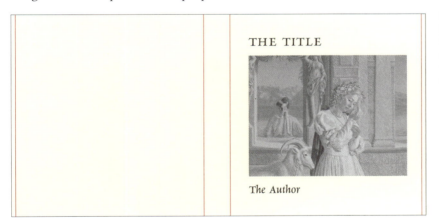

Framing the picture, leaving margins around the panel may be the only way to maintain the best elements of the original composition.

Can the image be 'flipped'? This may be the only way of fitting the central part of the image to the format. Flipping a work of art is not likely to be allowed.

This action has hidden pitfalls with human figures, such as rendering wedding rings on the wrong hand or hair partings on the wrong side – beware.

If the image is a commissioned artwork, has the artist been supplied with the jacket or cover dimensions? If not, corrections may be time consuming and expensive. Supplying a layout grid before the artist starts work will reduce any possible confusions.

Can the image be manipulated by colour changes? The image owner may object to any colour treatment. The process of rendering a black and white photograph into a sepia hue is usually an acceptable change. Works of art have to be approached carefully with such changes and the owner's permission should be sought with trials of any proposed treatments.

Is it possible to add to the image by cloning extra areas? This may be the only way to change the proportions of the image to fit the format's proportions. *Cloning* is a procedure carried out in Photoshop® by which, using several processes, matching areas can be added to an image, as in this example:

The available portrait photograph does not fit the format without increasing its size and reducing the areas in which to place the calligrapher's lettering. The areas of background wall and dark sweater are cloned to extend the image above and below the head. This allows space for the lettering.

Obviously the image itself should not be distorted in any way.

What is the text to be fitted onto the image? Keep constantly in mind the position, extent and size of the lettering that is to be fitted within the image. It is necessary to confirm the exact wording with the publisher from the outset.

Is there a copyright or reproduction limitation which restricts running text over the image? The owners of an image may not allow text over the image. Such a limitation reduces the possible layout solutions and the sooner you become aware of any restrictions the better.

Can the image be made more acceptable by using a ghosted area? This will sometimes allow the text – especially if it contains many words – to be placed in an area which would otherwise be unsuitable. The image owner may also object to this.

Ghosting is an effect which fades out the image. It can be applied to the whole image or as a gradient over a portion of the image. A panel can be ghosted into which text is placed. Black and white are commonly used though any colour can be employed.

Left:
white ghosting in a gradient from the picture's top.

Right:
black ghosting in a gradient from the picture's top.

The original image, on the left below, is complex and the legibility of the text is reduced when placed onto it. The images in the middle and to the right have ghosted areas in the top third of the image, out of which the text reads clearly.

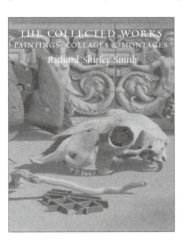 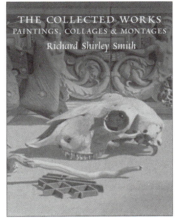 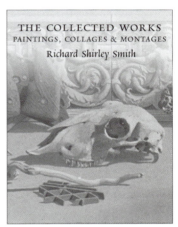

What is the full extent of the wording to appear? You may be asked to add to the titling, using such text as quoted reviews, which may arrive late in the layout process. Marketing departments may add early reviews of the book at a late stage.

On the left an early review – a *shoutline*; on the right a *strapline* announcing a prize for the book. Such elements seldom add to the overall look of the cover or jacket.

Commissioned jacket and cover artwork

Original artwork commissioned by a publisher from an illustrator may come as drawn or painted artwork or in digital form. Immediately check for fit within the format of the jacket. Ensure not only that the image fits but, if the image is to be bled out, sufficient extra drawn or painted area exists to achieve this. Cloning extra areas to create a bleed is time consuming. If you have supplied a grid, ensure that it has the exact spine bulk. This avoids late corrections. The example below shows a jacket illustration drawn up on a supplied grid – here all the elements fit the jacket layout and the bleed is filled.

See *Illustrated books*, p.296

This jacket, drawn by Chris Corr, is an excellent example of a work done to a pre-set grid with sufficient area allowing for bleeds.

Now the text elements, including the barcode and publisher's logo, are added:

Areas have been left by the artist for the titling on both front and back panels and the spine. The only figure on the spine has been placed to allow space for the author, title and publisher's logo.

Calligraphic lettering

The original artwork may also include lettering. If this is originated in a digital program such as Illustrator® it should be checked for compatibility with the layout program. If it is drawn, it should be scanned at a minimum of 1,000 dpi and at the final size of use. The lettering is cleaned of any extraneous marks, the background made white, and then converted to a bitmapped form for use.

However white the paper appears, the scan will always pick up a background.

The scan before the background is removed and conversion to the bitmap below.

VERTIGO

If there is a need to refine the letter spacing this is better carried out in the bitmapped form, rather than with the original artwork.

VERTIGO
VERTIGO

During the course of developing a jacket or cover, the publisher may ask for marketing materials for the book. Here an A3 poster was laid out using the lettering and image.

A bitmap is a digital image in which the pixels are either 'on' (black) or 'off' (no colour). There are no tones or background. A bitmapped image can be printed in any colour or reversed-out.

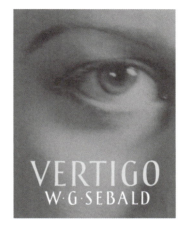

The finished cover. The bitmapped title was printed in silver. Lettering by Steve Raw

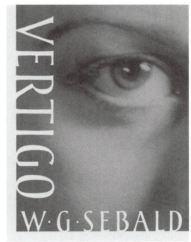

Late changes in artwork may not allow time for the artist to make revisions; you should be proficient in illustration programs so you can make any minor changes yourself.

Coloured text with images

It is possible for you to make any CMYK colour in layout programs but it is difficult to check the proof for colour accuracy. You are better advised to choose from industry standard colour guides. The Pantone® Solid to Process guide will give CMYK mixtures which can be checked for accuracy at the proof stage.

If you are using a tint of a colour as a background, it is better to refer to the Pantone® Colour Tint Selector. This will give you an industry standard. It shows examples of letters both black and reversed-out of your chosen tint.

Whether the lettering you want to colour is derived from typefaces or drawn sources, there are some basic principles that should be borne in mind. They apply both to the use of hues – the colour – and tones – the intensity of the colour.

Avoid conflicting hues: This is not just a matter of taste; some colour combinations create optical effects that are disturbing. Bright red lettering on a blue background of a similar tone causes the letters to vibrate unpleasantly; in smaller type sizes they may become illegible. There is no list of such conflicting combinations, but be alert to this possibility as you pick colours.

Avoid similar tones: The greater the contrast in tone, the more easily will the text be read. For instance, greens and blues of the same tone in combination do not read well.

Avoid fine typefaces: There is a tendency for the typeface area to be reduced by dot gain – effectively an increase in the spread of ink – in the four-colour printing process. The letters become even finer and less legible. This is especially the case if the lettering is in a dark hue against an illustration background of similar tone. Fine typefaces set in small sizes on a black background will suffer from glare which reduces legibility. Use larger bolder faces to minimize this effect.

Colour blindness: A substantial proportion of the male population is colour blind and may have difficulty seeing red type against some backgrounds.

Reversed-out lettering with images

Reversed-out lettering is effective if the background image is deeply and evenly coloured. Reversed-out letters cannot be run over images with light areas – as in the white blouse of the image opposite. If larger type sizes are used it is often better to use a light tint – a beige or grey – for the letters, to reduce the dazzle of the white unprinted area.

Trajan bold
In the right-hand example the type is in a tint of 15%.

Positioning lettering with images

Once an image has been chosen, it may be moved, cropped, reduced or enlarged. Try it in combination with various text positions to find an effective solution.

Each combination of the image and text will offer different solutions. The sequence below is an example of varying approaches using the same image:

Bear in mind the possible restrictions of the resolution of the original image. See *Digital images* p.311

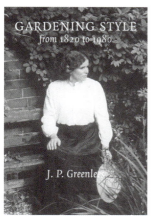

Centre set: the author's name is partially lost in the hat. No text can be put across the blouse.

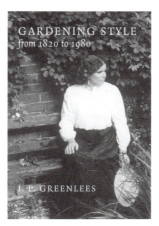

Text ranged left: that leaves the left side composition empty, the right fuller.

Centre set and lowered: this gives an increased picture content. A bolder sans serif type for the title

Enlarging the picture gives more drama but leaves the lower right area empty. An italic is used to match the intimate picture crop.

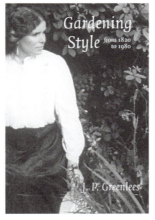

The picture is enlarged even more: the sub-titled date reduced in size. The text setting is close to a magazine style now.

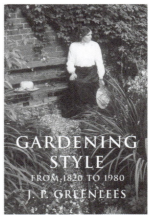

Using all the picture allows space for a more monumental lettering style suitable for an eminent author.

Typesetting jacket and cover copy

The jacket and cover text is essential promotional material for the book. Copy is supplied by the editor and may consist of some or all of these elements:

Front panel: Title/sub-title; author; foreword and author; review quotations; publisher or series title

Front flap: Synopsis of the book's contents; author's authority; the price

Spine: Author; title; publisher's name and logo

Back panel: Barcode; possibly another author photograph; further reviews; photographs for illustrated books; reviews of previous books by same author

Back flap: Author portrait; author/translator's biography; the ISBN number (International Standard Book Numbering); publisher's name and city (including a website address); name of artist or photographer whose work is used on the jacket. If necessary the back flap can be used for a continuation of the book's synopsis from the front flap though this may test the persistence of the potential buyer.

Having received the copy and indications of where it is to be placed, the design is laid out. If the book is part of a series, that style should be followed. Design styles will vary widely but attention should be paid to maintaining readability.

An acquaintance with the slang terms that are used for some of the text elements is useful when dealing with editors and marketing departments:

Blurb – any synopsis of the contents, author biography

Shoutline – emphasized and usually shortened review quote

Strapline – publisher's short announcement, for example, 'Short-listed for the Booker Prize'

Author biog – author's biography

A book first published in hardback form will frequently be later released as a paperback. The copy for the paperback cover is usually a reduced version of the hardback jacket copy with reviews of the book added. The contents of the hardback's front flap and back flap have to be fitted on the back cover. The paperback copy may also be rewritten for a different audience.

Jacket and cover front flap text layout

There is little difference between the layout treatments of jacket flaps and the flaps of a flapped paperback. A synopsis of the book and the price comprise the normal contents of the front flap. To that may be added a review quotation, or praise for the author. It has to be set in a style which makes for easy and speedy reading in a crowded bookshop. The margins should be generous, the type well leaded.

The available text measure for a flap is likely to be narrow. Ranged left settings are commonly used. If the text is lengthy, a justified setting can be just as economical with space, as below:

In his new bachelor flat, too close for comfort to his former family home, Mike Newall, Oxford don and Wittgenstein scholar seeks to rebuild his life, but feels increasingly weighed down by the past.

When Donovan O'Dywer, his colleague and fellow expatriate New Zealander dies, Newall attends the funeral. Afterwards, Newall reveals to his old friend Bertie Winterstoke the secret that O'Dwyer carried with him to his grave. During the battle for Crete in the Second World War, a soldier in New Zealand's Maori battalion died in harrowing circumstances. Believing his commanding officer, O'Dwyer, was responsible for the death, the soldier's family placed a makutu, a Maori curse, on him.

Winterstoke demands to be told all, and in the days that follow Newall obliges. But Newall's life and O'Dwyer's are curiously interconnected and Newall finds that he must interweave O'Dwyer's tale with his own – his childhood in New Zealand, his self-imposed exile in Oxford, his marriage and divorce, the pilgrimage recently made to Croatia and the promise of a new beginning that this may hold. Gradually, through a series of entwined stories, beautifully told, reflecting on decades of war and of peace, on memory and its failures, and on language and its limitations, Mike Newall comes to see a way of laying the ghosts of O'Dwyer's – and his own – past to rest.

Fiction
£13.99
US $23.00

The use of reversed-out type against a dark or black background is an easy design choice but provides poor readability for the reader and should be avoided. If a dark or black background must be used, semi-bold faces will increase legibility.

Gradually, through a series of entwined stories, beautifully told, reflecting on decades of war and of peace, on memory

Gradually, through a series of entwined stories, beautifully told, reflecting on decades of war and of peace, on memory

Left: Scala regular
Right: Scala bold
Both at 9 pt

An image that extends onto the flaps may result in a reduction of readability if the type is set over the picture. A panel will allow for the easier reading of the text.

The top half of the flap shows text reversed out of the illustration. The bottom half has a bordered frame and white background to allow the text to be readable.

Jacket and cover back flap text layout

The layout of the back flap should be consistent with the front flap in text measure and position. The contents are as listed on p.366.

Here the author's portrait and biographies of both the author and translator are the main elements. These are followed by a copyright attribution for the image used on the front cover and credit for the portrait photographer.

See p.177

The ISBN number is set out in numerals in four groups as here:

0 948021 61 6

At the foot is the publisher's name and city (important for bibliographical purposes), with their website address.

HARUKI MURAKAMI was born in Kyoto in 1949. His works of fiction include *Dance Dance Dance*, *The Elephant Vanishes*, *Hard-boiled Wonderland and the End of the World*, *A Wild Sheep Chase*, *Norwegian Wood*, *The Wind-up Bird Chronicle* and *South of the Border, West of the Sun*. His first work of non-fiction, *Underground*, is an exploration of the Tokyo subway gas attack. He has translated into Japanese the work of F. Scott Fitzgerald, Truman Capote, John Irving, and Raymond Carver.

PHILIP GABRIEL is Associate Professor of Japanese literature at the University of Arizona. He has translated Haruki Murakami's *South of the Border, West of the Sun* and *Underground* (with Alfred Birnbaum), as well as the work of Senji Kuroi and Masahiko Shimada.

Cover by Jamie Keenan
Photograph of Haruki Murakami by Marion Ettlinger

ISBN 1 86046 825 X

THE HARVILL PRESS
LONDON

www.harvill.com

Jacket back panel text layout

The back panel presents a marketing aid. If the author is well known or attractive a large portrait photograph will often be used. Reviews of the book or previous books by the author may also be used. An image on the front panel may be continued across the spine onto the back panel. Other elements may be chosen by the publisher and designer.

This back panel for a thriller uses two portions of the image on the front panel to reinforce the sense of mystery. These pictures frame a series of reviews of the author's previous books and an award announcement.

The barcode of the book's ISBN must be placed on the jacket back panel. Were it placed on the back flap, the book would have to be opened to allow machine reading; if the book is shrink-wrapped, the back panel is the only area available. There are strict rules about the display of this necessary but unattractive object. The contrast between the background and the bar itself must not interfere with the machine-reading. The sure way of achieving this is to place the barcode in a white box. If the background is a very light tone, the barcode can be used alone.

The barcode is created using a dedicated program. Do not be tempted to change it in any way or the retail machine-reading mechanisms will not function.

A fully sized barcode in a white box

A small reduction of the barcode may be allowed.

A barcode on an acceptably pale background

A barcode on this background will not read.

Ensure that the last right-hand bar is not placed too closely to the right border of the box or the machine will mis-read the code.

Spine text layout

The layout of text and other elements for the spine are the same for hardback jackets and paperback covers. The spine will carry the author's name, book the book's title, and the publisher's name and logo.

The type size must be large enough to be easily read on a bookshop shelf. Rarely will the title fit horizontally across the spine, except in bulky volumes. The alignment of the words to be set down the spine differs from country to country. In the UK, the tops of letters face the front panel so that the words can be read when the book is laid flat with its front panel showing. The opposite is the tradition in France; such variations should be noted for multilingual co-editioned books.

In the case of this cover spine, the publisher's logo at the top is placed just inside the width of the spine. This is to avoid any possibility of the logo slipping over onto the front or back panel if the binding machines fails to centre the printed cover exactly.

The spine of a book is often exposed to sunlight in a book shelf. Some colours, especially reds, tend to fade.

BEETHOVEN

Life&Times

AMIN MAALOUF PORTS OF CALL

HARVILL

Amin Maalouf *Les Echelles du Levant*

EDITIONS
BERNARD
GRASSET

As the spine increases in bulk it becomes possible to use words horizontally though the size may be limited. In the spine on the right the author and publisher are set horizontally. The title is set vertically in larger type.

It is easier to centre a title in caps than in upper and lower case. A title may contain no ascenders or no descenders, as on the left, and care has to be taken to centre it visually.

When binders wrap the jacket around the cased book, it may not be fitted to within 1 or 2 mm of dead centre. It is safer to avoid placing lettering too close to the vertical margins of the spine.

LUCY
ARCHER

EDWIN
SMITH

ARCHITECTURE IN BRITAIN & IRELAND

600–1500

HARVILL

Cover back panel text layout

The layout of a cover front panel is for all intents and purposes the same as that of a jacket. It is led by marketing demands and varies from the soberly typographic for reference books to the lurid for thrillers and romantic novels which can have gold-embossed titles and brilliantly coloured artwork.

If the paperback has flaps they are dealt with as jacket flaps. If there are no flaps, the back panel is the only source of information for the reader and will have to carry a synopsis of the book, an author biography, review extracts, barcode, price and publisher's details. Editorial skill is required to reduce these texts to fit into the panel. Colouring some of the text elements will assist the bookshop browser.

There is an option to print further information on the inside of the cover, usually only on the inside of the front cover. This does incur an additional printing cost.

Shown here – together with its spine – is a back panel layout in which a synopsis of the book is combined with a picture of the book's subject.

A review quotation follows with brief biographies of the author and translator.

The text contains only 180 words. To fit lengthier texts into this area would require smaller typefaces and reduce readability. If this is likely to be the case, the designer should contact the editor and point this out. The text may have to be shortened.

The publisher, logo and the website address are placed opposite the barcode and price.

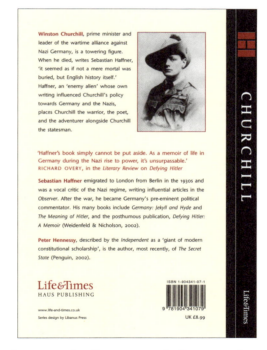

Winston Churchill, prime minister and leader of the wartime alliance against Nazi Germany, is a towering figure. When he died, writes Sebastian Haffner, 'it seemed as if not a mere mortal was buried, but English history itself.' Haffner, an 'enemy alien' whose own writing influenced Churchill's policy towards Germany and the Nazis, places Churchill the warrior, the poet, and the adventurer alongside Churchill the statesman.

'Haffner's book simply cannot be put aside. As a memoir of life in Germany during the Nazi rise to power, it's unsurpassable.' RICHARD OVERY, in the *Literary Review* on *Defying Hitler*

Sebastian Haffner emigrated to London from Berlin in the 1930s and was a vocal critic of the Nazi regime, writing influential articles in the *Observer*. After the war, he became Germany's pre-eminent political commentator. His many books include *Germany: Jekyll and Hyde* and *The Meaning of Hitler*, and the posthumous publication, *Defying Hitler: A Memoir* (Weidenfeld & Nicholson, 2002).

Peter Hennessy, described by the *Independent* as a 'giant of modern constitutional scholarship', is the author, most recently, of *The Secret State* (Penguin, 2002).

Life&Times
HAUS PUBLISHING

www.life-and-times.co.uk
Series design by Libanus Press

ISBN 1-904341-07-1

9 781904 341079

UK £8.99

CHURCHILL

Life&Times

In the example above there is no attribution to the illustration which was used on the front cover or the photographer of the back cover image. These are set on the imprint page of the book – an acceptable alternative. The barcode, however, *must* be placed on the back panel.

PART FIFTEEN
PRE-SETTING AND POST-SETTING

PREPARING TEXT FOR SETTING

The relationship between a book's designer and editor is an important one. It is the editor who supplies the designer with text and illustrations and oversees the design and proofing stages before the book goes to print. The aim of this section is to establish an understanding of how editors and designers work together through the various stages of producing a book. The process of preparing a text described here is based on the working practices of a wide range of publishers, so is not reliant on the tools offered by any particular software. These instructions are not absolute, and may be adapted to suit individual needs.

How editors supply text

Text is delivered to the designer in two formats, a disk and hard copy. It is crucial to have both. The hard copy serves as a check for the designer that nothing is missing from the disk, and that sections are in the correct order. It also contains information that may not be conveyed on disk, such as special characters.

Some editors prefer to mark up a hard copy rather that put coding for headings and extracts onto the text disk.

Editors have their individual way of preparing a text for typesetting, depending on how they have been trained and the demands of the sorts of text they work with. But there are two basic principles that both editor and designer should be aware of in order to make the transition as smooth as possible.

The first is consistency – use the same system throughout the whole text. This makes it possible to use the global 'find/change' or 'search' tool to make changes quickly and thoroughly. An example of this is indicating the start of a paragraph. This may be done by inserting a tab, or by leaving a line space, or by using a code. The important thing is to use the same method throughout using exactly the same keystrokes. For example, a global search for two line returns will not find them if an extra word space is inserted between them:

A global search for ¶¶ will not find ¶·¶

end of paragraph.¶
¶
Start of next paragraph

end of paragraph.¶
·¶
Start of next paragraph

The second principle is to keep it simple. The conversion from word-processing program to typesetting program may result in some features being lost or changed. This is especially true when it comes to paragraph formatting. Automatic indents and line spaces created by a word-processor's 'space before' and 'space after' settings do not always translate in a satisfactory way. Using simple keystrokes such as tabs and line returns in the word-processing document is a safer approach. These can then be changed globally by the designer.

Editors and authors can be over-helpful. In trying to make the typescript resemble the finished object as closely as possible, they create more work for the typesetter who has to strip out what they have done before formatting the text.

Italics, bold and small caps

Basic formatting, such as italicizing text, is done on the text disk by the author or editor. This formatting can be changed globally into the chosen font by the designer.

Some editors will use bold to highlight words on the text disk which they or the proofreader need to check. The designer should be told of this and given instructions as to whether to leave the bold in or to remove it.

If small caps are keyed in as capitals and put into a small caps font, they will stay as capitals; while if they are put into an expert font, they will change into expert characters such as ligatures or fractions, or disappear entirely:

lower-case	→	LOWER CASE	Minion to Minion expert
Small Caps	→	SMALL CAPS	Stone Print to Stone Print small caps
EXPERT FONT	→	fl ⅔⅓	Garamond to Garamond expert

Some layout programs have the facility to change keyed-in capitals to lower case, but if this is not available they will need to be re-keyed by the designer, which can lead to errors.

Ideally small caps should be keyed in as lower case and formatted by the author or editor into small caps using the formatting palette of the word-processing program. This can then be changed globally into the correct face by the designer.

Indicating headings

Some word-processing and layout programs will translate style sheets automatically. This means that the editor can apply the style sheets in the word-processing program and they will convert into the correct style in the layout program. This depends on both parties having compatible IT set-ups. If you wish to work in this way give it a trial run first.

Editors will sometimes apply some basic formatting to the headings on the text disk – putting them in a larger size and in bold, for example. For simple texts with only one or two levels of heading this is enough to show the designer where the headings are. In more complex texts with many levels of heading, using a code will make it clearer. Inserting [CH] for chapter headings and [A], [B], [C], etc., for each level in the hierarchy of sub-headings is the usual way of doing this:

> **[CH] Milling [CH]**
>
> **[A] Watermills [A]**
>
> **Water and wind were the only sources of mechanical power until well into the 18th century. Waterwheels were used in Roman Britain and increasingly from Saxon times on; the first**

These codes can then be deleted by the designer as the text is formatted.

Page breaks and line breaks

Page returns should be inserted wherever text starts on a new page. If all chapters are to start on rectos, this should be given as an instruction at the beginning of the text. If some section openings require recto starts and others do not, this may be indicated by inserting [recto] at the top of the appropriate pages.

Where line spaces are needed, it is preferable to use a code (to be deleted later), such as [#], which leaves no doubt that a line space is to be used:

> been preserved. There is also here the Clubhouse, Members'
> Restaurant, and Barnes Wallis's office.
> [#]
> The great refineries at Fawley and Grangemouth are not yet indus-
> trial archaeology, but are conspicuously part of the landscape, as

Simply leaving a line space may lead to confusion, especially if line spaces are being used anyway to indicate new paragraphs or space before and after extracts.

New paragraphs

New paragraphs may be indicated on the text disk by line spaces or by an indent. Either way is acceptable as long as it is done consistently throughout. The designer then changes these globally. Indents created by tabs convert better between programs than the 'first line indent' command.

Extracts

Extracts should be indented on the text disk. The indent should be large enough so that the designer can see it clearly when scrolling through the pages. If there are many extracts and possible confusion as to where they start and end, inserting [extract starts] and [extract ends] will make it clear. If a text contains prose extracts and poetry extracts, this may also be noted.

> announced Second Wrangler (a title given to those candidates who gained a first class in the mathematical tripos).
> **[prose extract starts]**
>> I always said from your early days [wrote his father] that such energy, perseverance and talent as yours, would be sure to succeed; but I never expected such brilliant success as this. Again and again I congratulate you. But you have made my hand tremble so I can hardly write. The telegram came here at eleven. We have written to W.[illiam] and the boys. God bless you, my dear old fellow – may your life so continue.[3]
> **[prose extract ends]**
>> George now admitted to his father his distaste for commerce:
> "I should prefer ... to be a poorer man and try and do something

Instructions should be given as to whether the text immediately following the extract is a new paragraph with the first line indented or set full out.

If extracts are to be set smaller this should be indicated at the start of the text.

If the editor does not have the facility to indent extracts on the text disk, they may be marked up on the hard copy instead.

See *Extracts and quotations*, pp.258–61

Notes

Word-processing programs help editors create footnotes automatically, and most editors use this function as it ensures that the numbering of the notes is correct. However, this process does not convert perfectly into layout programs. When the text is converted, these automatic notes will usually appear at the end of the text. The editor should instruct the designer on the following:

> Are the notes to be set as footnotes, chapter notes, or endnotes?
> Are the notes to be numbered continually throughout the book, or
> should they start from one for each chapter or each page?
> Does the book have a combination of footnotes and endnotes?

If the editor does not create notes automatically they may be supplied in a separate document, or, if they are footnotes, inserted into the text:

In this unformatted text, the footnote has been inserted in double square brackets with the coding 'FN', following the indicator. The note is then cut and pasted into a text box at the foot of the page.

> 'United' starts in upper case, and 'states' in lower; in the printed version that is reversed, but in both cases those states are declared as being 'in Congress Assembled'.[26] [[FN:26. J.R. Pole (ed.), *The Revolution in America, 1754–1788. Documents and Commentaries* (London, 1970), pp. 20, 29, 41.]]
>   Talk of union at this stage was as much animated by the practical need to hold together the forces of rebellion as by any

This makes it easy for the designer to see where they occur and place them in the appropriate position. If footnotes are supplied in a separate document, it is helpful if the editor highlights the notes' indicators in the main text so they can be found easily. Missing a footnote at the layout stage can take a long time to correct.

Special characters

Some characters which are not part of the standard Latin alphabet may not translate from the editor's word-processing program to the designer's layout program. This is because they depend on using particular fonts or combinations of keystrokes which will not be the same for all computer operating systems. These characters should be marked up on the hard copy. It is also useful if the designer is given prior warning so they can source or create the necessary fonts.

Illustrations

Where illustrations relate to a particular passage of text, this should be indicated by the editor. This may be done by marking up the hard copy or by inserting picture positions on the disk which are removed by the designer later. Putting these into bold or a second colour at the conversion stage will make them easier to spot. If the name of the picture file is known this is also helpful:

> Vestibule and the two main staircases **[Fig.2 SP88215]** and sets the basic pattern for the final designs. Comparing this plan to the survey drawing of the old house **[Fig.3 SP88217]** the direction of Soane's thinking is clear. The pre-fire plan was basically a series of interconnecting spaces, the structural skeleton of which had to be retained to avoid rocketing costs. Soane transforms

References to the pictures within the text may be used by the designer to place the pictures. Care should be taken if some illustrations are referred to more than once. The editor should use some method of highlighting those which indicate a picture placement to differentiate them from similar references to pictures which are placed elsewhere:

> made prior to Soane's meeting with Lord Grenville at Dropmore on 8 December 1820 (Fig.9 WP0021). 'Design B' had an oval plan similar to that at Tyringham (Fig.22), and 'Design D', which became Soane's favourite, shifted the whole arrangement to the eastern end of the room (Fig.10 WP0022). This last design incorporated a ring of columns at first-floor level inspired

The picture references for figures 9 and 10 have been highlighted in red indicating that pictures are to be placed here.

So the final text would look like this:

> became 'Design A', which is shown in two perspective views made prior to Soane's meeting with Lord Grenville at Dropmore on 8 December 1820 (Fig.9). 'Design B' had an oval plan similar to that at Tyringham (Fig.22), and 'Design D', which became Soane's favourite, shifted the whole arrangement to the eastern end of the room (Fig.10). This last design incorporated a ring of columns at first-floor level inspired by

The illustrations Fig.9 and Fig.10 would be placed close to this passage of text. Fig.22 would appear later in the book.

Converting text for use

When the text disk is supplied by the editor it will need to be converted by the designer from word-processing document to page-layout document. Before starting this process, the designer should go through the hard copy and make a note of editorial instructions to watch out for during setting, such as special characters or picture placements.

Possible problems in the conversion

The text file may be supplied as one big file or divided into smaller files. Joining these smaller files together when converted will mean having to go through the process just once.

Some formatting applied to word-processing documents may have unexpected and unwanted results when the text is converted. Once the text has been flowed into a new document in the layout program, select all, then check the following:

1 no unwanted indents on text
2 ICS is at zero
3 horizontal and vertical scaling are at 100 per cent
4 text is in black at 100 per cent (except coloured editorial coding)
5 there is no baseline shift on the text
6 lines or paragraphs do not have the 'keep together' option selected
7 there is no unwanted space or rules above or below paragraphs

Cleaning the text

If the editor does not have en dashes in their word-processing program, two hyphens should be used, which can be changed globally. Be careful when getting rid of unwanted superior characters that you do not lose indicators for notes.

The designer can then make the following changes in preparation for setting, most of which can be done globally:

1 Put the text into a uniform font, using italic and bold where appropriate
2 Put the body text into a uniform size and leading
3 Put the headings into a larger size with line spaces before and after
4 Take out line spaces between paragraphs and insert paragraph indents
5 Insert page breaks for new chapters (if they do not run on) and part-titles
6 Check that word spaces contain only a single space
7 Replace hyphens with en dashes where appropriate and unspaced ellipses with spaced ellipses
8 Replace lining figures with non-lining figures where appropriate
9 Remove unwanted superior figures created by default settings (th, rd, etc.)

The aim of this process is to create a text file that is consistent throughout, stripping out unwanted commands and styling. This clean text can then be formatted using a combination of global commands, style sheets and master pages.

Picture placements

If you are working on an illustrated book, and the editor has not highlighted the references for picture placement, it is worth taking the time to do this before you start laying out the book. Discuss any queries with the editor.

Footnotes

Preparing footnotes for setting depends on how confident you are about spotting indicators as you go. Putting footnotes into the text before setting means that you have more than a small superior figure to look for and you can see instantly the length of the note. These footnotes can be formatted into the correct font and size, ready to cut and paste into a text box as you go along.

See p.378

Formatting

Formatting text includes putting it into the chosen font and leading, setting the headings in the chosen size and style with the correct amount of space above and below, and applying indents to extracts. Some designers prefer to do this before the text is flowed into the final book layout. This makes sense if the text is not continuous and will be placed in unlinked text boxes.

Style sheets are a powerful tool for formatting text. They are particularly useful for texts with many levels of headings. However, using them for the main body of the text can result in the loss of italics and superior figures, so in some situations it is better to use a find/change mechanism.

The effect that style sheets have on the formatting of text will depend on how the program's preferences have been set up.

Putting in special characters

When the text has been formatted into the chosen font, special characters, such as non-Latin characters, fractions and symbols can be put in. These may involve a change of font and keystroke. Whether or not this can be done globally will depend on how the author or editor has keyed them in.

From production to design

Some publishing houses have a form filled in by the production manager, a copy of which is sent with the text to the designer. This ensures that both parties understand what is to be undertaken. The following is an example:

title	
subtitle	
author(s) / editor(s) translator(s) / compiler(s)	
project manager / editor	designer
ISBN hardback	paperback
format hardback	paperback
date passed to designer	date of publication
number of page proofs required	date required

Please indicate below which items are included with the edited text disk and which are to come (give dates if possible). Delete those that are inapplicable.

half-title	. . . .	acknowledgements	. . . .
author biog	. . . .	permissions	. . . .
frontispiece	. . . .	introduction	. . . .
title	. . . .	list of abbreviations	. . . .
title verso	. . . .	any other preliminary matter?	. . . .
dedication	. . . .	. . . .	
epigraph	. . . .	. . . .	
contents list	. . . .	appendices	. . . .
list of figures	. . . .	footnotes	. . . .
list of illustrations	. . . .	chapternotes	. . . .
list of maps	. . . .	endnotes	. . . .
list of tables	. . . .	glossary	. . . .
preface	. . . .	bibliography	. . . .
foreword	. . . .	index . . . . likely extent	

figures (indicate number)			illustrations (indicate number)		
on disk	. . . .	colour	on disk	. . . .
to scan	. . . .		to scan	. . . .
maps (indicate number)		b/w	on disk	. . . .
on disk	. . . .		to scan	. . . .
to scan	. . . .	captions . . . .

running heads/feet	recto
	verso

Please indicate page numbers on typescript for the following:

text headings	part	
	chapter	
	sub-headings	A
		B
		C
		D
	other	
chapter epigraphs		
poem epigraphs		
poem dedications		
extracts	prose	
	verse	
	correspondence	
	drama	
display matter		
tables		
lists		
marginals		
spaces in text		
special characters		
special instructions		

EDITORIAL RULES

The responsibility for the content of a book lies with the publisher who employs copy-editors to refine the text before it is typeset. Designers should not make corrections to the text unless instructed by the editor.

The purpose of this section is not to teach copy-editing – a huge subject – but to serve as a brief introduction to those areas which are relevant to book typography. The following list of rules is far from comprehensive, but deals with some common queries raised by designers. A final decision should always be sought from the editor. These rules are all covered more fully in specialist copy-editing manuals.

See *Reference books and further reading*, p.423

Italicization

When setting text in a roman font, the following should be italicized:
>titles of books, films, plays, long poems, works of art
>titles of ballets, operas, oratorios, overtures, song cycles,
>>symphonic poems
>names of newspapers, periodicals, ships
>words or phrases in foreign languages
>stage directions

The following should not be italicized, but set within single quotation marks:
>titles of chapters in books
>titles of articles in periodicals
>titles of short poems, songs
>popular titles of musical works, e.g. the 'Moonlight' Sonata

When setting text in an italic face, the opposite applies. Words normally italicized are put into roman. The term for this is *opposite font*.

Italics are also used for emphasis, or to show the reader that particular attention should be paid to the meaning of a word. In fictional works italics may be used more creatively, for example, to convey unspoken thoughts. They are often used to reproduce letters as the cursive forms are closer to those of handwriting.

Capitalization

Initial capitals should be used for:

For the
capitalization of
titles, see p.165

    proper names: John Smith

    titles which form part of a name: Sir Peter Jones, Mrs Andrews

    titles of office-holders: the Prime Minister

    names of institutions: Royal College of Art

    organizations and their members: National Trust, Democrat

    names of political and religious movements: Catholicism, Marxism

    geographical and topographical names: Mount Everest

    names of historical periods, eras and events: Renaissance, the Depression

    names of aircraft, trains, ships, etc: Flying Scotsman

    trade names: Mercedes, Dyson

    some adjectives derived from proper names: Shakespearian

Abbreviations and contractions

An abbreviation is a word that is shortened by taking letters from the end, for example, p. meaning page. A contraction is a word that keeps its first and last letter and removes letters from the middle, for example, Dr for Doctor.

Most British publishers will follow abbreviations with a full point – vol. p. l. – but not contractions – Mr Dr Mlle – unless confusion is possible, for example, no. for numero.

Full points are also omitted after the following:

    units of measurement: mm, kg

    abbreviations which consist of a string of upper case initials: BBC

    acronyms: wysiwyg

    plurals of abbreviations: figs, cats

Where abbreviations are followed by a number, for example, p.5, fig.13, cat.28, they may be set without a word space following the full point, but this depends on the preference of the publisher. When c. is used for *circa* it is usually italicized, *c.*1938.

Abbreviations and contractions should only be used in the text where requested by the author and should not be introduced to solve problems of typesetting.

Word division

Where words are divided between two lines, they should be divided according to their etymology – the derivation of words – or their pronunciation.

Divide between two consonants where possible, but two consonants forming one sound should not be divided:

> tele-phone not telep-hone   perish-ing not peris-hing

Divisions should not be made which create new words or lead the reader to mispronounce the first half of the word:

> oper-ation not opera-tion   digi-tal not dig-ital

Words containing hyphens should only be divided at the hyphen.

There should be a minimum of three characters before and after the division.

Compounds

Two words joined to form an adjective, adverb or noun are called a compound. Some are set *open* (with a word space between), some are hyphenated and some are set *closed* (with no word space between). This is not a subject that can be reduced to a few simple rules, but you should be aware of some common confusions.

A compound such as 'nineteenth century' is sometimes hyphenated and sometimes not depending on usage. When used as an adjective it is hyphenated:

> one of the great works of nineteenth-century literature.

When used as a noun it is open:

> it was written in the nineteenth century.

Compound numbers from twenty-one to ninety-nine are hyphenated.
For ages, use: three-year-old boy, thirty-two-year-old woman.

When the first part of the compound does not modify the meaning of the second, an en dash is used. This may mean 'and' or 'to':

> London–Brighton classic car rally
> Liberal–Labour alliance

Quotation marks

If using single quotation marks to denote speech, quotes within speech are set within double quotation marks:

> 'She said "that's him," but I don't believe it,' he said.

If using double quotation marks, quotes within speech are set within single quotation marks:

> "She said 'that's him,' but I don't believe it," he said.

The position of punctuation inside or outside the quotation marks depends on whether it is part of the sentence inside the quotation marks.

When a speech is more than one paragraph long, each paragraph begins with an opening quotation mark, but only the final paragraph ends with a closing quotation mark.

Apostrophes

Possession is indicated by use of 's :

> the town's main street, the dog's tail

Plurals nouns ending with s have just an apostrophe to indicate possession:

> the houses' front doors, the cars' headlights

Some singular names ending in s should be followed by 's :

> Thomas's, James's, Charles's

This depends on pronunciation, and there are exceptions to this, including some classical names. Editors' preferences may vary on this rule.

Some place names and institutions do not use apostrophes:

> All Souls, Earls Court

Apostrophes should not be used in plurals:

> 1950s not 1950's

References to bibliographical sources

It is not within the scope of this book to detail every one of the many possible permutations of bibliographical data, as this is the concern of the editor. Further information can be found in J. Butcher, *Copy-Editing: for Editors, Authors, Publishers* (Cambridge University Press, 1992). The following are simple examples used to explain the basic approach. References to multi-volume works and unpublished sources in particular become more complicated.

Short-title system

Abbreviations used in bibliographical references:

p.   page
pp.   pages
vol.   volume
l.   line
ll.   lines
ff.   following
col.   column
edn   edition
ed.   editor
tr.   translator

There are a number of methods for giving bibliographical information in text or in the notes. The most usual is called the *short-title system*. The first time a reference is given it takes the following form:

> Author, *Title: and sub-title*, translator or editor (edition (if not first),
> publication place, publisher, date) page

So it will look like this with elements separated either by commas or parentheses:

> G. Mak, *Amsterdam: A Brief Life of the City*, tr. Philipp Blom (London,
> Harvill Press, 1999) p.207

The Harvard system takes a similar approach, using the author, date and page. This example would then become:
Mak 1999, 284

Any subsequent mention of the same publication may be shortened. If this is the only book by this author it can be shortened to: Mak, p.284

If there is more than one book by this author it becomes: Mak, *Amsterdam*, p.284

In the bibliography, information is given in the same order – except that the surname of the author appears before the initials:

> Mak, G., *Amsterdam: A Brief Life of the City*, tr. Philipp Blom (London,
> Harvill Press, 1999)

Titles of essays of articles are put in quotation marks, with the publications in which they appear in italics:

> Hofman, W., 'A Captive' in *Henry Fuseli 1741–1825*, exhib. cat. by G. Schiff
> (London, Tate Gallery, 1975)

Lists of more than one reference are separated by semi-colons:

> Bell pp. 39–40; Whinney 1964 p. 176; Rosenblum pp. 30–31; Pressly pp. 48–9

Credit lines

Where permission has been given to reproduce an extract of text or an illustration from another source which is under copyright, a credit line should be given at some point in the book. This may be on the imprint page or on a separate page set aside for the purpose. In the case of illustrations, it may be the wish of the copyright holder that the credit is placed in the caption. Wording may be stipulated by the copyright holder, but if not, a consistent form of wording should be used throughout, for example:

Photograph: Jonathan Gibson / Country Life Picture Library

Spelling

Many words have alternative spellings, and most publishers will have house rules stating their preferred choice. If not, the author or editor may choose, and should then ensure that spelling is consistent throughout the book. One exception to this is quoted matter, where spelling, punctuation and sometimes spacing are kept the same as the original. The proofreader will be given a list of these choices, along with proper names, but it is unusual for the designer to receive such a list unless you are being asked to make global changes before setting the book.

Copy-editing manuals contain lists of difficult and alternative spellings. The largest group of words with two spellings are those which may end -ise or -ize.

American spelling

It is unusual for books published in the UK to retain US spelling, and the editor should revise American texts before sending them to the designer. It is a matter of editorial judgement whether to restrict this to spelling, or whether to change words according to usage – for example, sidewalk to pavement – which can change the authorial voice.

Transliteration of names

Established systems exist for the transliteration of names from most non-Latin alphabets. These are usually adhered to even when English equivalents are available. For example, the Russian Aleksandr would not be translated to Alexander.

In some languages, such as Arabic and Chinese, there are competing systems of transliteration. The distinction between them is a matter for the author and editor.

The marking up of proofs

When the first proof of your setting returns to you, it will have been marked up for corrections from both the author and editor. The symbols indicating corrections should be standard throughout the industry. The British Standards Institute publishes a complete list of them which it is wise to have to hand. Some publishing houses have their own standard set of symbols but you will find that the style of marking up varies from one editor to another. The key point is that you should be able to identify what is intended quickly and without ambiguity.

The marking up of a text uses a combination of marks within the text and symbols and words in the margin instructing the required changes. The list below contains the most commonly occurring symbols:

He hurried back to Cambridge	He hurried back to Cambridge	insert space
His lectures started again in	His lectures started again in	insert spaces
but wasted as a single woman	but *wasted* as a single woman	in italics – or
so *simple* and unaffected	so simple and unaffected	to roman – or
surprsingly, stuck to his	surprisingly, stuck to his	insert character
She came to twice us during	She came to us twice during	transpose words
She was mindful that alice	She was mindful that Alice	to a capital
during the sum mer holidays	during the summer holidays	close up
Erasmus must have walked	Erasmus must have walked	ignore correction
one of the best in Kent	one of the best in Kent.	insert full point
bangs and shouts to the cattle	bangs and shouts, to the cattle	insert comma
grazing on the Queens' Green	grazing on Queens' Green	delete word
on the castle battlements	on the castle battlements	remove extra space

The marking up of some punctuation corrections may look confusing but is usually straightforward in application, although the marks used may vary:

;	in late April a great event	in late April; a great event	insert semi-colon
:	started again in late April	started again: in late April	insert colon
⋀ ;	of dressmaking his lectures	of dressmaking; his lectures	delete, insert semi-colon
⸌ ⸍	I'll do it, William said.	'I'll do it', William said.	insert single quotes
⸌⸌ ⸍⸍	'I'll do it, William said.	"I'll do it", William said.	insert double quotes
⋀ !	'Look out', he said.	'Look out!', he said.	insert exclamation
⊢⊣	a tired looking man	a tired-looking man	insert hyphen
N	clouds – the ones I saw today	clouds – the ones I saw today	use en dash
⋯	moved forward...then back	moved forward . . . then back	use ellipsis
²	rattle of the butchers' traps.2	rattle of the butchers' traps.[2]	use superior figure
	rattle of the butchers' traps.2	rattle of the butchers' traps.[2]	use superior figure
?	Aunt Caera hoped that life was	a continuing editorial query – resolve with editor	

Corrections to capitalization and font changes will also form part of the marked-up proof and are frequently noted with additional abbreviations:

s/c	The painter had got hold	THE PAINTER had got hold	change to small caps
u/L	THE PAINTER had got hold	The painter had got hold	to upper and lower case
	The price was enormous and	The price was **enormous** and	change to semi-bold
lig	was very inefficient	was very inefficient	use ligature
wf	accumulation of work awaited	accumulation of work awaited	wrong font, change

If the change cannot be dealt with using any of the symbols, is unusually complex or gives a choice, then it is better spelt out and circled to distinguish the comment from any text additions:

Would it be better in bold ?

There may also be marked-up corrections to spacing, leading, indentation and the setting. If any additional matter is to be inserted, it is usually supplied as separate hard copy or written on proofs.

<table>
<tr><td>

correct over-spacing

turn back word   *t/b*

insert additional matter supplied   ⋏ Ⓐ

paragraph indent

transpose words   *trs*

new paragraph   *np*

run on sentence

turn over word

check leading

set full-out

use en dash   <u>N</u>

insert hyphen   ⊢

</td><td>

The reservist was unable to answer; this Red Army clerk smelt of soap and sweat, and also of some sweet life unknown to his heart – a heart that was used to hiding away in its own solitude, its own barely smouldering warmth. He bowed his head and began to cry because things were so miserable for him, and Moscow Chestnova let go of his hand in bewilderment. The reservist stood there for a while and then, glad that he was not being detained, disappeared to his unknown dwelling, to keep himself going one way or another up to the edge of the grave, without registration or danger.

But Moscow found his address on the re-registration form and, some time later, went to call on him.

She wandered for a long time in the depths of the Bauman district before she found the small housing co-operative where the reservist lived. This was a building with an incompetent management committee, and with accounts that were in deficit; the walls had not been painted years for, and the grim, empty yard, where even the stones were worn down from the games of children, had long been in need of proper attention. Moscow felt sad as she followed the walls of the building, then made her way down dimly lit corridors; it was as though she had been hurt by someone or as though she herself were to blame for the careless, unhappy lives of other people.

When she emerged on the other side of the building, which faced a long, blank fence, she saw a wet stone porch, with an iron awning and an   *t/o* electric lamp shining above it. She listened closely to the noise in the surrounding air: behind the fence, planks of wood were being thrown to the ground and she could hear spades cutting into the earth; beside the iron awning was a hatless, bald man, standing there on his own and playing a mazurka on the fiddle. Lying on a stone slab was the musician's hat – it had lived, on his head, through long misfortunes of every kind. Once it had covered a youthful head of hair, and now it was collecting money for the sustenance of old age, for the support of a feeble consciousness in a bare, decrepit head.

</td></tr>
</table>

A thin red pen is best used for corrections. A thick pen may cover more characters than intended and reduce the accuracy of the marks. Do not use pencil as it is difficult to see against the black text and the marks may not photocopy.

Up to now the correction marks shown cover straightforward texts. We strongly recommend that you buy the British Standard Institute's *Guide to Copy Preparation* BS 5261. This deals with more complicated texts, those in other languages and mathematical markings. It also contains notes on abbreviations, italicization and other useful copy treatments.

When all the corrections are done, send this *first revise* to the editor *together* with the marked-up version. It is absolutely necessary that the marked-up proofs can be seen to confirm the corrections. If you yourself have any queries, mark up the pages with your query circled and flag the page itself with a label. If the queries are numerous attach a list of those pages to the front page of the proof.

This proof will be checked by the editor and returned. At this stage the corrections should be minimal. Do the changes and send a proof, the *second revise*, with the marked-up first revise. Any editorial queries should have been finally resolved but in complex or academic texts there may be a few more changes or additions to achieve the accuracy necessary in such publications. Any changes in pagination will have to be reflected in the setting of the index.

You may expect further small but sometimes important corrections by phone, fax and email. Make these corrections and *confirm* by hard copy, fax or PDFs of the individual pages. This is a point at which confusion may occur; keep the faxes and emails concerning these late changes. Be absolutely sure that the changes have been approved.

Marked-up proofs for illustrated books

The proof will either be a greyscale, with the illustrations in black and white half-tones, or a four-colour digital proof. The text of the book will be marked up for corrections as described. Changes to illustrations are made by written instruction rather than by symbol. These will cover picture position, sizing and orientation, as overleaf:

Traditionally blue was a colour code for editor's or author's corrections and red for typesetter's errors. This coding was used to allocate charges. Generally this has now been abandoned.

First revise

Second revise

Final revise prior to output

Send a complete printout of the work you have output to the editor to further confirm any last-minute changes.

flip

Usually this means horizontally though with technical works or abstract art it may be vertical.

resize

with an indication of size and any refitting of associated text

rotate

with an indication of desired horizontal

fit picture to left

This easily happens if the scan has not been cropped to the image margin.

use detail

Enlarge picture to fit picture box as indicated.

Apart from these instructions, you may be asked to replace a misplaced or late arriving picture with the correct one. The position of the picture may be moved within the page or to another page. If this occurs at a late stage and affects the pagination, changes will have to be made to the index.

Output

The work is now ready for output. In the past a final hard copy printout would have been literally *signed off* with an editor's signature. This is no longer the case and the instruction to output of the work may be given over the phone or emailed. However, you would be wise to get a written authority to output to the printers.

This is a very important stage for the designer/typesetter. If the work is for a publisher, the output will be sent to their production department. If you are print-managing the work yourself, it will go to your selected printer. All output procedures require a set of laser proofs. It is wise to read these through carefully yourself to ensure that no minor errors have crept in during the last few revises.

Output of text-only books

1 as a layout document in your program
2 as a PDF file (a portable document format)

1 *A layout document*

You will need to send a hard copy of the work – a greyscale – at actual size, together with the layout itself in the program you used, on a disk. Check with the repro house that that program can be accepted. Not all layout programs can be translated into film or plate-making programs at the repro house. Legally, fonts may not be sent to the repro house. *See p.76*

2 *A PDF*

Your document can be translated into a PDF file. Most commonly the PDF output will be in single pages rather than spreads. These are then fed into an imposition program at the printers. There are many settings and profiles for creating print-quality PDFs. Before creating the PDF contact the printer to ensure that your PDF settings are suitable or ask for the printer's preferred profile and work with that.

As all the fonts are embedded there is no legal constraint on their use for a 'print and preview' PDF. If the PDF is 'editable' – that is further changes can be made to the document – the restriction on the supply of fonts applies.

Output of illustrated books

1   as a layout document in your program with original artwork
2   as a layout document with high resolution scans fitted
3   as a PDF file

See *The output of scanned images* pp.316–17

The treatment of the high resolution images at output has been dealt with already.

1 *A layout document*

The layout program document will be on disk, sent with a 100% greyscale printout and all the original transparencies and photographs. The repro house will scan the images to the sizes shown in the greyscale and fit them into your layout document.

2 *A layout document with high resolution scans fitted*

When scans have been fitted and sized, the layout document and all the high resolution scans are saved onto a disk. A 100% greyscale laser printout is also sent. If the book is heavily illustrated there may be several disks.

If the document involves complicated use of coloured texts as well as pictures, it is helpful to the repro house to have a coloured digital printout to ensure that all the colours have been translated to their system.

3   *A PDF*

Check that the PDF profile you use is compatible with that preferred by the repro house and convert the layout document to the PDF using that specification. This will usually be in a single page form, not in spreads.

It is also quite normal for the repro house/printer to request a set of full-sized colour digital printouts to accompany the PDF output. Although this is not used for direct colour comparison, it does ensure that all the four-coloured elements can be confirmed by the printers. This does involve a cost, which you should allow for.

See *Time and money* pp.414–15

The technology of printing evolves at a rapid pace. You are advised to keep abreast of advances. Ask your printers to keep you informed of these.

Checking the printer's proofs

If the output has been passed onto a publisher's production department it may be that no printer's proofs are passed back to the designer; checking is done by the production manager and editor. With text-only books, the proof from the printer will be a laser output. Check that the fonts have been correctly loaded and that no words have run over onto the following lines or pages.

An illustrated book requires careful checking. The printer should supply:

> A laser-printed proof of your output layout with pictures in place
>
> A set of high resolution digital colour proofs of the pictures
>
> A set of *wet proofs* if requested after the high resolution proofs are checked

Laser proofs are also known as *plotters.*

Wet proofs are also known as *machine proofs.*

The laser proof is checked to ensure that the fonts have loaded correctly and the images are in the right position. Coloured text treatments which have been created out of the four-colour process should be checked to ensure that the text is coloured as planned. This is also the stage at which last-minute text corrections can be made. You may see a word that has not been coloured as planned and which you over-looked when checking the greyscale at output; there may be an ugly overcrowded line which can be easily corrected by turning over a word. Mark up the proof, flag it and write a note pointing it out. Do not make a habit of extensive late changes; they will try the printers' goodwill and extra costs may be incurred. The colours of the laser-produced images may be denser than you expect – this can be ignored.

If the type size of any four-coloured text is small, it may 'lose' colour if the screening is not very fine. Try to avoid using too small a type size.

The digital colour proofs are produced on large sheets with irregular placing of the images at the final picture size. These proofs are called *scatter proofs.* They should be checked with the originals to hand. Any extraneous marks should be noted and their removal requested. If the colour balance of an image is not as the original, make notes against the image. As experience is gained you will know how to make comments such as 'reduce the magenta' or 'increase the cyan'. It is always sensible to leave the repro house to judge how such instructions are carried out.

The names given to these digital processes changes as technical improvements occur. Ask the repro house for details of the process they use and what can be expected of it.

Wet proofs are printed from plates on press using the chosen paper. This form of proof gives the most accurate view of what the final work will look like. Check the colour values against the originals. Changes at this late stage are expensive to make.

Paper and presses

In conversations with printers, papers are referred to as *stock*.

The choice of papers for printing is a complex subject and what follows can only be a brief introduction. Printing presses are designed to use particular sizes and paper-feeding mechanisms which places constraints on the designer's choices.

Other printing processes such as screen printing and letterpress printing may be used to produce covers and jackets but are seldom used in book production.

There are two common printing processes and two paper-feed mechanisms:

Offset lithographic, either sheet-fed or web-fed

Digital printing, either sheet-fed or web-fed

Sheet-fed presses use large separate sheets cut to the maximum size for the plates of the press. The printed sheets are then transferred to separate binding machinery. These presses are used for a wide variety of work from simple brochures to high quality art books. Sheet-fed presses are built in a wide range of sizes and give the designer a greater choice of format.

Web-fed presses use rolls of paper that enter the press as a continuous sheet, and are only cut into separate sheets for binding after they have been printed on. Binding machines may be directly linked to the press, making for a single flow of paper to the finished book. Commonly such presses are used for newspapers and cheaper fictional works in single colours. These high-speed and economic presses have been specifically designed to deal with standard book sizes and the designer is unlikely to be able to change these formats.

It cannot be stressed enough that the proposed printer should be consulted at the earliest stage to discuss the format of a book you wish to design, especially if it is not to be to a standard size. The concerns are two-fold. Can the book's format use available manufactured sheet sizes efficiently? Does the chosen sheet fit the presses? There is little sense in choosing a paper manufactured to a size which allows only four pages of your format, instead of the eight pages that can be printed within the area available on the press. Equally a printer may only have small presses and a sheet with sixteen pages-to-view would be too large be fed through them.

There are significant economies to be made in choosing the appropriate paper size and the opinions of the printer should be taken into serious consideration. In asking for estimates for the printing of a book, always confirm that the format is efficient in its use of a sheet. Ask if an adjustment to the format, a millimetre here or there, would make for a substantial reduction in costs of stock – sometimes it will, especially in long runs.

The use of digital printing is increasing. Web-fed digital presses offer a speedy set-up and can print very small runs of books – *print on demand* – in a single colour without the complex mechanisms of plate changing and running up the press. The print quality of these presses, especially in the reproduction of images, is improving. Sheet-fed digital presses are now used for a wide range of commercial four-colour printing. The use of such presses to print quality four-colour books is a little way off at the time of writing, but improvement is inevitable and the digital route may take over from offset lithographic printing in the future.

Paper choices

An enormous number of papers is available and as many descriptions of them offered by the paper trade. But there are basic divisions between paper types which may help when you are faced with a sheaf of samples. The performance of a paper depends on several physical features:

Surface quality	Weight, thickness and bulk
Opacity	Grain direction
Tint and colour	Paper acidity

Paper surfaces

Paper starts off as mass of fibres, either cellulose or rag, which are pressed together into a sheet. At this stage the surface is rough. It can be smoothed either by being further pressed between rollers – *calendered* – or by being covered – *coated* – with minerals to give it a smooth surface.

Coated or *un-coated* is a basic division between types of paper. Coated papers have very smooth surfaces and are capable of accepting fine printed images, allowing for the delicate adjustment of four-colour ink densities. They are invariably used for illustrated books. The degree of surface 'shine' of coated papers ranges from the gleamingly bright – *art* – to the duller – *matt*, with intermediate forms variously described as *silk* or *satin*.

Un-coated papers are also referred to as *cartridges*.

This book is printed on an un-coated paper.

An un-coated paper may not perform as well as the coated paper in the reproduction of images and requires a greater density of ink to fill its irregular surface. For text-only books this is no drawback and indeed the textured surface with its reduced glare makes it easier to read extended texts such as novels.

Paper weight, thickness and bulk

The weight of a paper is expressed as the weight in grams of one square metre of the paper, expressed as a number of 'gsm' or 'g/m²'. The imperial system used in

A ream is 500 sheets.

America is based on the weight in pounds of a ream of paper of a certain size. American companies importing paper to Europe will give a metric equivalent.

When you pick up a piece of paper, your fingers will get an impression of its thickness. Not all paper is made up of fibres: papers may include a *loading* of other materials, usually clay based, which are used to increase the thickness of the paper without using more fibres. So it can be the case that a paper which feels quite thick may have a large amount of loading, which is light. Thus the weight of a paper is not a complete guide to its thickness. Manufacturers also offer an exact measurement of the thickness of a paper expressed in microns – thousandths of a millimetre. This is more useful to a printer.

If a book is being printed 16-to-view, it will be folded into 32-page signatures. The choice of a bulky paper may create problems with folding machines or wrinkling in the gutter of the fold. To avoid this, either reduce the paper bulk or print 8-to-view with a 16-page signature

The combination of a paper's weight and thickness create a paper's *bulk* – which may also be referred to as its *volume*. The volume of a paper is the thickness of 100 sheets of the paper. For example, if 100 sheets of a 100 gsm paper have a bulk of 18 mm it is referred to as an *18 volume* paper. In the production of trade paperbacks the overall width of the spine of a book – its bulk – is calculated from tables of volumes and page extent. These will be supplied to you by the printer.

These technicalities may be a little overwhelming, but from the point of view of the designer they will give an indication of what paper to choose. If you have an exhibition catalogue of only 96 pages, a paper of 170 gsm and some bulk will make the book more impressive. A novel of 416 pages would need a much less bulky paper of 80 gsm or the bound book would be too thick.

To make a paper choice, get samples of possible papers, seek the printer's advice and look at books in similar papers. Have a dummy binding made with your choice.

Paper opacity

The degree to which the printed text and images on a page can be seen when looking at the other side, is known as *show-through*. If the show-through is very marked
it begins to affect the legibility of the printed words. The more opaque the paper,
the less the show-through to distract the reader.

See *The text panel*
p.41

There is no classification of opacity offered by manufacturers. If a particular paper
is suggested, a printed sample of it will give an indication of its opacity. If you only
have an unprinted sample to hand, placing it on top of any printed page and seeing
how much you can see through the sample will give you some idea of its opacity.

Paper grain

With the exception of hand-made papers, all papers have a grain direction – the
direction along which most of the fibres run. The paper folds most easily parallel
to this direction. If the gutter of the pages run parallel to the grain, the pages lay
comfortably flat when bound. If the spine is at right angles to the grain, the
book opens badly and the pages tend to curl, especially if exposed to moisture.
Check with the printer that the grain of the sheet you have chosen is correct for
the format you are using.

Most papers have the
grain running along
the longest dimen-
sion of the sheet and
are referred to as
long-grained. If the
grain runs along the
shorter dimension
of the sheet it is
called *short-grained*.

Paper colour

The colour or *tint* of a paper will affect both the quality and the readability of the
print. A very white paper will give the best reproduction of four-colour images
but at the same time produce a glare which can be uncomfortable to the eye
when reading text. An off-white paper is preferable for long texts. It is quite possible to print images on un-coated and tinted papers and the effect can be attractive
if colour accuracy is not an overriding issue.

Paper acidity

The acidity of a paper is expressed as its *pH*. A paper which is acidic will become
discoloured and brittle over time. A paper with a neutral pH – pH7 – is of an ideal
archival quality although it is more costly. In choosing an archival paper, judgement must be made of the enduring (or otherwise) value of the text itself.

Publishers may wish
to advertise their use
of archival, neutral
or renewably
resourced paper
on the imprint page.

PART SIXTEEN

TIME AND MONEY

The production sequence

An awareness of the production process in which you are involved is helpful. Editorial work is usually carried out before the book's design is commissioned.

The 'MS' is the final edited text.

Initially this progression can look complicated. All these stages have been dealt with in more detail elsewhere in the book.

The book's jacket production is often done to an earlier schedule to assist marketing.

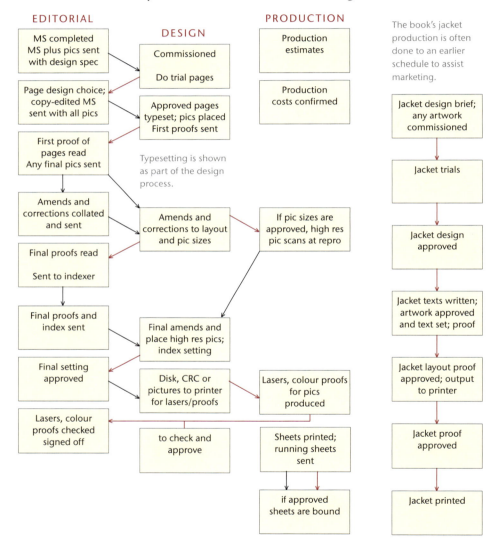

EDITORIAL

DESIGN

PRODUCTION

MS completed
MS plus pics sent
with design spec

Commissioned

Do trial pages

Production
estimates

Page design choice;
copy-edited MS
sent with all pics

Approved pages
typeset; pics placed
First proofs sent

Production
costs confirmed

First proof of
pages read
Any final pics sent

Typesetting is shown as part of the design process.

Amends and
corrections collated
and sent

Amends and
corrections to layout
and pic sizes

If pic sizes are
approved, high res
pic scans at repro

Final proofs read

Sent to indexer

Final proofs and
index sent

Final amends and
place high res pics;
index setting

Final setting
approved

Disk, CRC or
pictures to printer
for lasers/proofs

Lasers, colour proofs
for pics
produced

Lasers, colour
proofs checked
signed off

to check and
approve

Sheets printed;
running sheets
sent

if approved
sheets are bound

Jacket design brief;
any artwork
commissioned

Jacket trials

Jacket design
approved

Jacket texts written;
artwork approved
and text set; proof

Jacket layout proof
approved; output
to printer

Jacket proof
approved

Jacket printed

This progression of work may follow other routes which will be indicated by the editor. If you are working as a freelance rather than in a publishing house, early contact with the editor before the final brief may help to refine the specification and agree the schedule for the work.

Receiving and understanding the brief – and avoiding pitfalls

You may be approached at an early stage when there exists only an outline idea of the book: conditionally accept the work and await the detailed brief. The brief from the publisher's commissioning editor should include the following details:

> The person in overall charge of the book's production
> The print specification of the book
> Any stylistic or marketing preferences for the work
> A list of materials to be supplied and by whom
> The schedule for each part of the work
> Responsibility for amendments and corrections
> Output and print management responsibility
> Any additional marketing requests
> Fee for the work, stage payments and detailed contracts

Who is in charge?

If you are a freelance working away from the publishing house it is important that you deal with only one person, who will usually be the commissioning editor. This will cut out any possible confusions. If there are technical details, such as scanning specifications, and you need to talk to someone in other departments or suppliers' companies, ensure that the editor has a knowledge of these conversations.

The print specification of the book

Even if you have had earlier discussions about the specification, a finalized brief should be provided. It may only note those areas in which you are involved and omit such things as copy-editing procedures or the binding details. The specification may come as a simple written list or in a form used by the publishing house. In a perfect world you would want to know all the details shown on the following page. You are unlikely to get a complete list but keep this list in mind while discussing the job, the amount of work you are being asked to do and the fee. Editors may take some functions – such as low resolution scanning for positional picture placement – for granted, forgetting the time it can take you to scan the pictures.

Many of the brief points noted here can be dealt with in greater detail in letter form.

The abbreviations 1/1, 1/4 and 4/4 are printers' terms for printing colour combinations. 1 refers to a single colour, 4 to a four-colour printing.

Trimmed page size:

_____ mm x _____ mm

Stock: _____ gsm

Extent: _____ pp total, of which

    Pages 1/1: _____ pp

    Pages 1/4: _____ pp

    pages 4/4: _____ pp

    Prelims: allow _____ pp

    Endmatter: _____ pp

Finishing:

    Perfect bound: ☐

    Limp-sewn/soft-back: ☐

    Cased: ☐

Text sources:

    Format supplied: _____

    Hard copy: ☐

    Disk: ☐

      copy edited ☐

      from author: ☐

Illustrations:

None: ☐

Plate section of _____ pp

Scattered: ☐

    Number of illustrations: _____

    Full page: _____

    Half page: _____

    Quarter page: _____

Supplied as:

    Originals to be scanned as low

    resolution positionals: ☐

    High resolution scans to be sized

    and cropped: ☐

Cut outs needed: ☐ Number _____

Jacket/cover: ☐

Four colour: ☐ other: _____

Marketing additionals: ☐

Overall style: Series: ☐ Original: ☐

When you receive the specification, read it carefully and comment on anything that is not clear. You may feel that the format suggested is not suitable or that work is requested that you cannot carry out, such as print-quality scanning. You may ask for additional fees, for example, to do picture cut-outs or make other digital alterations, if these were not mentioned in the initial specification. The earlier you raise any queries the better; it will avoid later confusion.

Style preferences

You may be given an idea of what the publisher has in mind for a particular book. If it is part of a series you will be supplied with a book in the series or a template to work to. The influence of marketing in the publishing trade cannot be underestimated and their directions in the matter of style may be emphatic. It is useful to know at what market the book is aimed. This will help you develop an appropriate style and avoid producing trials that would not appeal to the intended audience.

Materials to be supplied

You will need to know in what form the book's text will be supplied. This would normally be in digital form on disk. Will it come directly from the author or in an edited form from the copy-editor? It is always preferable to do your trial layouts with the complete text though this may not always be available. Having the complete text enables you to come to a closer estimate of the extent of your suggested designs.

The manner in which illustrations are to be supplied should be made clear. Do you receive original transparencies, photographs and artwork, or photocopies of them, or just estimated picture numbers and sizes? Unless you are to be sent high resolution scans, the sooner you have the real thing in front of you the easier it is to get on with the work. Many of the illustration sources will be unique and sometimes valuable. Publishing houses may send *acceptance of delivery* forms with the artwork to be signed and returned. Keep a log book of their arrival and the dates when you send them back or on to the printers. *Keep good care of all artwork.* It is surprising how few objects go astray between the publishers, designers and printers but such occasional losses can be much resented. You should have an insurance for your workplace which covers the loss of such materials. If you work from home a normal house contents insurance will not cover them.

Work schedules

The commissioning editor should give you a schedule with deadlines for each of the stages. Ensure that you can meet these times. The schedule should consist of a date when it is planned for you to *receive* necessary materials as well as the date on which the editor expects each stage returned. This is important: if the delivery of materials is delayed, you may be expected to turn round a given stage quickly to maintain the schedule. If the delay is long, talk to the editor and re-schedule the stages or consider charging an extra *rush fee*.

Be careful not to create a style which involves you in over-complex formatting, the time and cost of which may not be appreciated by the client.

See *How editors supply text* p.374

Amendments, changes and corrections

Corrections after first proofs will vary from the occasional inserted comma to added paragraphs that require repagination. Publishers have the right to charge the author for extensive corrections at proof stage but rarely invoke it. The use of a percentage figure, say the commonly quoted 10 per cent for corrections that can be made to a text without an extra typesetting fee, is a contentious area. What is it 10 per cent of? It can't possibly mean changing 10 per cent of the words. The best that can be made of this figure is to take 10 per cent of the original setting time: when you have spent more than that time on corrections, other than correcting any errors you may have made, extra charges should be levied. If you fear that a particular book is likely to be subject to many changes, it is wise to let the client know your hourly cost for corrections at an early stage. If there is a contract for the work make sure this point is clear.

Considerable amendments to the text or picture positions after the first proofs can be very time-consuming and the brief should make clear who is responsible and who should bear the costs. If you have to carry out extensive changes made by the author or editor after the first proof, these create an extra cost which you should charge for. The number of times corrections, changes and amendments occur can be numerous. Telephoned, emailed and faxed changes are now commonplace, with PDF files being emailed as revised proofs instead of hard copy proofs. Sometimes the final illustrations may arrive late in the process.

You have to make a judgement as to whether you charge for late changes and if so, how much. Keeping the client happy has to be kept in mind but it is always worthwhile pointing out to an editor or client how much time has been spent on such work. If you decide not to charge for this time, it will at least make the point and avoid the editor thinking that such changes can be made in future work without an extra charge.

Output and print management responsibility

See *Output* pp.395–6

The form of output should be made clear. Do you output text layout disks and the original artwork to the printer directly or send all the material to the editor for forwarding? Has artwork been supplied at high resolution for pictures to be sized and cropped by you? Do you output PDFs with or without coloured proofs? What are your responsibilities following output? Are you required to check laser and colour proofs – even to sign them off for the printer? If so, such work should have been reflected in the fee. Having thought that the job was finished it can be galling to be asked to do more than you reckoned on or allowed for in your fee.

Additional marketing requests

Over and above the design of the book you may be asked to produce promotional material, such as posters, advertisements and leaflets, for the book's marketing. Such requests are reasonable at this stage in the production as you will have both text and illustrations to hand. This work should be subject to an additional fee.

Fees

You may be offered a fee for design and typesetting in one of several ways:

An overall fee: for the entire specified work. Be sure that the work expected of you is clear to both sides. Negotiate extra fees if you are asked to do work in addition to the original specification.

A fee based on a cost-per-page: This is an attractive proposition for books that are not illustrated – you know where you stand and can set your own target for getting the work done quickly and effectively. If the texts contains additional matter such as footnotes or illustrations ensure that the page rate is adequate for what you know will be a more time-consuming task.

A fixed fee based on the client's budget: This figure may be less than you normally expect. It is for you to make the decision to accept it. Either do the hours of work that the fee covers or accept that you will do more than those minimum hours, uncharged, to ensure that the work satisfies you.

A negotiated fee: which you propose after seeing both the specification and schedule. If the client expects you to drop everything else you are doing there must be an understanding that the fee will be higher than usual.

A fee using an hourly rate charge: which you agree with the client. In an open-ended situation with a particularly difficult piece of work where the specification is vague at the outset, the work involved unclear and the timing of publication unknown, this is a solution which you may have to adopt. Work out a cost ceiling for the client and keep in touch as the work proceeds.

Budgets and print management

Clients who are not familiar with the publishing or printing worlds may ask you to undertake a project completely and deal with all aspects within a fixed budget. This can be an attractive proposition offering you total control. The repro and print costings require careful research to ensure that you have covered all eventualities. Accept the budget only if you are sure that the project can be completed within it. Any possible problems should be foreseen and a note of these made to the client before the work starts. If a production element runs over the budget this may represent a loss to you as you cannot increase the fee without further negotiations.

Stage payments

The design stages of a straightforward book may be speedy. More complex books, especially co-editioned illustrated books, may take many months from the trial stages to final output. If you can negotiate *stage payments* – that is a portion of the fee paid at agreed stages of your work – it will ease your cash flow. If the project is abandoned, and regrettably this does happen in publishing, you will have a smaller amount of outstanding unpaid work to be collected.

Contracts

The simplest form of contract is a letter from clients confirming their wish to go ahead. If you have already established in writing what work is involved, then this letter is sufficient. To be doubly safe, you may be advised to reply. Check what work has been agreed in past letters and meetings and put a resumé in your letter of acceptance. If the client merely phones you with the go ahead, ask for a letter in confirmation. All of this may sound rather formal but it will resolve any possible misunderstandings at the outset. Larger publishing houses may well provide you with a legal contract. Look at it carefully and if there are any points that confuse you or do not reflect what you have understood to be the case, discuss it with the editor and resolve these concerns. Rarely, if the contract is for a large fee or contains penalty clauses that disturb you, take it to a lawyer for approval.

Keep all the paperwork until the final cheque clears and the book is in the shops.

Design and typesetting work progression

After the brief is received the materials will be sent to you to start the project. In outline the work will follow these stages:

1 Trial spreads and extent calculations
2 Response to trial spreads
3 Modification of trial spreads
4 Formatting, typesetting and layout – the first proof
5 Corrections and changes to first proof – second proof or *first revise*
6 Final changes to second proof – third proof or *second revise*
7 Output
8 Checking printer's proofs

The working details of all these procedures have already been dealt with in this book. The purpose of this section is to look at the way in which you will have to deal with editors and printers at each stage of the production.

Trial spreads and extent calculations

The brief will have indicated the format, extent and possibly the style that the editor wishes to see. You will have to design text panels and illustration treatments within these parameters. Format the text disk with correct chapter turns and line breaks; any illustrations are scanned in, probably at low resolution. Make sure you have enough material to do trial spreads. If the whole text is to hand you should confirm that the extent is reasonable and achievable. If the suggested extent cannot be achieved within the bounds of producing a readable text then talk to the editor as soon as this is evident.

You may be competing with other designers for the commission – a procedure called *pitching*. You will have to submit a proposed fee and trials for the work. To protect the design element make your copy-right note on all the trials.

Publishers may expect to see three trial spreads using different combinations of font and text panel. Do spreads of each dealing with such points as chapter openings, footnotes and illustrations, as well as the main text. You may also be asked to provide trial spreads for title or contents pages. Do *not* do a deliberately poor spread in order to persuade an editor to choose from the others. This will always backfire on you – it may be chosen. If you anticipate a particular difficulty, such as a request for chapter openings on a recto with a large illustration, deal with it at this stage. Complex books, especially exhibition catalogues, require more detailed information from the editor to create the trial spreads of illustrated sections, as in this example below:

> Long catalogue entry (type A: 2pp, 600 words facing pic)
>
> Medium catalogue entry (type B, 1p, 250 words beneath pic)
>
> Short catalogue entry (type C, 2 works per page, 250 words under caption)

This is a necessary guide to laying out trial treatments of the illustrated pages.

Produce these pages either cut to final trimmed size or with a keyline to indicate the trim. Using a frame will leave enough space around the spread to annotate the types used and write comments on the suggested design. If the book is illustrated or has colour text treatments you will need to provide digital colour spreads.

When you send the trials, as well as annotating the trial sheets, write an explanatory letter. Detail the typefaces you used and your reason for the choices in both the letter and on the trials – frequently the letter is mislaid, separated from the sheets or not read by everyone.

Response to and modification of trial spreads

You will need to have a detailed and positive response to the trials. Be sure that both you and the editor understand what the final choice is. Frequently the choice will involve a 'pick and mix' conclusion – one heading style from one trial and a main text style from another. If you feel that the choices represent a poor typographical solution, explain your case as clearly as you can without adopting too much of a *prima donna* stance.

If you feel that there is any possibility of confusion as to what has been decided, do a second modified trial spread showing the choices and ensure that everyone is clear about the style before starting the layout.

Formatting, typesetting and layout of the first proof

Check that you have all the materials, both text and pictures that you need. (If the book has an index this will not be produced until the later stages – make allowance for it in determining the extent.) If the book has footnotes and sidenotes it is especially important that you have them to hand. If you are short of any material, discuss this with the editor immediately. If there is an unavoidable delay, usually it is an illustration or two, you will have to leave a space in the layout. If there is any point which is not clear contact the editor and resolve it; don't make guesses about what might or might not be intended. The more details that are sorted out at the first layout, the fewer late changes will be required.

You will be asked for sets of proofs. How many will depend on the nature of the book. If it is a straightforward work of fiction it is unlikely to be more than two – one for the editor and one for the author. For books with several contributors, editors or translators, you may be asked for several copies. For long books this can be expensive and should have been noted in the specification. If you are asked during these stages for additional sets of proofs over and above the agreed number, keep a note and inform the client if you wish to make an extra charge. The editor circulates the proofs, keeping one set on which all the corrections and changes will be collated and returned to you. Resist any suggestion that you receive several sets and collate them yourself; this can result in several competing solutions to one problem and may lead to errors on your part. It is also more time-consuming than you might think.

Corrections and changes to the first proof

When the first proofs are returned, you should be told if there are any major changes that affect pagination, or illustrations that are to be re-positioned. Go through all the pages and get an idea of the level of corrections and the reasons for them. If you feel that they are excessive refer to the specification and talk to the editor straight away. Carry out the corrections and double check them. If there is any point at which they cause a page to run over or text to be moved away from an illustration, make a note when you send the revised proof.

Note: There is a possibility of confused terminology here. Your second, third and fourth proofs may be called by the editor respectively the first, second and third revises. See diagram right.

Corrections to the second proof

There should be only a small number of minor corrections at this stage. If the book has an index it will be supplied at this stage as there should be no changes to the pagination of the main text. On the editor's advice, you will have set aside some

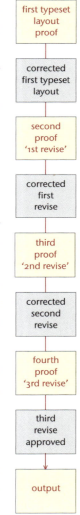

first typeset
layout
proof

corrected
first typeset
layout

second
proof
'1st revise'

corrected
first
revise

third
proof
'2nd revise'

corrected
second
revise

fourth
proof
'3rd revise'

third
revise
approved

output

blank pages at the end of the main text to accommodate this. There may be other small additions or corrections to the preliminary pages that can be made without affecting pagination. Any late illustrations must also be dealt with at this point.

See *Indexes*
pp.194–7

This third proof is then sent off. It is unlikely that any more changes will be made, barring the odd misspelt proper name or incorrect picture caption. These may be organized by telephone or fax and confirmed with PDFs of specific pages. If you have been supplied with high resolution pictures these will have been fitted and sized by you. The book is now ready for output.

Output of signed-off proofs

See *Output*
pp.395–6

Previously the final set of proofs would be physically *signed-off* by the editor as ready for press. More commonly these days only a telephone call may be made. The various mechanisms of output to the printer have been covered earlier. The output should be sent either directly to the printer or to the editor for forwarding.

You may be asked to send a high resolution PDF version directly to the printers. In the case of four-colour illustrated books this will have to be accompanied with a set of full size colour digital printouts. If the book is lengthy, this is a costly print-out and you should check with the editor who pays for this.

Checking printer's proof prior to press

A basic rule is that whoever is responsible for meeting the costs should finally sign the work off.

It is important that you establish at the outset who holds the responsibility for checking these proofs. In publishing houses it is usually the joint responsibility of the editor and the production manager and you may not see the work again until it has been printed and bound. If you are working for a smaller house or an individual client you may be responsible for checking the proofs. They may be in one of several formats. With text-only books, proofs will be limited to laser printouts for you to check for the possibility of reflowed text or the use of incorrect fonts. For four-colour books you may be supplied with a coloured laser output – to check text and picture position – and a set of colour proofs digitally produced by one of the many colour proofing mechanisms. Where the colour reproduction is of great importance, for example in the reproduction of artworks, wet proofs may be supplied. These are sheets printed on the press using the plates, paper and inks that will be used in the final printing. For work of importance or where a judgement is required, you and the editor may be asked to *pass on press*. This involves you watching the sheets as they are printed, commenting on the final ink values and colours. This increases your familiarity with printing processes which is an advantage but far from being an attractive proposition it can be very time-consuming, taking at least a whole day. If the presses are abroad, you are more likely to spend your time in an industrial park on the outskirts of a Italian town rather than the romantic centre of a famous city. If you are asked to pass on press, make a note that you will charge a separate fee and travel expenses.

Previously photographic film was produced and used to create printing plates. The *Computer-to-plate* (CTP) process uses computers to directly produce the plates, cutting out the film stage. The ease with which PDFs can be used in the output of work is economically attractive both for printers and publishers. But it can be unnerving for the designer, who may not see printer's proofs at all or only see colour laser proofs. Be sure that the editor sees whatever proofs the printer supplies and is responsible for checking and passing them.

If you are in charge of the production process and the final quality is particularly important it is wise to ask the printer for a set of *running sheets*. These are a set of loosely folded sheets from the finished print run. This is your last chance to check for any errors or issues with print quality. If there is an error it will only be necessary to reprint one of the sheets. If you only discover a fault after the book has been bound there is little to be done except reprint the whole book.

File copies

The printer should supply you with two or three file copies of the book. If these can be delivered to you before the delivery to the client it gives you the chance to make one last check to ensure that the work is perfect. If a problem has arisen, it will give you some time to discuss it with the printer before approaching the client.

Do make sure that you have file copies. A contract will normally specify the number of file copies to expect and also offer you the right to purchase further copies at a discounted price. The file copy is the only sample of the work you have done; it is important and enables you to show past work to future clients.

Wet proofs are also known as *machine proofs*. This was an expensive process but the use of *CTP* – computer-to-plate – technology, has made it less costly. Even so it is an additional costing which should be built into the overall production cost.

Time sheets

If you are working as a freelance you will need to keep an accurate record of the time you spend on each stage of a project. Even if the fee you will receive is fixed this is a worthwhile exercise and will give you a continuing insight into how much time you take with each task. It will also give you a record of any extra works you were asked to do. Even if you work in a publishing house you may be asked to record such times in order to help with the costing of an individual book.

A sheet with these sub-divisions is sufficient and notes stage schedules if known:

In the early stages of your career it is likely that you will not be able to set your own fee. When each book is finished, review the time spent and work out the final hourly rate. Keep this in mind and always try to build in the capital cost of equipment, font purchases, insurances and other overheads.

Title: Trials: 8/4/05			1st proof: 23/7/05 pub date:							completed	hours
ISBN: 2nd proof:			output: output format:								
Consultation/tel calls:	1.5									✔	1.5
Trial spreads:	2	3	1	0.5						✔	6.5
Text conversion:	3.5									✔	3.5
Type formatting:	7									✔	7
Scanning low res:	8									✔	8
Scanning high res:											
Layout to first proof:	6										
First revise:											
Second revise:											
Place/size high res pics:											
Third revise:											
Output disk:											
Output pdf:											
Output colour proofs:											
Additional works:											
Additional proofs:											
Post/courier:											
Travel:											
Supply costs:											
Total:											

You can design your own time sheet to meet your own needs. If you use any outside suppliers, such as repro houses or digital printers, keep invoices from them.

Print management

If you are organizing all the repro and printing for a client you will need to get quotations for this work from one or more printers. The form below enables an outline specification to be speedily put together and passed to the printers:

Print/repro house   **Your company**
Contact: Contact:
Company: Company:
Address: Address:
Tel: Tel:
Fax: Fax:

Job specification: **Title:**   **Quote required by:**

Trim size: x   mm   Portrait / Landscape   Bled pages ☐

Extent: ___ pp   Colour: Black only ☐   Four colour ☐   Other ☐

Cover: Colour: Single only ☐   Four colour ☐

Other: ☐ Specify:

Jacket: Colour: Single only ☐   Four colour ☐

Other: ☐ Specify:

Text: supplied as:
PDF ☐   Quark ☐   InDesign ☐   Other ☐   Specify:

Illustrations:
Number: B/w: _____   Colour: _____   Line: _____   Cut-outs: _____

Repro/printer:
To scan high res ☐   Low res image supply for OPI ☐   Repro to fit ☐

You will: Supply high res scans ☐   Sized and fitted at output ☐

Proofing requirements:
High res digital proofs for colour: ☐   Bromides for line: ☐
Lasers for text and picture position: ☐   Wet proofs: ☐

Materials:
Text: Cover: Jacket:

Finishing:
Limp sewn ☐   Perfect bound ☐   Saddle-stitched ☐   Cased ☐   Other ☐
Flaps ☐   Width: _____mm   Laminate: Gloss ☐   Matt ☐   U/V ☐

Quantity: _____   Run-on: _____   Delivery to:

The form of high resolution colour proofs is a technical area that is constantly developing. Check with printer to see what process is used.

Apart from the single cost of printing, you will need to discuss and agree other aspects of the project, the paper stocks to be used, binding styles and materials, and the schedule itself. Try to resolve as many of these details as early on possible.

Paper stocks

The advice of the printer on the choice of paper stocks for a project is usually invaluable. Printers will have strong views on what paper suits what job. Frequently stocks of commonly used and tested papers will be held by them and will have been purchased in large quantities giving a favourable costing.

Collect samples of papers which you like and always ask the printers to consider using them. As mentioned before there may be good reasons for not using a paper of your choice such as the size and grain of the sheet or the printing surface. If you want to use a particular paper which the printer finds difficult to deal with, discuss the printing limitations which may arise and listen to the printer's advice.

Binding materials

See *Jacket and cover components* pp.352–5

When the paper stock has been decided, the style and materials of the finishing has to be chosen. For a cased hardback binding, the following need to be defined:

> The cloth or paper for the boards and the weight of the boards
> An endpaper choice – manufacturer, colour and weight
> The head and tail bands; the text and artwork for the spine blocking
> The choice of round-backed or flat-backed spine

For a paperback, the choice of either limp sewn or perfect binding must be made. If flaps are to be incorporated, check the maximum width available on the printer's presses before you specify their dimensions.

Dummy bindings

If there are any modifications or errors in the dummy, make the correction clear. If there are many ask for a revised dummy.

Whatever kind of binding you choose, it is imperative that the printer supplies a dummy – a bound set of sheets of the correct size and extent – using the paper and binding materials you have specified. After you have reviewed it yourself, show this to the client. This ensures that there is no misunderstanding about the finished product. Return the approved dummy to guarantee that the finishing is done using the same materials.

Invoicing and VAT

Invoicing

If you are a freelance, having done the work, you now have to invoice for it. Your invoice should detail the stages of the work in short simple terms. At this point it will remind the client of the work you have done; if it stretched over a lengthy period make a note of the date at which work started. Do not delay in sending the invoice – do it while the book is in everyone's mind. Publishers may take a standard period of two to three months to settle their invoices and that period starts from the date of your invoice. For individual clients you should make a note of your *terms* – that is, when you expect your invoices to be paid.

If you take on a project as a production manager you must reassure yourself of the credit-worthiness of your client. If it is the first time you have dealt with the client, do whatever credit checks you can, ask for a deposit towards the work and raise stage payment invoices as the work proceeds. This will ensure that at no point is there any large amount outstanding. You can reduce any possible liability by asking the client to pay major suppliers' invoices, such as the printer's bill, directly. The printer will also make credit checks. All this may seem to be over-cautious but one bad debt takes a lot of earning back.

VAT

At the time of writing, the production of books is not subject to VAT but all the suppliers of the preceding stages involved – artwork, photography, typesetting and design – may be subject to VAT. Publishers will claim back the VAT on those stages as an input tax. If you, as the designer or typesetter, are not VAT registered, your fee is not subject to VAT; if you are registered for VAT, you must apply VAT.

If you are acting as a print manager for the whole project and are VAT registered you will not charge your client VAT on the finished book. You can reclaim the VAT input taxes from any supplier and printer you have used. This is a very simplified review of what can be a complex subject and you would be wise to contact Customs & Excise if you have any doubt about your position in regard to VAT. They will supply you with information which deals with printing and its allied trades.

ACKNOWLEDGEMENTS

We are grateful to many people in the publishing and printing trades who have helped in myriad ways and given us the opportunities over the years to work on diverse and interesting books. We owe a special debt to our editors, Jon Cannon, Dr Rowan Whimster and Susie Whimster, who have patiently assisted us, turning our points of technical jargon into plain English. Publishers and editors, including Christopher MacLehose, Bill Swainson, and Sue Palmer encouraged us to continue with the book.

For the provision of texts and illustrations we are grateful to The Harvill Press, Tate Publishing, the National Gallery Company, Sir John Soane's Museum, Haus Publishing, Reaktion Books, Ulysses, Broadway Publishing, The Foundling Press and Browse & Darby. Our thanks also go to Hampton Printing Ltd for resolving the fugitive cream ink colour and to Butler and Tanner for approaching the reproduction and printing with enthusiasm and skill.

We must express our gratitude to our friends and families, and especially Michael's wife, Caroline, who have supported us in this project and put up with its intrusion into their lives.

CREDITS

The majority of text extracts used throughout the book are from the following publications by The Harvill Press:

Lucy Archer, *Architecture in Britain and Ireland 600–1500*, 1999

David Bellos, *Jacques Tati: His Life and Art*, 1999

Rick Bragg, *Redbirds*, 1997

Raymond Carver, *Call if You Need Me*, 2000

Jean Cocteau, *Les Enfants Terribles*, 1999

Ernesto 'Che' Guevara, *The African Dream*, 1999

Midas Dekkers, *The Way of All Flesh*, 2000

Jean Echenoz, *I'm off*, 2001

Marcello Fois, *The Advocate*, 2001

Jean Giono, *Second Harvest*, 1999

Thomas Glavinic, *Carl Haffner's Love of the Draw*, 1999

Dermot Healy, *Sudden Times*, 1999

Peter Høeg, *Tales of the Night*, 1997

Bohumil Hrabal, *Dancing Lessons for the Advanced in Age*, 1998

Georges Ifrah, *Universal History of Numbers*, 2000

Ismail Kadare, *The General of a Dead Army*, 2000

Ismail Kadare, *Three Elegies for Kososvo*, 2000

Jean-Paul Kauffmann, *The Dark Room at Longwood*, 1999

Jean-Paul Kauffmann, *Voyage to Desolation Island*, 2001

Andrey Kurkov, *Death and the Penguin*, 2001

Björn Larsson, *Long John Silver*, 1999

Halldór Laxness, *The Fish can Sing*, 2000

Amin Maalouf, *On Identity*, 2000

Amin Maalouf, *Ports of Call*, 1999

Claudio Magris, *Microcosms*, 1999

Geert Mak, *Amsterdam*, 1999

Fosco Maraini, *Secret Tibet*, 2000

Javier Marías, *When I was Mortal*, 1999

Myra Montero, *The Messenger*, 1997

Haruki Murakami, *Norwegian Wood*, 2000

Haruki Murakami, *Underground*, 2001

Haruki Murakami, *After the Quake*, 2002

Daniel Pennac, *Passionfruit*, 1999

Daniel Pennac, *Write to Kill*, 1997

Georges Perec, *Three*, 1996

Arturo Pérez-Reverte, *The Fencing Master*, 1999

Per Petterson, *To Siberia*, 1998

Mazarine Pingeot, *First Novel*, 1998

Andrey Platonov, *The Return*, 1999

Andrey Platonov, *Happy Moscow*, 2001

Anna Politkovskaya, *A Dirty War*, 2001

Manuel Rivas, *Butterfly's Tongue*, 2000

Manuel Rivas, *The Carpenter's Pencil*, 2001

Peter Robb, *Midnight in Sicily*, 1998

Jay Rubin, *Haruki Murakami and the Music of Words*, 2002

St John of the Cross, *The Poems*, 2000

José Saramago, *The Tale of the Unknown Island*, 1999

Michael Schmidt (ed), *The Harvill Book of Twentieth-Century Poetry in English*, 1999

W. G. Sebald, *The Rings of Saturn*, 1996

W. G. Sebald, *Vertigo*, 1999

Nicholas Shakespeare, *Bruce Chatwin*, 1999, in association with Jonathan Cape

Robert Solé, *The Alexandria Semaphore*, 2001

Frances Spalding, *Gwen Raverat*, 2001

Andreas Staikos, *Les Liaisons Culinaires*, 1998

Sebastiano Vassali, *The Swan*, 1997

Luis Fernando Verissimo, *The Club of Angels*, 2001

Eric S. Wood, *Historical Britain*, 1995

Ilya Zbarsky and Samuel Hutchinson, *Lenin's Embalmers*, 1998

Additional covers, jackets, title pages and text extracts are from the following publications:

Sebastian Haffner, *Churchill*, Haus Publishing, 2003

Martin Geck, *Beethoven*, Haus Publishing, 2003

Rick Gekoski, *Tolkein's Gown*, Constable & Robinson, 2004

A New Description of Sir John Soane's Museum, Sir John Soane's Museum, 2001

Saving Wotton, Sir John Soane's Museum, 2004

Hooked on Books, Sir John Soane's Museum, 2004

Thomas Banks: 1735–1805, Sir John Soane's Museum, 2005

Simon Whistler, *On a Glass Lightly*, Libanus Press, 2004

D. Fountain and D. Robins, *Cool Rules*, Reaktion Books, 2000

A. Wilton and T. Barringer, *American Sublime: Landscape Painting in the United States, 1820–1880*, Tate Publishing, 2002

R. Godfrey, *James Gillray: The Art of Caricature*, Tate Publishing, 2001

J. Townsend (ed), *William Blake: The Painter at Work*, Tate Publishing, 2003

D. Bomford and others, *Degas: Art in the Making*, National Gallery Company, 2004

J. Dunkerley, *ISA Inaugural Lecture*, ISA, 2004

and our thanks to artists, illustrators and photographers for their work used in the book:

Richard Shirley Smith, Simon Brett, Ian Beck, Steve Raw, Chris Corr, Marion Ettlinger, James Mitchell, John Pasmore, Maggie Whistler, Graham Herbert, Paul Barker/Country Life Picture Library and the Estate of Mervyn Peake.

REFERENCE BOOKS AND FURTHER READING

Reference Books

Dictionaries

Collins Dictionary of the English Language; *Chambers Twentieth Century Dictionary* or *The Shorter Oxford English Dictionary*. It is also useful to keep a selection of French, German, Spanish and Latin dictionaries.

Reference books

Aitchison, James, *Cassell's Dictionary of English Grammar*, Cassell & Co, London, 2001

Burchfield, R. W. (ed), *New Fowler's Modern English Usage*, 3rd edn, revised by Sir Ernest Gower, Oxford University Press, 1996

Butcher, Judith, *Copy-editing, The Cambridge Handbook for Editors, Authors and Publishers*, 3rd edn, Cambridge University Press, 1992

The Chicago Manual of Style, The University of Chicago Press, 14th edn, 2001

Hart's Rules for Compositors and Readers at the University Press, Oxford, 39th edn, Oxford University Press, 1983

Oxford Dictionary for Writers and Authors, Oxford University Press, 1991

The Times Guide to English Style and Usage, Times Books, London, 1998

Writers' and Artists' Yearbook, A & C Black, London, 2005

The Oxford Companion Series to *Art, Music* and *English Literature* is also helpful.

Further Reading

Bringhurst, Robert, *The Elements of Typographic Style*, 2nd edn, Hartley & Marks, USA, 1996

Brown, Derek, *Designing a Book*, Primrose Hill Press, Bicester, 2003

Carter, Sebastian, *Twentieth Century Type Designers*, Trefoil Publications Ltd, London, 1987

Friedl, Fredrich, Ott, Nicolaus, and Stein, Bernard, *Typography – when who how*, Könemann, Cologne, 1998

Gordon, Bob, *Making Digital Type Look Good*, Thames & Hudson, 2001

Horn, Barbara, *The Effective Editor's Handbook*, Pira International, Leatherhead, 1997

Hochuli, Jost, and Kinross, Robert, *Designing Books: Practice and Theory*, Hyphen Press, 2003

Kinross, Robin, *Modern Typography*, Hyphen Press, London, 1992

Lee, Marshall, *Bookmaking*, 3rd edn, W. W. Norton & Co, New York, 2004

McLean, Ruari, *The Thames & Hudson Manual of Typography*, Thames & Hudson Ltd, London, 1980

Perfect, Chistopher, and Rookledge, Gordon, *Rookledge's International Typefinder*, Serama Press, 1983

Powers, Alan, *Front Cover*, Mitchell Beazley, London, 2001

Tschichold, Jan, *The Form of the Book*, Hartley & Marks, Washington, 1991

Upton, Ellen, *Thinking with Type*, Princeton Architectural Press, New York, 2004

Historical background reading

some of these titles may be out of print

Bartram, Alan, *Five Hundred Years of Book Design*, The British Library, 2001

Carter, John, and Muir, Percy H. (comp/ed), *Printing and the Mind of Man*, 2nd edn, Karl Pressler, Münich, 1983

Dreyfus, John, *The Work of Jan Van Krimpen*, Sylvan Press, London, 1952

Gill, Eric, *An Essay on Typography*, 3rd edn, J. N. Dent & Sons Ltd, London, 1936

Glen, Duncan, *Printing Type Designs*, Akros Publications, Scotland, 2001

Harling, Robert, *The Letter Forms and Type Designs of Eric Gill*, Westerham Press, 1976

Hutt, Allen, *Fournier; the Compleat Typographer*, Frederick Muller Ltd, 1972

Isaac, Peter, *William Bulmer*, Bain & Williams, London, 1993

Lewis, John, *The 20th Century Book*, 2nd edn, The Herbert Press, London, 1984

Lowry, Martin, *The World of Aldus Manutius*, Basil Blackwell, Oxford, 1979

Morison, Stanley, *Four Centuries of Fine Printing*, 4th edn, Ernest Benn, London, 1960

Morison, Stanley, *A Tally of Types*, Cambridge University Press, 1973

Mosley, James, *The Nymph and the Grot*, Friends of St Bride Printing Library, 1999

Neuman, Eckhard, *Functional Graphic Design in the 20s*, Reinhold Publishing, 1967

Steinberg, S. H., *Five Hundred Years of Printing*, 3rd edn, Penguin Books, London, 1974

Tracy, Walter, *Letters of Credit*, Gordon Fraser, London, 1986

Tschichold, Jan, *Treasury of Alphabets and Lettering*, Omega Books, Hertfordshire, 1985

Updike, Daniel Berkeley, *Printing Types*, 2 vols, Dover Publications, Inc., New York, 1980

Williamson, Hugh, *Methods of Book Design*, Oxford University Press, 1956

GLOSSARY AND INDEX

characters-per-line 33–7, 237

chronology 343

CIP (cataloguing-in-publication) data 177

CMYK (cyan, magenta, yellow, black) 312, 315
the colour of inks used in four-colour printing

coated paper 399
paper with a coating derived from minerals to give
a smooth finish

coding, editors' 376–9
a system of codes used by the editor to specify
different text treatments to the typesetter

co-edition 300, 330–1
book produced jointly by two or more publishers,
usually in different languages

colon 248–50

colour, text 84–6
the overall tonal value of a panel of text

colour 139, 141, 155, 207, 300, 364
    adjustment of 315

column 274, 340–3

comma 248–50

compound 386
two words conjoined by a hyphen to form a single
word

condensed 67
form of font with very narrow characters

consistency 19

contents page 181–5
page listing the sections of a book

continuous text
prose text, set in lines to form a block
see 'text', 'text panel', 'typesetting'

contracts 410

contraction 385
word shortened by removing letters from the
middle, e.g. Dr

copyright 176–8
legal right of the author of a text or owner of an
image

copyright statement 176–8

cover 146–7, 352–71
card cover of a paperback book
    combining text and image 358–61
    copy for 366–71
    flaps 352–3
    extension of cover folded inwards

coverage 43, 228–31
area of page covered by text

crop 304–7
to cut off unwanted areas of an image

credit line 191, 389
line naming author, owner or publisher of material
reproduced in a book

cross-fold bleed 297
image that extends across the gutter of a spread
onto the opposite page

CTP (computer-to-plate) 415
process of producing a printing plate direct from a
digital file without using film

cursive 68
form of italic based on handwritten characters

cut-out 285
removal of extraneous background from an image

cyrillic alphabet
alphabet used for Russian and Serbian languages
see 'non-Latin alphabets'

decimals 275

dedication 180
inscription by the author dedicating their work

demy 28
a standard book format, approx. 216 x 136 mm

descender 76–7
part of a lower case letter which extends below the
main body of the letter, on characters such as g, j,
and y

detail 175, 307
small portion of an illustration enlarged

dialogue 237

diary entries 265

digital images 310–17
pictures rendered digitally, to be manipulated by
computer
    colour adjustment of 315
    management of 313–15
    output of 316–17
    resolution of 310–12
    scanning 311
    size of 317

digital photography 315

digital printing 398–9

display font 62, 67, 142–57
font designed for use in display settings

display settings 142–57
a small number of words designed to catch the
attention, e.g. chapter headings and title pages

displayed text 258–67
text differentiated typographically from the main
text, e.g. diary entries, correspondence

DPI (dots per inch) 310–13
unit of measurement of the resolution of digital
images

format *continued*
   progressive formats 334–6
   text books 29
   trade formats 28
   a range of standardized formats used
   throughout the publishing trade

formatting text 381
putting text into the chosen typeface and size

four-colour printing
process of reproducing colours out of four colours
– cyan, magenta, yellow, and black – printed in
small dots
   planning of 293

fractions 276

frame 150–1

frontispiece 170
illustration placed opposite a title page

full out 55
a line of text set with no indent

full point 250–1
full stop

function 16–19

ghosting 361
lightening or darkening of an area of an image,
usually to allow text to be placed over it

global changes 374–5
changes which are automatically applied to an
entire text document

glossary 192
definitions of technical words and terms used in
a text

Greek fonts 333
fonts used for setting Greek and in some
mathematical settings

grid 56–9
underlying layout which indicates where text and
images are placed on each page

guides 56–9
non-printing lines drawn up in a layout program to
aid the accurate positioning of elements on the
page

gutter 44–7, 338
inner vertical margin of the page

half-title page 172
first page of a book, containing only the title

half-tone 312–13
the rendering of continuous tone in a black and
white image using small dots

handwriting, re-creation of 265

hanging-out 247, 263
the opposite of indenting. Setting a character or
word outside of the text area

hardback 350
book bound between hard boards

hard copy 374
printed copy of a digital text file

head of page 48, 202–3
top of the page

headings, chapter 114–25
typographic treatment indicating the beginning of
a new section
   chapter drops 116, 137
   space from top of the text panel to the first line
   of text of a new chapter
   chapter epigraphs 121
   chapter numbers 119–20
   coding for 376
   in extent calculations 116, 235
   position of 117
   run-on chapters 110, 123–4
   chapters which do not begin a new page, but
   follow on below the text of the previous chapter
   size of 118
   small caps 122
   type style of 115
see also 'sub-headings'

headwords 195–7, 263, 338
words listed alphabetically in an index or
reference book

house rules 19
set of conventions applied to the production of
text, some of which are specific to individual
publishing houses

hyphen 252
punctuation mark used in the creation of
compounds and in the division or words between
lines

hyphenation 98, 104, 386

ICS (inter-character spacing, tracking) 83
space between characters in a line of text
see also 'letter-spacing'

illustrated books 282–301
   format of 289
   grids for 286, 291–2
   output of 316–17, 396
   prelims in 185–6
   revision of 393–4
   typography in 294–5
see also 'co-editions'

illustrations
   bled-out 296–7
   cropping of 304–6

ranged left setting 52–3, 100–1, 111, 344–7
text setting which aligns on the left-hand side but
not on the right-hand side

ranged right setting 213, 295
text setting which aligns on the right-hand side but
not on the left-hand side

readability 18, 20–5, 33–4, 38–9, 65, 98
the ease with which text may be read
    characters-per-line 33–4
    inter-related elements 24–5
    leading 23
    letter-spacing 23
    regularity and rhythm 21
    type size 22
    word-spacing 23

ream 400
500 sheets of paper

recto
right-hand page
    recto starts 110, 125

reference works 337–8

regular 66
roman form of font used for text setting,
e.g. Albertina regular

repro (reproduction) 395–7
the process by which the final layout and artwork is
converted into printing plates

resolution 310–12
number of pixels per inch in a digital file
    high resolution 312–14
    resolution of digital image necessary for
    satisfactory printing
    low resolution 312–14
    resolution of digital image inadequate for
    satisfactory printing

reversed out 364–5
white type (unprinted paper) on a black or
coloured background

revision of proofs 390–4

RGB (red, green, blue) 312, 315
colours out of which digital images are produced

river 33–4, 345
line of white space running down through a text
panel as the result of loose word-spacing

roman 66, 130, 244
an upright form of a typeface

roman numerals 119, 163, 201, 278–9

rotation of pages 188

royal 28, 334
a standard book format, approx. 234 x 156 mm

rules 149, 275, 342
printed straight lines

running foot 204–5
book or chapter title repeated at the bottom of
every page
    and margins 48–9
    when to delete 206

running head 202–3, 206–7, 337
book or chapter title repeated at the top of every
page
    and margins 48–9
    shortening of 207
    when to delete 206

running shoulder 205
book or chapter title repeated in the fore-edge
margin of every page

run-on 110, 123–4, 129
following directly on, not starting a new line,
paragraph or page

sans serif 62, 65, 69, 133, 202, 344–7
letterforms with no serifs

'satin' paper 399
coated paper with a slightly reflective surface finish

scaling, horizontal and vertical 241
the process of distorting a character, by stretching
or squeezing it

scanning 311–12
process of rendering artwork into a digital image

scattered illustrations 282–7, 293
illustrations placed throughout a book, not
grouped together in a plate section

scatter proofs see 'proofs'

screen 312–13
pattern of dots out of which four-colour images
and halftones are printed. The fineness of the
screen is measured in lines-per-inch

script 143, 267
typeface designed to resemble handwriting

section break (line break, white line space)
54, 109, 376
space of one or two lines in the text panel

section opening see 'part-title'

semi-bold 66, 70, 139, 263
typeface with thicker strokes than a regular face,
though not as thick as a bold face

semi-colon 248–50

series 57
a range of books produced to the same format and
design

serif 62, 65, 69
additional horizontal and oblique strokes which
terminate the main strokes of a character